PRETENDERS
TO THE
ENGLISH
THRONE

PRETENDERS
TO THE
ENGLISH
THRONE

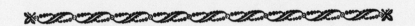

JEREMY POTTER

BARNES & NOBLE BOOKS
TOTOWA, NEW JERSEY

First published in the USA 1987 by
BARNES & NOBLE BOOKS
81 Adams Drive
Totowa, New Jersey, 07512

ISBN 0-389-20703-9

Library of Congress Cataloging in Publication Data

Potter, Jeremy.
   Pretenders to the English Throne.

   Bibliography: p.
   Includes index.
   1.   Great Britain—Kings and rules—Succession.
2.   Great Britain—History. 3.   Great Britain—Politics
and government.   4.   Imposters and imposture—Great Britain
—History. I. Title.
DA28.1.P68 1987   941'.009'92   86-26483
ISBN 0-389-20703-9

First published in Great Britain 1986 by
Constable and Company Ltd
10 Orange Street London WC2H 7EG

Copyright © 1986 by Jeremy Potter

Printed in the United States of America
M 9 8 7 6 5 4 3 2 1

CONTENTS

Introduction 9

1   Duke Robert and William Clito   13
2   Empress Matilda, Lady of England   31
3   John of Gaunt, King of Castile   46
4   Yorkists, Lancastrians and Henry Tudor   65
5   Lambert Simnel, Ireland's King   80
6   Prince Perkin   91
7   Queen Jane   113
8   The Queen of Scots   128
9   King Monmouth   137
10 James III, Old Mr Melancholy   158
11 Charles III, The Bonnie Prince   178
12 Henry IX, King Cardinal   196

Conclusion 206
Select Bibliography 211
Sources and References 219
Index 221

ILLUSTRATIONS

Lambert Simnel as a royal turnspit 88
From an 18th-century engraving

Perkin Warbeck's autograph 112
British Library

                              between pages 60 and 61

Robert of Normandy
From 13th-century effigy in Gloucester Cathedral

Empress Matilda's Seal
British Museum

John of Gaunt
*By kind permission of The Duke of Beaufort.
Photo: Courtauld Institute of Art*

Henry Tudor as a young man
Library of Arras Ms. 266

Henry Tudor as Henry VII
National Portrait Gallery

Perkin Warbeck
Library of Arras Ms. 266

Lady Jane Grey
National Portrait Gallery

Mary Tudor
National Portrait Gallery

Pretenders

between pages 156 and 157

Mary Queen of Scots
National Portrait Gallery

Arbella Stuart (*identification unconfirmed*)
City of Bristol Museum and Art Gallery

Duke of Monmouth
National Portrait Gallery

James II
National Portrait Gallery

James Stuart, the Old Pretender
National Portrait Gallery

Charles Edward Stuart as a young man
National Portrait Gallery

Charles Edward Stuart as an old man
National Portrait Gallery

Henry Stuart, Cardinal York
National Portrait Gallery

The author is grateful to Geoffrey Wheeler
for assistance in obtaining illustrations.

GENEALOGICAL TREES

		page
A	THE NORMANS	16
B	HOUSE OF LANCASTER	48
C	HOUSE OF YORK AND THE TUDOR CLAIM	66
D	THE TUDOR SUCCESSION	116
E	STUARTS AND HANOVERIANS	160

INTRODUCTION

THIS is a book of alternative kings and queens; a portrait gallery of losers; a record of those who failed to succeed.

Lives of kings and queens of England abound: in history as in sport the spotlight is on the winner who sits on the throne or stands on the podium. But in this re-enactment of dramas of the past, winners are relegated to secondary roles, while members of English history's supporting cast are drawn from the wings to occupy the centre of the stage.

In more than 900 years since the Norman conquest most of England's 39 sovereign lords and ladies have succeeded to the throne without dispute, although others faced challenges not easily overcome. A few of those who competed with them in vain for the crown achieved the consolation prize of lasting fame in history or legend; others suffered a traitor's death and the further indignity of burial in footnotes to the chronicles of their time. Both are to be found here.

In exploring these byways of the past a distinction should be drawn between a pretender and any candidate for a throne. To qualify as pretenders candidates must be public claimants in their own names or publicly accept the candidature thrust upon them. Royal pretenders, it should be stressed, do not pretend in the modern sense of the word. Rather, they have pretensions. They are the real or imaginary victims of usurpation. Their claim may be hollow or it may be just.

They may be impostors or they may be princes. Plausibility is the overriding qualification: it alone can attract a following and recognition.

Victory in battle is what history applauds; defeat is the unforgivable sin. But in the struggle for a crown, whatever the winner may allege and his chroniclers dutifully record, right does not always prevail. Without the means to realise them, even valid aspirations to sovereignty remain no more than pretensions. Armies are not defeated by rightful claims. Usurpers can be enthroned by force of arms. Truth and justice, no less than imposture, must submit to the supremacy of the sword.

What then does a pretender require, in addition to a plausible claim, if he is to attain success and succession? First, it must be recognised that the most famous of kings have rarely been the best or kindliest of men. In a dark age scruples and compassion can be fatal flaws in a ruler. Pretenders who are honourable and good-natured do well to abandon their claims; only the ruthless should stay in the game. Next, an army or the finance and facilities to raise and equip one is an indispensable requirement. This presupposes some measure of popularity or at least sympathy at home coupled with the backing or at least connivance of a foreign power in making resources available and providing a springboard for invasion. Other essentials include sound political advisers and experienced commanders in the field, good diplomacy, good intelligence (in the military sense), good judgment, good timing, good weather and, above all, good luck. No wonder the record of pretenders is so dismal.

Indeed it may be argued that pretenders cannot succeed. They have much in common with traitors, and just as none dare call it treason if treason prospers, so a successful pretender is known to history as a king. William, Duke of Normandy, for example, was a pretender to King Harold's realm on the eve of the battle of Hastings. The next day he was the king and has been so recognised ever since. Similarly, for thirteen days after Edward VI's death Mary Tudor was a pretender to what had become Queen Jane's realm, but she won the contest for the crown to become Queen Mary. Short-term pretenders of such a kind have been excluded from this selection, but it seemed appropriate to relieve the gloom of a roll of history's losers by the inclusion of one long-standing claimant who became a winner against the odds. The shining example of Henry Tudor serves to demonstrate that, however forbidding the prospect, there may always be some pretender clever, lucky and unscrupulous enough to surmount all obstacles to the throne.

To exclude other monarchs it has been necessary to overlook the regrettable fact that every king and sovereign queen of England for more than four and a half centuries was a pretender. A futile claim to sovereignty over a foreign country where their writ never ran was maintained with extraordinary persistence by successive kings of England styling themselves kings of France.

It was Edward III who first quartered the three French fleurs-de-lys with his three English lions (passant guardant) in staking a claim as heir general to the royal house of Capet. It was argued that although his mother Isabella, daughter of Philip IV, could not, as a woman, succeed to the French throne when her uncle Charles IV died, her right could be transmitted to her son. The claim was advanced as a tactical manoeuvre, not to be taken too seriously (Charles IV had died twelve years earlier), but it was retained for bargaining during the Hundred Years War and reinforced by Henry V's marriage to Charles VI's daughter. Their son achieved the unique distinction of being crowned in Westminster and Paris, but he never reigned as King of France and after his death the pretence became meaningless. It lingered on nonetheless until 1801, when France had ceased to be a kingdom.

As this example suggests, pretenders do not conform to a pattern. They come in many guises; which adds to their interest but defies any tidy arrangement into categories. Between them those included in this selection straddle some 800 years between the eleventh and nineteenth centuries and have little in common apart from their pretensions. Here are the eldest son passed over (Robert of Normandy), an early protagonist of women's rights (the Empress Matilda), the grandee reaching for a foreign crown (John of Gaunt), the lucky winner (Henry Tudor), the disinherited or their impersonators (Lambert Simnel and Perkin Warbeck), the child victim (Lady Jane Grey), the rival queen (Mary Queen of Scots), the eldest but illegitimate son (Monmouth) and the legitimate but rejected heirs (the Old and Young Pretenders and Cardinal York).

There are also some lesser knowns: Edgar Atheling, William Clito, Edward of Warwick, Edmund and Richard de la Pole, Arbella Stuart and those comic frauds, the Sobieski Stuarts. But, like King John, I have eliminated Arthur of Brittany, the son of his elder brother Geoffrey. Richard I willed England to John, and England, like

Normandy, accepted him: Arthur's real claim to a share of the Angevin empire was confined to Anjou, Maine and Touraine. Omitted too are Charles II's years as pretender (or king in exile) during the Commonwealth period and his contemporary unmajestic shoulderers of sovereignty, Protector Cromwell and his son Tumbledown Dick.

In today's world – republican, communist, egalitarian – the age of monarchy is almost done. Thrones have become presidential and surviving hereditary sovereigns reign without ruling. Yet such is the magic of monarchy that hopes of restoration die hard. Kings may be few, but pretenders are many. In Europe there are recognised Bourbon, Hapsburg and Romanov pretenders to the long vanished thrones of France, Austro-Hungary and Russia. There are acknowledged claimants from the houses of Savoy and Braganza to the crowns of Italy and Portugal. There are exiled kings of Greece and Afghanistan and aspiring successors to the last royal rulers of Yugoslavia, Albania and Iran. All are awaiting a turn in the tide such as occurred in England after Cromwell and after Franco in Spain.

So the following assortment of 'might-well-have-beens' – and in one case an eventual 'was' – may perhaps offer some lessons of relevance today as well as drawing a thread through one aspect of English history in offering glimpses of the past from an unusual point of view: that of the exile, the underdog or, if it is permissible to adapt a modern term, His Majesty's disloyal Opposition.

Shadows and puppets, focuses of treachery and intrigue, often the seared victims of injustice, pretenders are among the least fortunate of men and women, soured by ambition unfulfilled and rarely shown pity or mercy. Although sometimes reckless players for high stakes and, through delusions and ill judgment, their own worst enemies, they should not be despised except by those who despise failure.

PRETENDERS
TO THE
ENGLISH
THRONE

I

Duke Robert and William Clito

SOME pretenders are well known despite history's verdict that they were no more than impostors. Lambert Simnel and Perkin Warbeck are as familiar to schoolchildren and the public at large as Henry VIII and his six wives. Yet few have even heard of William the Conqueror's eldest son, Robert of Normandy, or of Robert's only legitimate son and heir, William, named the Clito (or prince).

Disowned by his father, outwitted by his younger brothers, Robert was twice passed over for the throne of England, which should have been his by right of birth. Robbed of his due fame as King Robert, he is remembered, if at all, as a hero of the first crusade and the founder of Newcastle-upon-Tyne. He died in prison and his son in exile. Neither body lies in royal state at Westminster or Windsor, but a thirteenth-century effigy of Robert is one of the glories of Gloucester cathedral, formerly the abbey church, where he was laid to rest.

In the eleventh century the Normans were the conquistadors of western Europe, fierce warriors from Scandinavia who had settled in northern France. 'The Normans are an untamed race,' confessed their chronicler, 'and unless they are held in check by a firm ruler they are all too ready to do wrong. In all communities, wherever they may be, they strive to rule and often become enemies to truth and loyalty through the ardour of their ambition. This the French and Bretons and Flemings and their other neighbours have frequently experienced; this the Italians and Lombards and Anglo-Saxons have suffered to the point of destruction.'[1]

The most prominent of the 'firm' Norman rulers of that time were William the Bastard, who conquered England, and Robert Guiscard, who made himself Duke of Apulia in southern Italy. Firmness in the case of these formidable warriors is a euphemism for ruthlessness and unspeakable cruelty in the pursuit of power. By their standards William's eldest son was unfit to rule, for it was said of him that if a weeping man was brought to him for justice he would weep with him and set him free.

The most attractive member of a grim family, Robert was a short, thickset, jolly man of great charm and courage. Cheerful, chatty and chubby-faced, he was a companionable and open-handed *bon viveur*. An evening with Robert would have been an evening agreeably spent, memorable for the conviviality and the hangover. Lazy and indulgent too, he inevitably became the black sheep of a clan renowned for energy, brutality and 'ardour of ambition'. The nicknames by which he was commonly known were *gambaron* (plump legs) and *brevis-ocrea* (short greaves), and history would have captured his nature and physique better if, instead of Robert Curthose (short stockings or breeches), it had opted for the first and passed him down to posterity as Robert Fatlegs.

He was born in or shortly before 1054. The duke his father had married above himself, for his mother, Matilda, boasted of royal blood on both sides: her father was Baldwin, Count of Flanders, a descendant of kings, and her mother the daughter of the King of France. From Matilda he inherited his shortness. She stood no more than four foot two inches high, but that proved sufficient for the production of nine children healthy enough to reach adulthood. Four of them were boys: after Robert came Richard (killed in a hunting accident), William (Rufus, the red-faced) and Henry.

At the age of nine, as a result of his father's conquest of territory long in dispute between Normandy and Anjou, Robert became Count of Maine. Three years later, just before the invasion of England, he was formally recognised as heir to Normandy. The barons swore an oath of fealty to him and during his father's absence he was associated with his mother in the regency of the duchy. Later, in accordance with the practice of the age, he became associated in the dukedom itself as his father's deputy and perhaps even as joint holder of the title.

The honour was flattering to a boy, but the Conqueror was not a man to part with real authority, however pre-occupied with his newly acquired kingdom. By his mid-twenties Robert believed himself fitted for, and entitled to, an independent role in Normandy and Maine. This was curtly refused, and after a quarrel between his followers and those of his younger brothers in which his father took sides against him, he left court to head an opposition party of disgruntled scions of the Norman nobility. An attempt to take over Rouen, the capital, was frustrated, but the dissidents were soon joined by other enemies of his father, not only from within the duchy, but also from the neighbouring hostile territories of France, Brittany and Anjou.

With the connivance of Philip I, King of France, Robert's rebel force established itself in the French castle of Gerberoi, near Beauvais, on the border between France and Normandy. But when the Conqueror angrily demanded his overlord's assistance in suppressing the rebellion, the French king weakly complied and they laid siege to the castle together.

The campaign lasted for three weeks during the Christmas of 1078. It ended when the beleaguered broke out and won a pitched battle outside the castle walls. In the fighting the Conqueror was wounded in the arm and unhorsed – by Robert himself, according to one report. The wound was to heal, but never the humiliation. Gerberoi was among the worst defeats inflicted on the proud duke who had made himself a king, and he is said to have cursed his son on the spot and vowed to disinherit him.

Immediately, however, he was forced to negotiate. The pope and the King of France intervened to make peace. The Norman barons and bishops acted as mediators to effect a reconciliation. In 1080 Robert was confirmed as heir to Normandy (but not to England) and in return agreed to aid his father by leading an army against the Scots, who had invaded Northumbria. Malcolm, the Scottish King, was compelled to accept terms which acknowledged that his kingdom was subject to William's, and halting beside the Tyne on his return Robert gave orders for the construction of a new castle as a protection against further raids from across the border.

Father and son then crossed to Normandy and joined forces to recover Robert's county of Maine from the Count of Anjou. Their apparent amity continued until 1083 when Robert's name inexplicably disappears from the Norman records and he is reported to be wandering in exile through France, Germany and Italy. He had always been on affectionate terms with his mother, and it may be her

A. THE NORMANS

This is a simplified genealogical tree. It includes all William the Conqueror's legitimate sons and their legitimate children, but omits members of the family not relevant to Chapters 1 and 2.

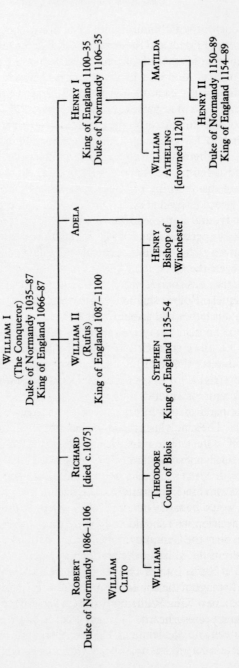

WILLIAM I
(The Conqueror)
Duke of Normandy 1035–87
King of England 1066–87

ROBERT
Duke of Normandy 1086–1106

WILLIAM
CLITO

RICHARD
[died c.1075]

WILLIAM II
(Rufus)
King of England 1087–1100

ADELA

THEODORE
Count of Blois

STEPHEN
King of England 1135–54

HENRY
Bishop of
Winchester

WILLIAM

HENRY I
King of England 1100–35
Duke of Normandy 1106–35

WILLIAM
ATHELING
[drowned 1120]

MATILDA

HENRY II
Duke of Normandy 1150–89
King of England 1154–89

death which brought family unity to an abrupt close. This time the breach never healed, and Robert was still abroad four years later when the Conqueror fell mortally wounded while burning to the ground the French town of Mantes, which had incurred his displeasure.

He was carried back to Rouen to die, but Robert, unwanted or unwanting, did not hasten to his bedside. If custom had been observed, the Conquerer's lands and possessions would have passed undivided to his eldest son, but the absent heir had never been forgiven: Gerberoi was to cost him England.

Indeed it fell to the Archbishop of Rouen to dissuade the dying king from disinheriting his eldest son entirely: had the barons not already sworn fealty and paid homage to Robert as the next Duke of Normandy, and at the king's own command? How, the archbishop argued more persuasively, could he administer last rites until the king had forgiven all his enemies, including his eldest son? Faced with this threat, even the Conqueror's normally inflexible will crumbled. A compromise was found, based on a distinction between patrimony and conquest. Robert should have what his father had inherited, but not what his father had acquired.

'I name no man as my heir to the kingdom of England; instead I entrust it to the eternal Creator to whom I belong and in whose hand are all things. For I did not come to possess such a dignity by hereditary right.'[2] These are the words of a chronicler put into the dying Conqueror's mouth. If he did indeed utter this pious sentiment, then the hand of the Almighty was quickly steered in the desired direction. The king's last act was to bequeath the realm of England, its sword of state and jewel-studded sceptre, to William Rufus, his second surviving son. Along with the sword and sceptre, Rufus was armed with a letter to Lanfranc, the Archbishop of Canterbury, and supplied with money and an escort to ensure that by the time his father died he would be safely out of his elder brother's reach.

The decision who should be king then rested with Lanfranc, who chose to obey the Conqueror's dying wish. The coronation ceremony in Westminster abbey on 26 September 1087 included a formal election of Rufus by church and people, his anointing with holy oil, and the homage of the nobility. England had solemnly and in due form accepted a new King William before Robert and his supporters could make their protests heard.

At Rouen, no sooner had the last breath left his body than the Conqueror's corpse was abandoned by his councillors and household as they scrambled for loot and rode away to secure their positions. It was Robert, returning too late, who ordered that his father's last wishes be honoured, in gifts of charity to the poor and the church and in the release of prisoners, to ease the passage of his soul through purgatory. It was Robert who arranged for the burial of the old King William with due honour and piety in his abbey at Caen, while the new one was consolidating his hold on England.

The new king was strong-willed and violent like his father. If permitted time for deliberation and a free choice, the Norman barons would almost certainly have expressed a preference for Robert, the easy-going and pliable. It was important to them, too, that whoever was duke should be king. The separation of England from Normandy left those with estates on both sides of the Channel owing a double allegiance. How could they remain loyal to both Robert and William?

The most powerful and turbulent of the barons was the Conqueror's half-brother, Odo, Bishop of Bayeux, who had fought at Hastings with a mace because men of God were forbidden to carry swords. For this secular activity he had been appropriately rewarded with the earldom of Kent, but had then developed ambitions to lead a Norman army to Rome and have himself made pope. A four-year stretch in captivity was the outcome, and he was the most eminent of the Conqueror's prisoners whom Robert set free. Appointing himself kingmaker, he sailed at once for England to plot Rufus's downfall and re-unite Normandy and England under Robert.

In Normandy an era of harsh government and ducal terror had ended. The Conqueror's guards were expelled from baronial castles, and private wars between rival magnates erupted unrestrained across the length and breadth of the duchy. Chaos and anarchy prevailed, and the incapacity of the affable Robert to rule the unruly was disastrously exposed. Under Duke William 'no man dared do anything against his will'[3] and, despite his cruelty to some, by others he was remembered as a lion of justice, a pillar of law and order, a protector of the weak against the strong. Under the new duke pillage and rape went unpunished, for 'all men knew that Duke Robert was weak and indolent, therefore trouble-makers despised him and stirred up loathsome factions when and where they chose'.[4] Robber bands, unlicenced castles, adultery, sodomy – according to the record of an unfriendly monastic chronicler every evil and vice was encouraged by the inertia, incompetence and licentiousness of 'the sleepy duke'. 'The earth was watered with the blood of many men',[5] and the

Conqueror had been right to predict that 'any province subjected to his rule will be most wretched'.[6]

However that may be – and parti-pris monks moralising in their cells some years after the event are not the most reliable of witnesses – in England a full-scale rebellion broke out on Robert's behalf in the spring and summer of 1088. Odo, the bishop earl, and his companions among the Anglo-Norman baronage had spent the Christmas of 1087 bargaining with Rufus. Among them was a trio as frightening as Odo himself: his brother, Robert of Mortain; Roger of Montgomery, Earl of Shrewsbury; and Geoffrey, Bishop of Coutances. Finding William a much tougher proposition than Robert, they had left dissatisfied to assert their interests and Robert's by force. They seized the channel ports in his name, and even the Tower of London itself. Once kindled, the flame of insurgency enveloped the country from Kent and Sussex to the Welsh marches, from the East Midlands and East Anglia to the north, where the princely Bishop of Durham became the torch-bearer.

All that was missing was Robert himself, whose endeavours to assemble an invasion force were hampered by lack of funds. For a second time William's presence and Robert's absence decided the issue. William moved with speed and determination to extinguish the flames and isolate Odo, until only the south-east remained in arms against the royal army. Soon the bishop was reduced to holding out in his castles at Tonbridge, Pevensey and Rochester. An inadequate force from Normandy sent to relieve Pevensey was destroyed at sea, and one by one the castles fell.

When the fighting ended in July Robert had still not put to sea. Although eager for the crown of England, of which he felt defrauded, mounting an expedition had proved beyond his resources. His treasure squandered, he had failed through mismanagement – and not even made the gesture of coming to claim his kingdom with what men he could muster, however few. His rival, on the other hand, had won new respect as a man of decisive action. To the English he had shown himself as their own king defying the threat of another Norman invasion. His master-stroke was to win over the beaten but still powerful rebels by treating them with a rare leniency.

Not only had Robert botched his chance of England. Conditions in Normandy and Maine, where the administration and law courts ceased to function, had plumbed such depths that William's aid was urgently solicited and he was able to take his revenge by launching a counter-invasion. Most barons and churchmen still believed that a united Anglo-Norman kingdom would serve their interests best, but their choice now fell on William, and he, far from impoverished like his brother, used the riches of England to sweeten their preference with bribery. In 1090 Robert was hard pressed to defend Rouen itself against an assault by his brother, and in the following year William returned with an even greater force.

This time there was no fighting. An agreed settlement suited all parties; so a treaty was negotiated to regularise relations between the brothers and their realms. As the weaker character in the weaker position Robert was obliged to concede his right to the English crown, but not irrevocably. The two rulers became, in effect, each other's heirs presumptive. Both were bachelors, but while Robert fathered bastards, the bisexual William preferred male company. Thus if Robert could outlive his brother England was likely to be his in the end. Meanwhile the brothers would be each other's vassals – an arrangement which enabled William to retain a large part of Normandy which he had overrun and the barons to hold land in both countries whichever brother they supported.

Under the terms of the treaty William was to assist Robert in pacifying Normandy and Maine and re-establishing his ducal authority, while Robert was to assist William, as he had assisted their father, in bringing Scotland to heel. After William had honoured his side of the bargain in Normandy (although not in Maine), the brothers crossed to England together and Robert travelled north for a second time to threaten King Malcolm into an act of submission.

As a mediator in his negotiations he had an ally in Malcolm's brother-in-law. This was Edgar Atheling (a grandson of Edmund Ironside), who qualified as the Saxon pretender to the English throne if he ever thought fit to make a claim. As Edward the Confessor's true heir and the choice of the thanes after Harold's death at Hastings, he had twice had to take refuge in Scotland, once from the Conqueror and once from Rufus. With Robert, whom he seems to have re-sembled in indolence and bonhomie, he struck up a lasting friendship. After settling their business in Scotland peacefully and before return-ing to Normandy together they spent a Christmas holiday at the English court, when it is safe to assume that a good time was had by all. William Rufus may have been a forceful ruler and dangerous antagonist, but he was not the ogre often portrayed. He is likely to have entertained hospitably and proved himself as boisterous a drinking companion as his guests.

Fifteen months later the crown of England almost fell into Robert's lap. Stomach disorder laid William low in Gloucester and he was rumoured to be dead. In fact, he was so near death's door that his iron resolve melted and he allowed himself to be persuaded that the salvation of his soul depended upon filling the archishopric of Canterbury which had scandalously been left vacant for nearly four years since Lanfranc's death. Most reluctantly he consented to the election of Anselm, who most reluctantly accepted, and they both lived to rue the day.

Later the same year (1093) Robert, with good reason, sent his brother a formal defiance, charging him with faithlessness and perjury in breaching the terms of their agreement. William responded in true Norman fashion with another invasion (*from* Hastings). Fresh negotiations ensued and arbitrators were appointed, but when they found in Robert's favour William, again in true Norman fashion, denounced the treaty. Sending to England for reinforcements and rallying his dependants in Normandy, he looted and devastated large areas of the duchy. The Count of Flanders moved in for a share of the pickings, and Robert was only rescued by the intervention of his overlord, the King of France, alarmed at the prospect of Normandy being repossessed by the King of England. A still uncertain issue was resolved by William's enforced departure to deal with troubles nearer home. Robert had Wales, Scotland and the tiresome Anselm to thank for unwittingly helping him save his duchy.

Eight years after his father's death he was precariously a duke and, with William in rude health and riding high, further than ever from becoming a king. So when on 27 November 1095 Pope Urban II preached his historic sermon at Clermont enjoining Christians to make war on the heathen instead of each other, it fell on ready ears in Normandy. When the first crusade was launched Robert decided to abandon his ungovernable duchy and his futile attempts on England and follow Peter the Hermit to Constantinople. Adventuring in the east was tempting, and its rewards included the forgiveness of all his sins, which may well have been considerable.

As usual, his problem was financial. Normandy was no longer a country in which it was possible to collect taxes. In England, however, the treasury was well stocked and William, although burdened with the most heinous of sins, had higher priorities than rescuing

Jerusalem from the infidel. A mutually satisfactory arrangement was negotiated through the medium of a papal envoy. William made his contribution to the Christian cause by agreeing to finance a crusader army for Robert. All he asked in exchange was Normandy.

The money came as a loan, not a gift, and the duchy was not to be surrendered permanently, only mortgaged for five years during the duke's absence. But few can have believed that Robert would return safely from the Holy Land with the ten thousand marks necessary to redeem his pledge. William brought the money over in person, shipping 67 barrels of silver coin, each containing £100, and paying the whole sum out in hard cash in Rouen. Robert then left with his followers and William took immediate possession of the duchy, where most of the barons chose to remain to keep a close eye on their property and a wary one on their new lord.

Bishop Odo, Edgar Atheling, the Duke of Brittany and the counts of Flanders, Boulogne, Aumale and Blois were among Robert's noble company. They marched in splendour through France and Switzerland and over the Great St Bernard pass into Italy, where the holy sites of Lucca and Monte Cassino were visited en route for the southern port of Bari. There they fortunately arrived too late to embark before the onset of winter and Robert enjoyed a convivial and extended Christmas holiday with the Norman Duke of Apulia. The short crossing of the Adriatic to Salonika was safely accomplished in March. In Constantinople he was royally welcomed and entertained by the Emperor Alexius II.

The first crusade was dogged by quarrels between the rival Christian leaders, among whom Bohemond, Prince of Taranto and Raymond, Count of Toulouse established themselves as joint supreme commanders with Robert staking a claim to third place in the hierarchy. A Turkish army was routed at Dorylaeum, where the duke's valour turned the tide of the battle, and after a slow march across Asia Minor for three and a half months it was Robert who led the vanguard in the advance on the beckoning prize of Antioch. But the defences seemed impregnable and, when it looked as though the besiegers were more likely to perish from starvation than the besieged, Robert withdrew to more comfortable and better provisioned quarters beside the sea at Laodicea, offering the excuse that he was protecting the inhabitants from Saracen marauders. Robert never flinched from danger, but discomfort was to be avoided. It took a threat of excommunication to get him back to the siege at Antioch.

Thereafter all was glory. The city fell through bribery, and Robert was one of the battle commanders whose army defeated an enemy relief force. He was one of the few to press on to Jerusalem itself and take a leading part in the victorious assault, not to mention the ensuing slaughter and pillage. He was prominent in the triumph at Ascalon over a Saracen army from Egypt, killing the emir's standard-bearer with his own hand. Legend even has it that, as a reward for his services, he was the first to be offered the crown of Jerusalem and only after his refusal was it given to Godfrey, Duke of Bouillon. By spurning this gift from God, the chronicles alleged, Robert brought on his own head the sorrows to come: a man who had rejected the honour of becoming King of Jerusalem had thereby forfeited any claim to another kingdom. It is a curious argument and the story is not supported by any reliable historical evidence.

Characteristically Robert was in no hurry to get home. He returned to Constantinople to sample more of the emperor's hospitality and accept tokens of his gratitude. Then he called again on his kinsmen in Sicily and southern Italy where, at the age of 47, he married at last. His bride Sibyl, daughter of Geoffrey of Conversano, lord of Brindisi, is said to have been young and pure and pretty. Their union cemented an alliance between the Italo-Norman barons and the duke of their homeland. Sibyl's dowry would provide him with the means to recover the duchy, and Sibyl herself would provide him with an heir.

A homecoming which stretched to twelve months proved too long by a few weeks. While Robert was still travelling north with his newly wed wife the judgment of God fell without warning on the impious William, who died impenitent and unshriven. During a hunt in the New Forest at Lammastide (2 August 1100) an arrow which should have brought down a deer struck the king. Mortally wounded in the chest, he expired where he fell, the third member of the family to die from a hunting accident in the same forest. Richard, the brother between Robert and William, had been crushed against a tree while chasing a deer, and only three months before William's death another Richard, a bastard son of Robert, had been killed accidentally by another huntsman's arrow. On that occasion, to avoid reprisal and expiate his sin, the archer had taken refuge in Lewes priory and become a monk. In William's case the bowman was Walter Tirell, Count of Poix, and he fled straight home to France.

Since they were so common, this is usually presumed to have been a hunting accident. Yet a repetition in August of what had occurred in

May, when combined with the timeliness of William's death in once more cheating Robert of the crown, must arouse suspicion of a plot and foul play. The man who seized the crown in his stead was a member of the hunting party, and so were some of his closest friends. They left the king's body lying on the ground to ride immediately to Winchester and take possession of the royal treasury.

Henry, who now became King Henry I, was the youngest and cleverest of the sons of the Conqueror; also the cruellest and least trustworthy. To his dying father he had complained about the division of Normandy and England between his elder brothers to his own exclusion, and the Conqueror had ordered him to be given £5,000 in silver. This he used to buy himself a lordship in the Cotentin from a complaisant Robert, while claiming from William estates which had belonged to their mother. In the disputes between his brothers he sided mostly, but not invariably, with William, who had more to offer. However, the parts of Normandy ceded to William under the treaty of 1091 included Cherbourg and Mont St Michel, which belonged to Henry, and the elder brothers had had to combine forces to besiege him in Mont St Michel and compel him to accept the terms of their agreement. It was typical of Robert's irresponsible chivalry that when Henry and his garrison were in danger of dying of thirst he allowed a party through the lines to replenish their water supply. Nothing could illustrate better than this act of graciousness why the quixotic Robert – a man who refused to go to any lengths to achieve an objective – remained a pretender and never became a king.

At the treasury at Winchester on the day of William's death there was a tense debate over the succession. The treasurer, William of Breteuil, an old friend of Robert, bluntly reminded the company that all present, including himself and Henry, had done homage to Robert and promised him fealty. Was the duke not the Conqueror's eldest son and a hero of christendom? Robert, he declared (in the chronicler's words), 'has toiled for years in the service of God, and now God restores to him without strife of battle both his own duchy, which he left as a crusader for Christ's sake, and his father's crown.'[7]

In reply Henry drew his sword. In justification of his claim he argued, first, that he was English (born at Selby in Yorkshire) and Robert a foreigner (born in Normandy). Secondly, he asserted the superiority of porphyrogeniture over primogeniture. Being born in the purple was a Byzantine concept barely recognised in the west, but it suited Henry's circumstances: he alone of the brothers had been born the son of a king. It can hardly be doubted that the sword, not the argument, carried the day.

After securing the treasure Henry's next step was to obtain the assent of council and church. Again the barons and prelates would probably have chosen Robert if he had been in England, but in his again crucial absence – whereabouts uncertain – only one candidate presented himself. Henry was to prove a skilful politician and a guileful diplomat, a thoughtful administrator and a ruthless exponent of the use of force. At this critical moment he demonstrated his ability by not putting a foot wrong.

William's disagreements with the church had left the clergy depleted. In default of archbishops (Canterbury banished and York vacant) the council agreed to a coronation by the Bishop of London. Henry responded by inviting Anselm to return and at once filling the numerous vacant sees and abbacies. He arrested and imprisoned William's unpopular chief minister, Ranulf Flambard, Bishop of Durham, and swore to put an end to the abuses and injustices perpetrated during his brother's reign. He issued a Charter of Liberties and bolstered his *bona fides* as an Englishman by marriage to a Saxon princess of the old blood royal (much as Henry Tudor was later to seek legitimacy in a union with Elizabeth of York). All this was a small price to pay for successful usurpation: promises could later be broken with impunity.

Although William's premature death had cost Robert another royal opportunity, it had in compensation given him back his duchy, which it is doubtful if William ever intended to relinquish. The heroic captor of Jerusalem received a rapturous welcome home, and soon half the Norman barons in England who had taken oaths of allegiance to Henry were plotting to replace him with the more congenial and amenable duke. The pattern of events which had followed William Rufus's accession thirteen years earlier was to be repeated, but this time a lucky addition to his following gave Robert a better chance. In February 1101 William's gifted minister Flambard escaped from the Tower of London to Normandy and offered Robert his services in organising an invasion. Under Flambard's direction there was no repetition of financial or organisational inefficiency and 'no small multitude of knights, archers and foot soldiers'[8] were soon assembled.

The army, which had been expected at Pevensey, landed un-opposed at Portsmouth and marched on Winchester. Henry hastened from London to intercept it and a confrontation took place at Alton. Robert's army was the larger but, as usual, the interests of influential barons on both sides demanded a negotiated settlement. The two brothers and their supporters parleyed and Robert foolishly allowed himself to be talked out of a battle. The barons who had determined to exchange a cruel regime for a mild one were persuaded that Henry would mend his ways, and by failing to press home his advantage Robert, ill advised (not least perhaps by the adroit Flambard, anxious to be pardoned and retrieve his rich prince-bishopric), threw away the crown which was at last within his grasp.

Under the treaty of Alton he formally surrendered his claim to England and recognised Henry as king in exchange for some almost worthless promises. Henry bound himself to pay his brother an annual subsidy of 3000 marks of silver, to give up all his estates in Normandy (except the castle of Domfront), to assist in the recovery of Maine from the Count of Anjou, and to grant a free pardon to all Robert's friends and allies in England who had deserted Henry but would now return to their former allegiance. The pact was sealed, and Robert spent several months making merry in England as Henry's guest.

He had, of course, been deceived. The strange notion of keeping his word probably never so much as entered Henry's head. Once Robert was back in Normandy and his army dispersed, the disloyal barons to whom Henry had promised an amnesty were fined, dispossessed and exiled. The earls of Surrey and Shrewsbury and other magnates of immense wealth and power were rewarded for not fighting Henry at Alton by being declared outlaws. They fled to Normandy, which under Robert's continuingly feckless rule had once more relapsed into anarchy, and there they found their fellow barons looking wistfully in the direction of England where those who had not offended Henry were enjoying the benefits of law and order, albeit hard-fisted.

Chroniclers and historians favour strong rulers. Those of the twelfth century make light of Henry's faithlessness, barbarous cruelty and dissolute private life, reserving their moral strictures for the unfortunate Robert, who is said now to have 'sunk beyond redemption in indolence and voluptuousness, which made him an object of contempt'.[9] Henry refused to honour his obligation to help him recover Maine, and when Robert incautiously paid another fraternal visit to England he was not permitted to leave before agreeing to forgo his annuity. Then 'King Henry crossed to Normandy and laid claim to the heritage of his fathers, which was being trodden under foot by traitors and brigands and rascals'.[10]

Henry's first invasion of Normandy deprived Robert of most of the duchy. Bayeux was sacked and Caen surrendered without resistance. Incapable of putting an army into the field, the duke was forced into the humiliation of following his younger brother to England to beg for the return of his inheritance. Henry's predictable reply was a second invasion to finish the job. Another confrontation between the brothers' opposing armies took place at Tinchebrai, and this time, since Henry had the advantage of numbers, the terms for an agreement were pitched too high for acceptance. Robert had already conceded England. He must now surrender Normandy, in return for a pension equivalent to half its revenues (payable, it must be presumed, at Henry's discretion).

Robert chose to go down fighting. The battle of Tinchebrai which reunited England and Normandy under Henry lasted less than an hour (on 29 September 1106). Already diplomatically outmanoeuvred, Robert fought without allies and his small army was quickly overwhelmed by Henry's, which had been reinforced by contingents from Maine and Brittany. With the duke a prisoner, Rouen and Falaise capitulated to the king and all Normandy made its peace with the new conqueror. Worsted by his younger brothers in a contest which lasted for nearly twenty years, Robert had suffered his final débâcle. 'For fear that dissidents might molest simple and peaceful folk under pretext of helping' him, the hostile chronicler recorded, Henry 'sent him to England and kept him for 27 years in prison, providing him liberally with every comfort'.[11]

The liberal provision of every comfort may be doubted. The fallen duke and royal pretender was held in custody first at Wareham and then in the Bishop of Salisbury's castle at Devizes. Later he was transferred into the safe custody of one of Henry's illegitimate sons, Robert of Gloucester, who kept him prisoner in his castles at Bristol and Cardiff. In Cardiff, where he was to end his days, he composed a poetic lamentation in Welsh, one line of which runs in translation: 'Woe to him that is not old enough to die'.

By the conventions of the age Robert's incarceration was improper, although not without precedent (Alfonso VI of Spain had imprisoned his elder brother Garcia for life – a 17-year stretch). The pope pleaded for the crusader's release, but in vain. By never using the title of duke himself, Henry implicitly conceded that he had unjustly deprived his brother of his rightful inheritance of Normandy, whatever the rights and wrongs over England. But lest his conscience were troublesome, there were those to reassure him that the union was God's will. One chronicler dubbed him *Rex Normanglorum*, for the vested interests of the barons since the Conquest had made England and Normandy inseparable. By failing to gain the first, Robert had inescapably lost the second.

Sympathy for Robert of Normandy as an honourable and at times romantic might-have-been of English history must be tempered by the acknowledgement that most of his misfortunes were of his own making and by serious misgiving for the condition of England had he become its king. No such qualifications apply to his son, William Clito, the shadowiest of pretenders, of whom little is known.

On the surrender of Falaise Henry committed one of his rare errors of judgment. The child heir to Normandy was discovered in the castle. Sibyl, his mother, had died, and Henry placed him in the care of Helias of Saint-Saens, Count of Arques, whose wife was one of Robert's illegitimate daughters. When later he realised his mistake and sent for the boy to be taken into his own custody, William was snatched from his bed by his half-sister and carried off on horseback into the night while the king's messengers were kept waiting below.

The rest of his life was spent eluding capture, as Helias escorted him through the courts of Europe. Louis VI of France and the dukes of Brittany, Burgundy and Poitou were in turn solicited on behalf of the disinherited refugee who was the only legitimate son of the eldest son of the conqueror of England. Fulk, Count of Anjou betrothed his daughter to him and granted him the disputed county of Maine. He became a rallying point for all who kept faith with his father and all who were ill-treated by Henry.

In 1117, when he was fifteen, Louis (the Fat), Fulk of Anjou and Baldwin, Count of Flanders formed an alliance to drive Henry out of Normandy and establish William as duke. Many of the Normans rose in support, but Henry won a decisive victory against an invading French army at Brémule. Despite this setback Louis persisted. He pleaded the Clito's cause at a papal council in Rheims, and Pope Calixtus consented to go to Normandy and negotiate in person with Henry for the restoration of the duchy to Duke Robert and his son.

But Calixtus was no more a match for Henry than Robert had been. The king represented himself as the saviour of Normandy from chaos and as a benign uncle with the kindliest of intentions towards his nephew, who had (so he said) the offer of three counties in England. Henry was a persuasive talker and his arguments are reported to have been 'well seasoned with gifts'.[12] The young William received no further papal support, and later, at Henry's urging, his marriage to the Count of Anjou's daughter was annulled by the pope on grounds of consanguinity.

In 1120 the drowning of Henry's only legitimate son, William Atheling, brought William Clito close to the English throne. If his father's renunciation at Alton was upheld, the Clito had become heir presumptive to the crown. Loss of his Angevin wife was more than balanced by marriage to a half-sister of the French queen and the grant of large estates in France on the borders of Normandy. From there he rode into the duchy to defy Henry and lay a formal claim to possession.

It was an empty gesture. After a further defeat, at Gisors, Louis had been forced to recognise Henry as Duke of Normandy. The marriage of his daughter to Henry's son had detached the Count of Anjou from the Clito's cause. Henry's daughter was married to the emperor, and the pope, already in Henry's pocket, was chary of offending imperial interests. This diplomatic isolation was reflected within Normandy, where Henry's men were firmly in control and dissident barons lay under threat of the seizure of their estates in England. Most decisive of all was the hard fact that the King of England had the resources of a wealthy realm at his command while his nephew was a penniless dependant existing on the good will of France.

After the fruitless foray into Normandy, however, Louis compensated him with a county at his disposal. Nominated as Count of Flanders, the Clito at last enjoyed a power base from which to make good his claim – first to Normandy and then, when Henry died, to England itself. Unhappily his brightening prospects were short-lived. A wound inflicted during a siege at Aalst, where he was engaged in putting down an insurrection, turned gangrenous. On 27 July 1128 this would-be King of England died and was buried in St Omer without ever seeing the realm which should rightly have become his on the death of his father.

Robert himself lived on to the vast age of eighty or thereabouts, dying on 3 February 1134, a prisoner still. Other eldest sons of English kings were never to be crowned, but (with the exception of Edward VIII, who abdicated before his coronation) always because they predeceased their fathers: the Tudor prince Arthur, who might have made a worthier monarch than his younger brother, Henry VIII; the most talented of the Stuarts, Prince Henry, who would certainly have made a better job of kingship than the unfortunate Charles I; and the Victorian Duke of Clarence (elder brother of George V) whose early demise may have been a blessing. Robert of Normandy, after 800 years, still suffers the unique distinction of being deprived of the crown, not by death, but by younger brothers.

It was the ultimate triumph of Henry the throne-snatcher to outlive both Robert and Robert's son. He died on 1 December 1135 and was buried with royal honour in Reading abbey, which he had founded. The struggle for the succession to his crown was to be the most bitterly contested in English history.

2

Empress Matilda, Lady of England

AMONG English monarchs Henry I takes the prize for marital infidelity. The number of his illegitimate children established a record never surpassed, more than twenty being publicly acknowledged. In the marriage bed, however, he was not prolific. His Saxon wife, Edith re-named Matilda, gave him three children: one who died in infancy, then Matilda and William.

William's early death was a tragedy. Before sailing from Barfleur in Normandy for England in December 1120 he ordered the dispensing of liberal quantities of liquor to sustain passengers and crew in good spirits during the winter passage. The crew became so fuddled that, on leaving harbour at dusk, the ship hit a rock and sank in the darkness with the loss of the heir to the throne and all aboard, except for a butcher from Rouen who swam ashore to tell the tale. After the wreck of the White Ship Henry, it is said, never smiled again. His first queen had died and his second marriage, to the beautiful Adelisa of Louvain, proved childless.

Matilda (or Maud), Henry's remaining legitimate child, has the distinction of being the only empress in English history before the assumption of the title of Empress of India by Queen Victoria seven and a half centuries later. She had been born in 1102 to a father who was brutal even by Norman standards and a mother who was the daughter of a saint (Margaret of Scotland) and saintly herself. The Conqueror had chopped limbs off rebels; Henry put eyes out, even

31

blinding two of his own grand-daughters held as innocent hostages. Queen Edith/Matilda (descended from fourteen generations of Saxon kings) wore a hair shirt during Lent, kissed the sores of beggars and embraced lepers.

While still at nursery school in Wilton nunnery, the young Matilda was betrothed to the Holy Roman Emperor Henry V, overlord of most of the kingdoms, duchies and counties of central Europe between France and Russia. At the age of seven she was despatched to Germany, responsibility for her upbringing and education (Latin, theology, sewing and embroidery) formally passing out of the hands of Anselm, Archbishop of Canterbury into those of the Archbishop of Trier. Her enormous dowry necessitated a special levy of three shillings on every hide of land in England. Four years later, in June 1114, she was married in the presence of five archbishops and thirty bishops. It was enough to turn the head of any twelve-year-old.

Unfortunately her husband's character was no better than her father's. His father, Henry IV, was the emperor who quarrelled with Pope Gregory VII over the lay investiture of bishops and abbots and died excommunicated after his humiliation at Canossa. Matilda's Henry, in an unfilial act of treachery, had imprisoned his father and seized his crown, posing as a champion of the church. After quarrelling with the pope and being excommunicated himself, he set matters straight by marching on Rome, kidnapping the holy father and keeping him prisoner until he had agreed terms. These included crowning Henry as emperor in St Peter's.

What Matilda thought about all this is unrecorded. Husband and wife were not much together. In 1116 he took her with him to Venice, where they stayed with the doge, but when he returned to Germany she remained in Italy as his viceroy. When he died in 1125 she was still only twenty-two and childless. In Germany her reputation was for 'prudent and gracious behaviour',[1] not in evidence later, and she may well have wished to continue living there in state as empress dowager.

This her still marriageable state did not permit, and her father had more ambitious plans for her. He summoned her to England to be recognised as his heir. On Christmas day 1126 the royal council was ordered to swear allegiance to her as his successor to the crown. All the magnates of the realm knelt to her: the Archbishop of Canterbury at the head of the bishops and abbots, followed by David, King of Scotland (her uncle), Stephen, Count of Mortain and Boulogne (her cousin), Robert, Earl of Gloucester (her half-brother) and the rest of the barons. It was an established custom for an ageing king to secure the succession for his son by this means, but not a normal procedure in the case of a daughter. There were no queens regnant in the twelfth century.

If this ceremony flattered Matilda, her father's next move outraged her and was to become a serious obstacle to the achievement of the crown which he was determined she should wear. An alliance with Normandy's disagreeable neighbour and hereditary enemy, the Count of Anjou, had become essential to the security of the duchy and Matilda was summarily bundled off to Rouen to be betrothed to his son. In Normandy the Angevins were despised and feared as barbarians who ate their meat raw and killed priests. The empress was now to be degraded to become daughter-in-law of their count. The woman of twenty-five was to be mated with a boy of thirteen. She stormed and had to be locked up. Matilda was obstinate, but Henry as inflexible as his father.

She married Geoffrey Plantagenet in Le Mans in 1128 and left him after a year to live by herself in Rouen. Later they were reunited and she bore him three sons, but they disliked each other and seldom lived together. After this second marriage Matilda's character grew more abrasive, as though soured by disparagement. Geoffrey was good-looking, intelligent and as well educated as herself, but descent from the imperial heights had been too abrupt. She waited impatiently for the reward of England and real power.

On Henry's death two strong rivals emerged. Robert of Gloucester and Stephen of Mortain and Boulogne were outstandingly the two largest landowners in England after the crown. There had been a dispute over which should have precedence in taking the oath of allegiance to Matilda. Both had been favourites of Henry and elevated by him to become leaders of his 'new men' who had been granted the estates of 'the disinherited', the supporters of Duke Robert and his son. In his anxiety to meet the threat from William Clito, Henry had put the means of dispossessing his daughter into other hands.

To his beloved bastard Robert he bequeathed a fortune of £60,000, twelve times his own legacy from his father, and Robert was already extravagantly well endowed. Through his marriage to the previous Earl of Gloucester's daughter he had become more powerful than the king in the west of the country. His royal blood and reputation for honesty made him a popular choice among the other 'new men', but as a man of honour he was reluctant to break his oath and put himself forward as a candidate for the crown, 'saying it was fairer to yield it to his sister's son, to whom it more justly belonged'.[2] This was the infant Henry Plantagenet, favoured by others who believed that, although a right could not be exercised by a woman, it could pass through her to a male heir. A lot of bloodshed would have been saved if acceptance of this argument and Henry as king had not been delayed for eighteen years, but his claim suffered from the same drawback as his mother's: the Angevin connection. If Matilda were to become Queen of England and Duchess of Normandy, Geoffrey of Anjou would become king and duke. If the infant Henry were to become king in name, Geoffrey would be king in fact.

The claim of the other competitor, Stephen, also came through his mother: Adela, a daughter of the Conqueror. Like Matilda, she is described by a contemporary chronicler as a 'virago': if she had borne arms, he reported, she would have equalled her father in valour. Instead she showed her mettle in family affairs. When her husband, Stephen, Count of Blois and Chartres, returned to Europe in disgrace after deserting his army at the siege of Antioch she sent him straight back to redeem his honour. This he obediently did, losing his life in the battle at Ramlah. She then arranged the succession to Blois by passing over her eldest son, William, in favour of the second, Theodore. Whether William was physically deformed, simple-minded or just not his mother's favourite is not known, but his supersession is another illustration of the practice of the period in striking a balance between hereditary and elective principles of succession. A member of the family customarily succeeded, but not invariably the eldest son or the most direct heir if considered unsuitable.

As a grandson Count Theodore was in line for the Conqueror's kingdom and duchy, and his candidature was backed by the barons in Normandy, with whom he shared a common interest in blocking a take-over from Anjou. But, perhaps at the insistence of his mother, he surrendered the claim to make way for his younger brother, Stephen (who paid him for his forbearance with a generous pension). For Theodore it was a better deal than becoming embroiled in the cauldron of Anglo-Norman politics.

Reputed to be the handsomest man in Europe, Stephen had great charm and impeccable manners. His mother had sent him as a boy to England, where he had charmed his uncle Henry, who had showered him with forfeited estates. He received the honours of Lancaster and Eye and, in Normandy, the county of Mortain. Henry arranged, too, for his marriage to the heiress of Boulogne, who also held large estates in England which became Stephen's. By the time of the king's death his nephew was lord of half a million English acres in addition to his counties overseas.

On learning the news he acted with the same turn of speed as William Rufus and Henry had shown in similar circumstances. While Matilda stayed in Normandy, handicapped by pregnancy, Stephen sailed immediately from Wissant, the port of Boulogne. The towns of Dover and Canterbury, which were in the hands of Robert of Gloucester's men, denied him entry, but London received him. With no Calais, Dunkirk or Ostend yet in being, the Count of Boulogne controlled the main continental port of entry for English wool and cloth en route to the Flemish market. There were sound commercial reasons for the city of London's support for a man who could sever a vital trading artery.

The youngest of the Blois brothers, Henry, was already in England enjoying a splendid plurality as not only Abbot of Glastonbury but also Bishop of Winchester – a see reputed at one time in the middle ages to be the richest in christendom after Rome itself. (A later bishop was to spurn preferment to Canterbury because its income was too low for his standard of living.) Bishop Henry's aid was crucial to Stephen in preventing Matilda's succession. He hurried on to Winchester to enlist it and take possession of the treasury, so that when the royal council met it was faced with a *fait accompli*.

To the Archbishop of Canterbury's announcement that they would all be committing perjury if they broke their oaths to crown Matilda, Bishop Henry replied that an oath taken under duress was not binding. He was supported by Roger, Bishop of Salisbury, King Henry's justiciar or chief minister, who argued that Matilda's marriage to a foreigner without the consent of the council also invalidated the oath. Hugh Bigod, Earl of Norfolk arrived from Normandy, where the king had died, to swear – falsely – that *in extremis* the king had changed his mind and nominated Stephen as his successor. This evidence quietened the archbishop's conscience and gave the council the excuses it was looking for to deprive Matilda. In Normandy the barons who had been about to elect Theodore as their duke switched allegiance to Stephen when they heard what had happened at Winchester. Those who expressed misgiving, foreseeing that the choice of either of the rival magnates, Stephen or Robert, would mean civil war, were soon proved right.

The salient facts behind these manoeuvrings were that Matilda should certainly have succeeded her father and that no one whose opinion mattered wanted her to. Her crown was stolen because she was a woman, because she represented the Angevin enemy, because she was slow off the mark, because she was personally unpopular, and because Stephen had all the appeal she lacked. Above all, he represented the 'new men' who were in power on both sides of the Channel, while her supporters were the dispossessed adherents of Duke Robert or their heirs, who looked to Angevin intervention to redress their wrongs and restore their estates. Thus Matilda's doomed claim stood in a line of descent from Robert's and William Clito's. As in Robert's case too, it had been a misfortune that she was on bad terms with her father and therefore not at his bedside when he died. Prospective heirs should be close at hand when death approaches.

In character, however, it was Stephen who resembled Robert. Friendly and easy-going, generous and tolerant, he had more than a touch of Robert's fecklessness and his rule brought upon England the same disasters as Normandy had endured under Robert. Compassion was not a public virtue in that age, when only the merciless could bestow on their subjects the blessings of an ordered society. The Conqueror had established peace through brutality, and his sons Rufus and Henry were cast in the same mould. So was Matilda, and her deprivation was England's loss. The usurper was 'a mild man, soft and good, and did no justice'.[3] The usurped was an iron lady: in the words of the Archbishop of Rouen, 'a woman girt about with fortitude'.

Bishop Henry's next service to his brother was to argue his case successfully with the pope. In this he was seconded by the King of France, who had no wish to see England, Normandy and Anjou under a single ruler. With Stephen accepted at home and abroad, Matilda's cause seemed lost irretrievably, but the weakness of Stephen's position soon became apparent. The circumstances of his accession had put him in the power of others. He had become king, not as a hereditary ruler divinely appointed, but on approval by the citizens of London, as the choice of the church and after election by the barons, and all had to be bribed into allegiance: the barons with grants, the church and the city of London with special privileges.

When Robert of Gloucester eventually and reluctantly did homage to his new sovereign lord, he openly declared that his loyalty was dependent on Stephen behaving as he, Robert, believed a king should behave. Stephen was on probation, not God-given: what his subjects had decided once they could decide again – differently. Therein shone a ray of hope for Matilda, and it shone all the more brightly when Stephen's eagerness to please led him to promise more than he could deliver: 'though you admired his kindness in promising, you still felt his words lacked truth and his promise fulfilment'.[4]

His weakness was soon demonstrated. The first revolt in Matilda's interest broke out in the west country, always prone to rebellion and down the centuries fertile territory for pretenders. It was headed by Baldwin de Redvers, castellan of Exeter, who was forced to surrender after a siege by the king. In accordance with Norman practice his punishment should have been blinding or mutilation, but Stephen in a forgiving mood allowed his mind to be changed and the low cost of treachery was duly noted by other malcontents.

Stephen's good nature was flawed with a streak of treachery, and this turned Roger of Salisbury and other bishops against him. He also made two serious errors in attempting and failing to capture Robert of Gloucester in an ambush. As a result, acting with strict propriety, Robert sent Stephen his formal *diffidatio*, a word normally translated as 'defiance' but in this instance bearing its original meaning: a renunciation of fealty, a severing of the ties of homage. He was returning to his allegiance to his half-sister and thereafter remained unswervingly loyal to her through good times and bad.

To her he came as a godsend: a man and a leader of men, an Anglo-Norman potentate (Caen and Bayeux was his as well as Bristol and Gloucester) and one who could not complain of the Angevin connection since he himself had negotiated the marriage as her father's representative. He joined her in the summer of 1138 and it was not until his death nine years later that her hope of becoming queen was finally extinguished.

With Stephen floundering, coats were readily turned. When Matilda's husband invaded Normandy the king could not muster sufficient force to dislodge him. Geoffrey penetrated to within ten miles of the capital and had to be bought off with a pension (2000 silver marks a year). In England there were rebels in arms everywhere, and Matilda's uncle, David of Scotland, who had refused Stephen his homage, seized the opportunity to indulge in the time-honoured

Scottish custom of ravaging Northumbria. These attacks by foreigners rebounded against Matilda. Sympathy drained from a cause
associated with Angevin and Pictish barbarians, and the northern
barons united to win a great victory for Stephen over the Scots at the
so-called Battle of the Standard, fought near Northallerton.

In other respects the tide was running strongly in Matilda's favour.
Robert's castle at Bristol, which was to become an impregnable
headquarters for Matilda throughout a long civil war, defied
Stephen's attempt to reduce it by siege. Bishop Henry became
antagonised to the point of fury by his brother's refusal to endorse his
nomination to the now vacant archbishopric of Canterbury, and the
king gave more offence and made more enemies by arresting Bishop
Roger and the Bishop of Lincoln while they were attending a meeting
of the great council in Oxford. The two bishops were then accused of
treason and held as hostages for the surrender of their castles and
treasure. The episcopal ex-justiciar had accumulated a vast quantity
of worldly wealth, and with strongly fortified castles at Salisbury,
Sherborne, Devizes and Malmesbury his secular power inspired more
awe than his spiritual grace.

But, whatever the political justification, Stephen had abused both
the right to royal protection traditionally extended to those summoned to council meetings and the privilege of churchmen to be tried
in ecclesiastical courts. Henry of Blois may have been denied the
primacy but he held the appointment of papal legate and as such
summoned the king to Winchester to answer charges before a church
council. Kings do not usually take kindly to having their presence
demanded by subjects, particularly no doubt by subjects who are also
younger brothers, but Stephen judged it best to obey the summons
and concede nothing. The most pressing of his problems, which had
necessitated action against the bishops and was driving deserters into
Matilda's arms, was one which had been familiar to their uncle
Robert. Henry's well stocked treasury had been emptied: there was no
money left to pay an army and reward the faithful.

The invasion forces of pretenders are commonly late and numerically inadequate. Matilda's, long awaited, was no exception. After
landing on the Sussex coast on 30 September 1139 she arrived at the
gates of Arundel castle, the home of Henry's widow, her step-mother,
with Robert of Gloucester and 140 knights. When Stephen came to
besiege and capture her there Robert had already slipped away and the
king chivalrously permitted her a safe-conduct to join him in Bristol.

She was escorted there by Bishop Henry, who is suspected of having given his brother treacherous advice, Stephen's generous gesture being otherwise inexplicable. One puzzled chronicler concluded that he was either simple-minded or negligent.[5] It was not a misjudgment that would have been made by any of his Norman predecessors except the ill-fated Robert.

In the years which followed, as the iron-willed former empress strove to impose her might and right over the incompetent king her subjects had chosen and lived to regret, England was to experience the worst period of civil upheaval in its history. The quarrelsome barons lived secure in their numerous castles and, under weak and divided rule, behaved like bandits with impunity. Geoffrey de Mandeville, Earl of Essex and castellan of the Tower of London, for example, was too powerful and valuable as an ally to be suppressed or antagonised by either party. He changed sides several times to maintain and better his position and looted and pillaged at will as a freebooter. Little blood was shed in the Wars of the Roses or the conflict between Roundhead and Cavalier by comparison with the butchery perpetrated during the reign of the man who had usurped Matilda's throne.

Theft, torture and murder were commonplace. There were reports of 'slaughter, fire and rapine, cries of anguish and horror on every side'.[6] 'You could see villages with famous names standing solitary and almost empty because the peasants of both sexes and all ages were dead.'[7] Or in the more picturesque words of the Anglo-Saxon Chronicle: 'Christ and his saints slept'.[8]

Although it was said that she had 'nothing of the woman about her',[9] her sex precluded Matilda from wielding a sword for herself, or even a mace like Bishop Odo. No Amazon or Boadicea, she was well served instead by Robert of Gloucester and others whom she goaded fiercely into battle. At Lincoln Robert and Ranulf, Earl of Chester joined forces to rout a royal army. Stephen's barons fled and left him to fight alone until knocked from his horse and taken captive. Unlike Richard III's at Bosworth, his life was spared. He was taken to Gloucester as a prize of war and brought before Matilda, who ordered him into prison at Bristol. Accepting what seemed the verdict of God, nearly all the bishops and barons transferred their allegiance. Henry of Blois abandoned his brother to come to advantageous terms with Matilda: she would be queen and he would be her adviser and chief minister. At Lincoln Robert had won her the crown. To wear it she had only to consolidate his victory through the exercise of prudence and restraint and a spirit of reconciliation – none of which was in her nature.

A council at Winchester, presided over by the Archbishop of Canterbury, formally recognised the justice of Matilda's claim. The crown was handed to her and she was hailed as Lady of England and Normandy: *domina* but not yet *regina*. To be queen she must be crowned and anointed in a ceremony traditionally performed at Westminster. Had she heeded the example of her father, she would have ridden straight for London instead of bargaining at Winchester, for already some disappointed barons were wavering in their new allegiance.

If to play the gentle dove of peace, showing friendship, gratitude and good will, was beyond her, she might at least have dissembled, but that too seemed impossible. Uncaring of the consequences, she exposed herself as a haughty termagant full of fury and motivated by an uncontrollable desire for revenge. For an intelligent woman she behaved with unimaginable stupidity in overplaying her hand, insulting bishops and barons and Londoners alike, upbraiding them for their support of the usurper and threatening them with dire punishments. Instead of flattery and honeyed words and beckoning promises to win them over, they were lashed with abuse and treated to bad-tempered exhibitions of high dudgeon. The three men on whose good will she had most to rely – Henry of Blois, Robert of Gloucester and the King of Scotland – were openly humiliated by being kept on their knees in audience when she denied them the customary courtesy of rising to greet them. The London city fathers, who came to pay their respects before welcoming her to her coronation, were met with imperious demands for money and heavier taxation. Just as surely as Robert of Normandy's good nature, Matilda's ill nature cost her the crown.

Why did the woman who had won popularity in Germany choose to make herself so unpopular in England in what should have been her hour of triumph? No answer can be other than speculative. She was thirty-nine, frustrated and embittered at her come-down in the world after life as the consort of an overlord of kings. It may be that she was a victim of the menopause, exciting an already fiery disposition. It may be that, over-conscious of her father's success through strength and her rival's failure through weakness, she believed it good policy to flaunt her sovereignty by being rude to the most eminent men in the kingdom and treating their advice with unconcealed contempt.

It is possible, too, that there are arguments in her favour of which we are not aware, for she has not enjoyed a good press. Of the two major contemporary sources for the events of her time, one – *Gesta Stephani* – is a pro-Stephen chronicle and the hero of the other – William of Malmesbury's *Historia Novella* – is Robert of Gloucester. There is no surviving account told from Matilda's point of view in which her 'grim look, her forehead wrinkled into a frown, every trace of woman's gentleness removed from her face'[10] might have been replaced by some explanation of her apparently total lack of understanding and political nous.

After experiencing her 'unbearable fury'[11] the Londoners were spirited enough (and concerned enough about their trading link with Flanders) to retaliate by demanding Stephen's release. They could not have expected that this would be conceded, but the demand was a sign that London was too important to be browbeaten and would bargain for acceptable terms. Matilda at last entered the capital on 24 June 1141 and, although uncrowned, set to work repealing Stephen's grants and issuing her own charters as queen.

She had delayed too long. Stephen's queen (another Matilda), not to be outshone as a female militant, had raised an army in Kent and marched to the bank of the Thames opposite London. The citizens knew which Matilda they preferred. The church bells roused them to arms and they rushed out of the gates 'like bees out of a hive' to assault the ex-empress – the Countess of Anjou, as her enemies described her – while she was dining in state at Westminster. In the first of several dramatic escapes she had to abandon all her possessions, leaped on a horse and fled to safety in Oxford. From there she sent orders to Bristol that Stephen was to be put in chains.

London was not alone in tiring of her. Bishop Henry, who had hoped to rule England in her name, had written her off as unmanageable and was now seeking his brother's release and restoration. Incensed at his treachery, she led an army to Winchester and summoned him to her presence in the castle. It was not a summons a wise man would heed, and the bishop replied by barricading himself in Wolvesey, his own castle beside the cathedral. There Matilda besieged him, while Stephen's queen and a force of Londoners hurried to his assistance to besiege the besiegers. Their army was commanded by William of Ypres, leader of a rough band of Flemish mercenaries whose professional fighting skills carried the day. Matilda was forced to retire, and her retreat became a rout. As at Lincoln, few on the losing side stood their ground. Allegiances were fickle, and the self-interest of the barons demanded instant disengagement from a losing side.

The honourable exception was Robert of Gloucester. Regardless of his own safety, he fought a determined rearguard action to cover his half-sister's escape. Thanks to this gallantry she eluded capture and reached Devizes. When the castle there was threatened by pursuers she was carried exhausted all the way to Gloucester on a litter strapped between two horses. The King of Scotland made good his escape to the north, but at the expense of having to bribe three successive sets of captors. Robert was made prisoner and taken to Rochester castle. Offered his release and the next place in the kingdom after the king if he would change sides, he replied that his honour would not permit him to accept.

Defeat at Winchester closed the period of Matilda's rule which had been won at Lincoln. Her reign as queen in all but title lasted 32 weeks. She was now obliged to part with her most valuable asset and set Stephen free in exchange for Robert. Robert himself chivalrously opposed the exchange, but Matilda realised that she could never regain power without him. He was a man, well liked and respected, who could inspire loyalty. She was a woman, much hated, who could inspire none.

On Christmas day 1141, in order that there should be no misunderstanding who was the real ruler of England, Stephen had himself crowned for a second time. Matilda, who was nothing if not stout-hearted, took this for a challenge to renew hostilities. Robert's western strongholds at Bristol, Gloucester and Oxford remained loyal, her misfortune attracted sympathy elsewhere, and Stephen was soon making enemies again and once more demonstrating his incompetence. In May of the following year he became so ill at Northampton that God seemed to have intervened to restore England to its Lady.

When he recovered, Matilda sent for help to a quarter from which it had been strangely missing. During all her tribulations her husband had been noticeably not at her side. Probably she preferred his absence to the role of obedient and dutiful wife, and while Matilda's objective was England Geoffrey's was Normandy, which Anjou had long coveted. He responded to her appeal predictably, inviting Robert to Normandy for a council of war and making use of his services to capture some enemy castles, while depriving his wife's supporters in England of their leader.

Without him Matilda plunged quickly into trouble. Her high-handed ways offended the barons whom Robert had ordered to Oxford to protect her, and they deserted when Stephen brought an army to burn the town and finish the war by taking her prisoner. Robert returned hurriedly to the rescue and began to assemble an army to raise the siege, meanwhile attempting to entice Stephen away with a diversion. Wisely, Stephen was not to be drawn and after three months the garrison in the castle at Oxford was reduced to near starvation. Matilda's most daring and spectacular escape then snatched her and her cause from apparently certain defeat.

The castle at Oxford stands beside the Thames, and one freezing December night she slipped out of a postern gate – or, according to one account, was lowered down the wall on ropes – to cross the ice-bound river on foot. Wearing white cloaks as camouflage, she and her escort of three crept undetected through the enemy lines on the opposite bank and trudged through deep snow for six miles to Abingdon, where horses were found to take them out of danger to Wallingford castle before daybreak.

This exploit, for which Matilda is best known in history, sentenced England to further years of misery. She was beaten but, buoyed by an occasional success, would not give up. Robert brought her close to triumph by routing Stephen at Wilton and narrowly failing to capture him in the pursuit. Rouen at last fell to Geoffrey, who was acknowledged as Duke of Normandy. This meant that any English baron with an ancestral estate in the duchy would lose it through forfeiture if he renounced his allegiance to Matilda. Stephen kept the crown, however, and gradually her supporters were forced on to the defensive and isolated as an unEnglish pro-Angevin faction.

In 1147 a prodigy and portent entered the arena. A boy who was to become the dominant figure in western Europe during the latter half of the century made his first appearance at the head of an army. He was called Henry fitzEmpress or Henry Plantagenet and as Henry II of England was to win the crown to which Robert of Gloucester had wished him to succeed on his grandfather's death and which ever since had lain just beyond his mother's reach. But his invasion of England at the age of fourteen, at the head of an appropriately small army, proved a fiasco. It was his own idea and when the money ran out neither his mother nor his father would help. As a last resort he appealed to the king he had come to fight, and Stephen, ever courteous, indulgently funded his return home.

Later the same year the faithful Robert of Gloucester died, and with him the last of Matilda's dwindling hopes. A few months later she abandoned the struggle – and England too, taking up residence with her husband in the ducal palace in Rouen. After more than eight years of disappointment she was never to return. But when Stephen fell out with the church the pope kept her claim alive by forbidding the coronation of his son Eustace (Stephen's method of ensuring a pre-arranged succession) on the grounds that he, Stephen, was not a true king but a usurper.

Henry's second invasion, this time in alliance with the King of Scotland, was another resounding failure, although less ignominious than the first. But by his third attempt (in 1153 at the head of 140 knights and 3000 foot soldiers) he was a different man. In 1150 his father had given him the duchy of Normandy. In 1151, on Geoffrey's death, he had succeeded as Count of Anjou. In 1152 he had married the divorced Queen of France and in her right acquired Aquitaine, Gascony and Poitou – a wide swathe of France between the Loire and the Pyrenees.

After a successful initial foray into England he was confronted by Stephen at Wallingford. Since his previous incursion the barons had enjoyed a taste of peace. Like the country at large, they were exhausted by war. Neighbours with conflicting loyalties began to make private accommodations, agreeing to differ and concluding formal treaties without the involvement of the crown. One such was between the Earl of Leicester, who recognised Stephen as king, and the Earl of Chester, who recognised Henry. Wallingford was thus a re-run of Alton, with the barons insisting on negotiation. Both protagonists were angry at not being allowed to fight, but neither could persuade their reluctant followers. Stephen's heir, described as an evil and ungodly man, was so incensed that he went on a marauding expedition, burning and looting in East Anglia, where he fortunately and conveniently died.

As the king showed no interest in the succession of his second son, William, the way was clear for a settlement. Stephen agreed to adopt Henry as his son, heir and successor. Henry agreed that Stephen should be king for life and did him homage. The magnates of the realm did homage to Henry as their next liege lord. To discourage further conflict, castles erected since Henry I's death were ordered to be demolished: they were estimated to number a thousand. It was a tidily packaged solution if one ignored

Matilda, who was then over fifty but had fourteen more years to live.

Stephen died less than a year after the settlement, and Henry's succession was uncontested. On this occasion there was no frantic dash across the Channel. He was a busy and self-confident ruler and came for the crown as soon as he could spare the time. Whether his mother came with him and attended his coronation is not known, but it seems unlikely.

Until her death on 9 September 1167 she lived in retirement outside the walls of Rouen, devoting her old age to good works. As a matter of form she was associated with her son in the government of Normandy: her name appears with his on several charters. But her last years are best remembered for piety and generosity. She used her wealth in building monasteries and bridges across the Seine. Her only known participation in English affairs was to advise Henry not to appoint Becket to Canterbury and to attempt mediation when they quarrelled. Old age had brought selflessness and wisdom, but too late.

Like Duke Robert, she was a flawed loser with qualities which command respect. The same chronicler who condemned her for 'always breathing a spirit of unbending haughtiness'[12] could not refrain from admiration for a mind 'steeled and unbroken in adversity'.[13]

3

John of Gaunt, King of Castile

JOHN OF Gaunt was a direct descendant of Matilda, through six generations of kings – Henry II, John, Henry III and the first three Edwards. Famous as the overmightiest of subjects, he was the most powerful of Englishmen who never became king: it was his successors who achieved the sovereign status which eluded him. Nor did he even establish the duchy of Lancaster, which is inseparably connected with his name: his predecessors as heads of that house were also in their time the greatest magnates in the realm after the king. Duke John's own record is one of power without achievement.

Although uncrowned, he was acknowledged as the real ruler of England during the last years of Edward III's decline and the middle period of Richard II's inadequacy. But he chose neither to emulate Matilda's first husband in betraying his father's trust nor, like Richard III, to supplant an elder brother's son. Not once, despite constant suspicion, did he reveal himself openly as a pretender to the English throne. Yet he haughtily arrogated to himself the title of King of Castile and Leon (which covered most of Spain) although never recognised by those he claimed as his subjects and never able to establish his rule or right to the kingdom.

His royal pretensions became reality only for his children and descendants, and then in abundance. One daughter was crowned Queen of Castile, another Queen of Portugal. After his death his son took the crown of England. Prince Henry the Navigator of Portugal and Henry V of England were his grandsons, Queen Isabella of Castile his great grand-daughter. For nearly 600 years, from Henry IV to Elizabeth II, his blood has flowed in the veins of the sovereign kings and queens of England and all of them have borne his title, Duke of Lancaster. The marriage between Henry Tudor and Elizabeth of York was a union of two of his descendants. So too were the marriages between Henry VIII and Katharine of Aragon, Queen Mary and Philip of Spain, and William of Orange and Mary Stuart.

These posthumous triumphs were not matched during his lifetime. In a career of paradoxes he became one of the most celebrated warriors in a family renowned for fighting. His father, brother and grandson all won great victories: at Crécy, Poitiers and Agincourt. He himself ended a long military career as the most redoubtable campaigner in Europe; yet without a victory to his name.

His character is also in doubt. Extraordinary power and influence appear to have resided in a very ordinary man. The titles and estates with which he was loaded had not been won, nor even inherited, by himself. Like Warwick the Kingmaker, the overmightiest subject of the next century (and another descendant), he acquired them by marriage. Just as Richard Nevill became Earl of Warwick through marriage to the daughter of the last Beauchamp earl, so John of Gaunt became Duke of Lancaster in the right of his wife Blanche, the last surviving daughter and heiress of the first duke. Marriage, not merit, has always been the shortest cut to fame and fortune.

Nothing could seem less in character than the two actions for which the duke most deserves the gratitude of posterity. Not a man known for his cultural interests, he was the patron (and brother-in-law) of the poet Chaucer, the flowering of whose genius owed much to the privileged life which he was enabled to live as a protégé of the duke – in particular his acquaintance with French and Italian literature resulting from travel abroad on official business. Even more surprising is the protection extended by a man of orthodox piety to the heretic father of English Protestantism. Without the shield of Gaunt, John Wyclif, who incurred the undying wrath of Rome and the church establishment in England, is likely to have ended his days in prison or, like Huss, at the stake.

Gaunt is an anglicised version of Ghent, and John was born there in St Bavon abbey. He was the fourth son of Edward III and Queen Philippa (daughter of William, Count of Holland and Hainault), a model of grace and virtue among English queens. His elder brothers,

B. HOUSE OF LANCASTER

This simplified genealogical tree omits John of Gaunt's third marriage, which is included in Table C.

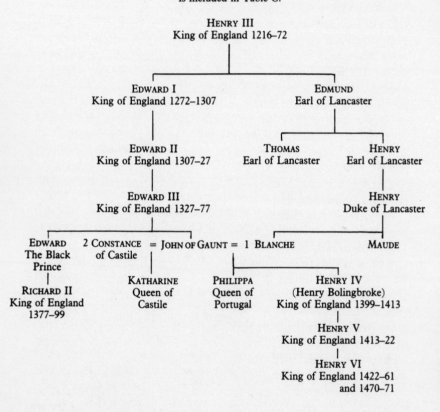

HENRY III
King of England 1216–72

EDWARD I
King of England 1272–1307

EDMUND
Earl of Lancaster

EDWARD II
King of England 1307–27

THOMAS
Earl of Lancaster

HENRY
Earl of Lancaster

EDWARD III
King of England 1327–77

HENRY
Duke of Lancaster

EDWARD
The Black
Prince

2 CONSTANCE
of Castile

= JOHN OF GAUNT = 1 BLANCHE

MAUDE

RICHARD II
King of England
1377–99

KATHARINE
Queen of
Castile

PHILIPPA
Queen of
Portugal

HENRY IV
(Henry Bolingbroke)
King of England 1399–1413

HENRY V
King of England 1413–22

HENRY VI
King of England 1422–61
and 1470–71

also identified by their place of birth, were Edward of Woodstock (later known as the Prince of England and, after his death, as the Black Prince), William of Hatfield (who had died in infancy) and Lionel of Antwerp (who became Earl of Ulster and Duke of Clarence). Lionel too had royal aspirations, with an eye on a kingdom in Italy, but died too early to do more than leave his descendants a claim to the English throne, in right of which they were to usurp Gaunt's.

In January 1340 a parliament in Ghent had sealed an anti-French alliance between the King of England and a league of counties and cities in Flanders. Since the Flemish had earlier sworn fealty to the King of France, the proprieties were observed by Edward reviving an abandoned claim to the French throne and riding into Ghent as king of both countries. The claim of English kings to the crown of France for the next 461 years sprang from this opportunistic sham. The Flemish dutifully did homage to Edward as King of France but, despite all the splendour and oaths of loyalty and friendship, on his departure for England he was forced to leave his pregnant wife and family behind as a surety for unpaid debts. Happily, he worsted a large French army lying in wait for him aboard warships at Sluys and was able to return in triumph to reclaim them. His son John had been born on 4 March during his absence, and the Flemish leader, Jacob van Artevelde, stood godfather to the new-born boy, holding him in his arms at the font. For John of Gaunt it had been an eventful entry on the European stage and an early baptism into a turbulent life of politics and war.

At the age of three he became Earl of Richmond. Too young for Crécy at six, he was granted his first taste of battle at ten, when the Black Prince took him on ship at Winchelsea 'because he loved him much'.[1] In this naval engagement against the Spanish there was some fierce.grappling and boarding and much bloodshed before victory was won. The Black Prince's ship with his young brother aboard had begun to sink when they were rescued. Life began, and often ended, early in the middle ages.

At fifteen John was campaigning with his father in Scotland, and at nineteen, in a great ceremony at Reading abbey followed by a tournament in London attended by the kings of England, France and Scotland, he was married to Blanche, younger daughter of Henry the Good, Duke of Lancaster. She was eighteen, tall and blonde and cultured, and was to bear him five children in a marriage which lasted for ten years.

Only two years after the wedding Duke Henry died of the plague, and in the following year his elder daughter and co-heiress (Maude, Duchess of Zealand) succumbed to the same disease. By this chance John succeeded, through Blanche's undivided inheritance, to all the Lancastrian honours and estates. He became Earl of Lancaster, Earl of Derby, Earl of Lincoln and Earl of Leicester. During the next year he was promoted to Duke of Lancaster during the celebrations held to mark Edward III's fiftieth birthday. With his elder brothers abroad as king's lieutenants – Edward in Aquitaine and Lionel in Ireland – he was without rival at his father's court for rank, wealth, power and increasing influence over the ageing king.

Dating from the previous century, the Lancastrian heritage provides an outstanding example of royal acquisitiveness. Edmund Crouchback (Crutchback or Crossback, the sign of a crusader) was the younger and favourite son of Henry III. At the age of nine, by agreement between Henry and the pope, he was awarded the crown of Sicily and Apulia, but since it was in the possession of the Hohenstaufens, his father was unable to make good the claim. Henry therefore determined that Edmund should be provided for at home, and the opportunity came with the defeat and death of Simon de Montfort at Evesham. Edmund received his earldom and honour of Leicester, which included the stewardship of England and land in twelve counties – and this was only a beginning.

The lands of Robert Ferrers, Earl of Derby, were seized, and the castles of Kenilworth, Monmouth, Cardigan and Carmarthen acquired. A royal grant of the honour of Lancaster followed. Edmund had become the leading magnate in the north and midlands and, being extravagant as well as rapacious, fell heavily into debt. Marriage to Aveline de Redvers (aged ten) brought relief with the earldom of Devon and lordship of the Isle of Wight. On her death he married the widow of the King of Navarre, and although Navarre itself escaped him he was able to gather in the title and estates of the Count of Champagne. From his mother he had a manor on the Thames which once belonged to her uncle Peter, Count of Savoy, and the Lancastrian palace built on this site between London and Westminster came to rival the palace of Westminster itself.

Edmund was succeeded by his son Thomas, who came to be worshipped as a saint but was no less ambitious for worldly power. As Edward II's cousin he took upon himself the protection of church and people against the king's wicked advisers, maintaining a private army of 500 liveried retainers, holding private parliaments and plotting to replace the king with a council of barons under his own leadership. He was among those who had the king's favourite, Piers Gaveston, executed and was later proclaimed a rebel and suffered the same fate himself. After his death he was hailed as a martyr who had resisted tyranny and the powers of evil in the cause of freedom and godliness. His effigy in St Paul's cathedral was said to work miracles, and three unsuccessful applications were made to Rome for his canonisation. He was not quite a pretender and not quite a saint.

Rome would have been aware that, like Edmund before him and John of Gaunt after, Earl Thomas had not neglected the worship of mammon. He made a not inconsiderable contribution to the growth of his Lancastrian inheritance by marrying Alice Lacy, an heiress with 10,000 marks a year who also brought with her the earldoms of Lincoln and Salisbury and the honours and castles of Pontefract and Bolingbroke (which were retained when she left for the more congenial companionship of the Earl of Surrey). But his death placed all in jeopardy. A rebel's estates are forfeit to the crown, and it took long, tortuous politicking by his younger brother and successor, Henry, to have them restored. This was eventually achieved through a petition in parliament which won an annulment on the grounds that Thomas was never permitted to answer the charge of treason nor accorded the trial before his peers to which he was entitled.

Henry's son, another Henry, who became the Good Duke and John of Gaunt's father-in-law, was a close friend of Edward III, who in 1351 rewarded him for feats of arms with the second dukedom in English history (the duchy of Cornwall dates from 1333) and quasi-regal authority in Lancashire. Henry was a hero of the Scottish and French wars, prominent at Sluys and Winchelsea and Crécy and the siege of Calais and a hard campaigner in Gascony and Poitou. When not fighting for England, he took to arms on behalf of the church: against the Moors in Spain, Cyprus and Rhodes and the heathen in Lithuania.

All this accumulation of a century of power and greed became John of Gaunt's inheritance through marriage when Henry and his elder daughter died. Others had created the sprawling duchy, but such is the magic of his name that theirs are forgotten and he stands alone as 'time-honoured Lancaster'. To itemise what he inherited would occupy a book in itself: no pretender before or since has had such resources of his own at his disposal. He held thirty castles in his own name as well as the wardship of three belonging to the king. His favourite residences were the Savoy palace and his castles at Leicester, Kenilworth, Hertford, Pontefract and Knaresborough. Important lords and members of noble families were on his pay roll and wore his livery: Nevills, Dacres, Scropes, de la Poles, Curzons, Dymmocks and Blounts among them. He had his own privy council, headed by a Chancellor (who was the Bishop of Salisbury), a Receiver General and the Steward, Chamberlain and Controller of his Household. His officers included treasurers and auditors, constables of castles, sergeants at arms and attorneys general. His stewards throughout the country acted as feudal lords themselves, collecting money and dispensing justice with the assistance of a regiment of bailiffs, feodaries, provosts and reeves.

His Chief Steward in the South was responsible for estates in thirteen counties from Kent to Monmouth and for lordships in Wales, and under him there was a steward for each county. In the midlands his Chief Steward was responsible for the counties of Derby, Stafford and Warwick and the honour of Tutbury, while the honour of Leicester under a Chief Steward of its own took in the counties of Leicester, Rutland, Nottingham and Northampton. His Chief Steward of the Northern Counties controlled estates in Northumberland, Yorkshire, Lancashire and Chester. There was a wholly separate administration for forest lands, with Lancashire, Yorkshire, Derby, Stafford, Dorset, Wiltshire and Sussex each having a Master of Forests supervised directly by the council. Later, when Lancashire became a county palatine again (Duke Henry's grant had been for life only), yet another elaborate administration was established.

Money flowed into the Duke's exchequer – from the receivers via auditors to treasurers – and flowed rapidly out again. The manorial and feudal revenues from lands and forest were enormous and they were augmented by pardons and fines, traffic in wardships, profits from wrecks and other perquisites. As well as sizeable manors, hundreds and wapentakes on the rent roll, there were numerous 'hamlets, meadows, pannage, herbage, fisheries, moors, marshes, turbaries, chaces, parks, woods and warrens, fairs and markets'.[2] But household costs were enormous too, and vast sums were spent on alms and presents as well as wages and personal aggrandisement. In the purchase of gold and silver and jewels John of Gaunt was lavish even for his rank and times. His public duties, too, involved prodigious expenditure: he personally financed foreign embassies and sometimes even armies. Despite wealth which attracted envy from all quarters, balancing the books at the end of each year was rarely an easy task for his hard pressed (but well rewarded) officials.

In the fourteenth century the Plantagenets, with their sovereignty over large areas of France, commercial links with Flanders and royal ambitions in Italy and Spain, were essentially a European rather than an English family. In addition to his English estates John of Gaunt held the lordships of Beaufort and Nogent in Champagne, a lingering asset from Edmund Crouchback's second marriage. (It was this Beaufort which provided a surname for his children by Katharine Swynford, although none of them was born there.) He had also succeeded to the lordship of Bergerac in Guyenne, granted to Duke Henry, and the Black Prince gave him Roche-sur-Yon. John of Gaunt was not only a prince of the blood with royal pretensions, but in modern terminology the proprietor and chief executive of a multi-national corporation.

After the blooding by his eldest brother his military education was taken over by his father, of whom it was said by a French chronicler: 'When the noble Edward first gained England in his youth nobody thought much of the English, nobody spoke of their prowess and courage . . . Now, in the time of the noble Edward, who has so often put them to the test, they are the finest and most daring warriors known to man'.[3]

Shortly after his marriage the young prince accompanied the king on a march of plunder and defiance through enemy territory from Calais to Rheims, but the French prudently refused the invitation to fight. The great victory won by Edward and his longbowmen at Crécy, followed by the Black Prince's similar triumph against a vastly superior force at Poitiers, had convinced the French that the English were invincible in the field. On the other hand, a strongly fortified and properly garrisoned town was virtually impregnable against fourteenth-century weaponry: after Crécy it had taken Edward many months to starve Calais into surrender. A prolonged siege of Rheims, so far from the Channel coast, would have been foolhardy, and king and prince returned from the campaign undefeated but unvictorious.

The stalemate was recognised by both sides in the terms of the treaty of Brétigny (1360), whereby Edward renounced his claim to the crown of France in exchange for full sovereignty over Gascony, Poitou, Calais and the other areas claimed by the Plantagenets. The French king was still held in captivity at John's Savoy palace in London and a ransom of three million gold crowns was agreed.

Brétigny would have set the seal on Edward's triumphs, but the terms were never implemented – probably the French never intended them to be – and from then it was downhill all the way as the once great king progressively withdrew from public life and lapsed into premature senility. For the last eleven years of his reign it was his favourite son, John of Gaunt, who assumed the responsibilities of government and became the *de facto* king of England in his place.

The heir to the throne, granted sovereignty over Gascony, had established a luxurious court at Bordeaux, where he ruled as Prince of England and Aquitaine. His courtiers included three crowned heads: the kings of Navarre, Majorca and Cyprus. In 1366 he took the disastrous decision to invade Spain on behalf of the dethroned King of Castile, Pedro the Cruel, a man who had murdered his wife to marry his mistress and fallen out not only with the French but also with the church and his own people. To restore a king to his throne and open a new front against France was an irresistible attraction for the prince. John of Gaunt was summoned from England and led an invading army across the Pyrenees safely through the dangerous pass of Roncesvalles. In the ensuing battle at Najera the Black Prince won another resounding victory, defeating one of the ablest French generals, du Guesclin, and *la fleur de toute la chevalerie du monde*. Duke John was in the vanguard with Sir John Chandos, whose men took du Guesclin prisoner. It was a feat soon to be soured. The prince was stricken with a sickness which was to cripple and kill him after years of debility, and Pedro's gratitude and new reign were both short-lived. Two years later his cruelty and treachery led to death at the hands of a bastard brother and French-backed rival, Enrique.

By that time John was back in northern France, leading a raid at the head of 600 men at arms and 1500 archers. On his progress from Calais to Harfleur, burning and looting, he outfaced a French army seven times larger. It paid him the unwanted compliment of not daring to attack, but after he was home a fleet crossed the Channel and burned Portsmouth in revenge.

Everywhere the outlook was darkening. While he was in Picardy his mother and wife had both died. With the death of the 'full noble and good' queen, Edward's once brilliant court deteriorated into vice and corruption as her place and influence (and jewels) were taken by the king's mistress, Alice Perrers. For Blanche, John of Gaunt erected a magnificent alabaster tomb near the high altar in St Paul's cathedral, where priests were paid to chant masses for her soul continuously and in perpetuity. Every year on the anniversary of her death he and his household attended a memorial service, and when he died the first injunction in his will was that his body should lie there beside hers. No one could accuse him of ingratitude for what she had brought him.

In the south, with the Black Prince broken in health, the struggle against France was all but lost. The expense of the expedition to Spain (for which Pedro had failed to provide repayment as promised) was recovered through heavier taxes imposed on the Gascons, and their resentment at having to pay for this as well as the prince's extravagances in Bordeaux led them to look more kindly on reconciliation with the King of France.

John came from England to the rescue, but too late. A hearth tax was revoked and the loyalty of some rebels bought back with pardons, but when its bishop treacherously surrendered Limoges to the French the Black Prince roused himself from his sick bed and swore a vengeance which was to blacken his reputation for ever. He joined John at Cognac and they marched together on Limoges, where he watched from a litter while his brother conducted one of the few successful sieges of the century. The wall was mined, the city taken by storm, and on the orders of the Black Prince every man, woman and child among the inhabitants massacred. John saved the lives of the garrison, satisfying his brother's blood lust by fighting a duel with their commander, and against his brother's wishes he contrived to spare the guilty bishop.

After this, his final solution, the prince appointed John his lieutenant in Aquitaine and returned home to waste away and die. Behind him he left an empty treasury and his elder son, Edward, dead and unburied. Undespairing, John buried his nephew with due ceremony and campaigned with his usual courage and vigour, but the French, as always, would not risk an engagement. They had no need, for time and geography were on their side. English rule in the principality was crumbling irrecoverably. After nine months of paying an army out of his own pocket the duke resigned the appointment and returned to England, frustrated but with his ambition still unquenched. Already the king's lieutenant in England, he had no wish for a like role in Aquitaine. His heart was set on suzerainty in his own right.

In Scotland he had a claim to the earldom of Moray, in southern France to the county of Provence, but neither lay on the path to a throne. What held most promise was the kingdom of Castile, which he had helped to win once by force of arms for another – the unworthy

Pedro. In September 1371, at Roquefort, he married Pedro's elder daughter, Constance, and ignoring Enrique, the sitting incumbent, assumed the title of King of Castile and Leon. Henceforward the Duke of Lancaster was to be addressed as 'my lord of Spain'. Later, when he made a treaty with his nephew Richard II, 'King of France and England', he was formally described as John, King of Castile, Leon, Toledo, Galicia, Seville, Cordoba, Murcia, Jaen, Algarve and Algeciras, Duke of Lancaster and Lord of Molina.

The hollowness of pretension of this kind has been the subject of critical comment: 'No proceeding can be less judicious, or afford less chance of ultimately redounding to the glory of him who adopts it, than this sort of speculative and dialectical claim to the supreme magistracy of a nation . . . What was the Duke of Lancaster to the Spanish nation? The majority of them scarcely knew of his existence; or, if they did, felt as much inclination to be governed by an emissary from the Grand Lama of Tartary.'[4]

To feudal magnates, however, the laws of inheritance and property took precedence over the wishes of common and ignorant people. To his own way of thinking, John of Gaunt's second marriage had brought him the proprietorship of most of Spain just as his first had brought him the ownership of so much of England. Whatever his personal shortcomings, Pedro had been the rightful King of Castile and when the usurping Enrique had been ousted John would rightfully take his place as the legitimate heir. In the furtherance of what he chose to see as a just cause, his first move was to form an alliance with Portugal. His second was fittingly grandiose: no less than the attempted conquest of France, whereby he would outshine his father and elder brother and strip Enrique of his only powerful ally.

It was midsummer madness, but his valour and vision were well supported. In the summer of 1373 he sailed for France with the finest fighting force to leave English shores during the whole of the Hundred Years War: it boasted 15,000 men, including 6,000 archers, many of them seasoned troops under experienced commanders, headed by Sir John Knollys and John of Montfort, Duke of Brittany. This, the greatest of the English *chevauchées* through France, was also the most foolhardy and calamitous. The army enjoyed the satisfaction of plundering and rape and the destruction of crops and vineyards at harvest and vintage time, but no answer had been found to the problem of getting the French to fight. Charles V cautiously pursued his policy of persistent inaction, thus ingloriously paralysing the invincible invaders. The Duke of Burgundy led a shadowing force which marched parallel to the English army at a safe distance and contented itself with picking off stragglers and pouncing on incautious foraging parties.

In this manner John of Gaunt marched like a conquering hero through Picardy to the county of Champagne which he claimed as part of his Lancastrian inheritance. But Troyes, strongly held, refused to open its gates, and he judged that a siege would be futile. To turn back would have been an admission of failure. The logic of his strategy, the best hope of forcing a battle, was to march on Paris itself. Instead he chose to press southwards through Burgundy and Lyonnois to complete an astonishing sweep across France from Calais to Bordeaux, pillaging goods and burning villages in the very heart of French territory to demonstrate the might of England and the inability of the French king to protect his own.

The army suffered for his pride scarcely less than the peasantry. As winter approached and they struggled across the mountains of Auvergne and rivers swollen with rain, thousands died of cold and starvation and disease. Casualties in battle would have been lighter, for when their destination was finally reached numbers had dwindled by half, and after such an experience many chose to desert from Bordeaux. The humiliation of France had cost England an army and brought John of Gaunt no nearer the throne of Castile: further away indeed, for he had paid for the expedition himself and it crippled him financially.

To achieve his ambition he now turned to diplomacy and proved surprisingly adept. His enemies may not have liked him, but they trusted and respected him. In Bruges, at lavish expense, he negotiated with the dukes of Anjou and Berri, and although no agreement could be reached on a treaty, the haggling ended with a one-year truce which was later extended.

At home the unsuccessful quasi-king was unpopular. In King Edward's high noon taxation had been justified by glory and the spoils of victory. Now Sluys, Crécy, Winchelsea, Poitiers and Najera had been succeeded by rebellion and defeat in Aquitaine and the fiasco of the long march. By 1375, when the truce was signed at Bruges, England's possessions in France had shrunk to the pale of Calais and a strip of coastland between Bordeaux and Bayonne, and John was blamed for the shame of the truce as well as the mortification of the war. His Castilian marriage and pretensions were disliked and, with

the king senile and the Black Prince a dying man, responsibility for
the government's corruption and incompetence was laid at his door.
He was the prime target of the so-called Good Parliament, which met
to air grievances in April 1376.

When the Black Prince at last died three months later, leaving a
ten-year-old heir to the throne, the self-styled King of Castile was
widely suspected of royal ambitions nearer home. Described as 'my
very dear and well-beloved brother of Spain', he was named in the
prince's will as principal executor, and the old king and his grandchild
were effectively under his protectorship and in his power. He had
already been the king's deputy for an unhappy decade, and a wary
parliament demanded that Richard of Bordeaux should appear in
open parliament to be formally recognised as the new Prince of Wales.
Calumnies were spread that the duke was holding the old king in
bondage, that he was plotting to have his nephew poisoned, and that
on his death bed the much mourned prince had made a last frantic
attempt to frustrate his brother's machinations.

But when the king died the following year, an air of conciliation
prevailed. 'My lord of Spain', a veritable Pooh-Bah, supervised all
the arrangements for his nephew's coronation. As Earl of Leicester
he performed the duties of the Steward of England. As Duke of
Lancaster he bore the great sword Curtana in the procession. As Earl
of Lincoln he was the king's carver. All other claims relating to the
ceremony were decided by him, applicants deferring to him as he sat
in state in the palace of Westminster. Afterwards he refused office
until parliament had formally acquitted him of all charges of treasonable intent. Only then did he accept nomination by the commons to
lead the new king's advisory council. Then he announced that he
would retire from public life rather than serve. His purpose was to
demonstrate publicly that those who said he would seize the young
Richard's crown were guilty of malicious slander.

Nevertheless, this voluntary retirement when most in demand does
not suggest a diminution of ambition. The mighty duke was disappointed and bitter and heartily sick of playing second fiddle. His
gesture signified 'king or nothing'. He may have expected a movement
in his favour: that he would be offered the crown, for which, through
loyal service and experience, he was best fitted. William Rufus and
Henry I had set a precedent for younger sons succeeding. But he must
have known that, even if initially successful, a coup like theirs would
have meant civil war. Whatever his intentions, he was, too, a man of

some principle, adhering to a code honoured in his age and class. Let his nephew and his country send for him if they wanted him. Meanwhile by holding no office he would be taking no responsibility and could attract no blame. His pride had been wounded by the canards, so he would let events take their course without him and play the part of king in waiting.

Others certainly regarded his move as no more than a tactical withdrawal. Suspicions were not allayed, and in the following year the commons were forced to apologise for slanderous accusations of treason. Even this did not appease him, and parliament was bullied into passing the statute *Scandalum Magnatum*, which provided for imprisonment for anyone spreading false rumours about magnates of the realm.

In addition to squabbling with parliament, John was on bad terms with the city of London and the church. William of Wykeham, whom he removed from the chancellorship in 1371, had continued to be his chief rival in government: the duke 'carried himself very imperiously to all his enemies, particularly to the Bishop of Winchester, whom he deprived of his temporalities and prohibited him to come within twenty miles of court'.[5] When Wyclif was summoned by the bishops for trial in St Paul's, the duke accompanied him and when the bishops threatened Wyclif, he retaliated by threatening the bishops. He told the Bishop of London that he would drag him out of his own church by the hair of his head – an insult which angered Londoners, who took the bishop's side. The duke's arms were hung up in the streets reversed like a traitor's, defamatory rhymes lampooned him, and a mob gathered outside the Savoy palace in murderous mood.

To have come out in the open as a pretender to the throne in the face of such hostility in the capital, in parliament and among churchmen would have been to invite a sentence of death. Nothing he could do or say or contrive would convince people of his innocence. A few years later, in 1384, a Carmelite friar took an oath on the sacrament that John 'had a design to destroy the king and usurp his crown'.[6] In his evidence he named the day, the place and other circumstantial detail, and when he was summarily executed while awaiting trial, this was taken as confirmation that his evidence was too dangerous to be heard in public and therefore likely to be true.

But John's country needed his services again when the truce with France expired and the south coast came under attack by enemy raiders. The Isle of Wight was overrun, and Rye, Hastings and

Gravesend were burned. The Prior of Lewes was surprised and taken prisoner of war in his own priory. In this emergency Duke John was the inescapable choice for commander-in-chief. He dutifully accepted appointment as King's Lieutenant and Captain-General in France, but his ill-luck persisted. When he took to sea the French adopted their usual tactics: the fleet was ordered not to engage him and the walls and garrison of St Malo withstood his siege. Once again his name became associated with failure.

The Peasants Revolt in 1381 offered an ugly revelation of the extent of his unpopularity. Its causes were various: the unjust burden of villein service, repressive legislation by a weak government, the 1380 poll tax levied to pay for the never-ending war against France, and discontent fanned by the preaching of egalitarian ideas and ideals. However often he answered the call to be the saviour of his country (and at least he kept the French at bay), the most powerful man in the realm inevitably became the scapegoat. He was haughty and had no skill or even interest in courting the public. Although open-handed and often a friend of the poor, he stood on his dignity and never condescended. To the have-nots he was the most conspicuous of haves, and particular odium attached to his pretence of Spanish royalty.

When the revolt broke out he was in Scotland negotiating a treaty, and rumours were spread that he was really negotiating on his own behalf and would be crossing the border to claim the crown with the backing of a Scots army. The rebels petitioned the king for his head. The Savoy, the most splendid house in the kingdom, was sacked and blown up with gunpowder. His duchess Constance had to flee from the sacking of Hertford castle and had the gates of Pontefract shut in her face. His physician was beheaded in the Tower. Corpus Christi College, Cambridge, was gutted because it was under his protection. The Abbot of Leicester refused to accept his treasures from the castle for safekeeping in the abbey. When he returned in haste he was treated as an outlaw at Berwick. Bamborough was closed to him on the orders of the Earl of Northumberland. Everywhere it was reported that he had been proclaimed an outlaw and traitor. With government, nobility, church and people united against him, he was forced to return to Edinburgh, where he was lodged in Holyrood abbey as an honoured guest.

From there he wrote to the king that he was willing either to go into exile or to return with an escort of one knight, one squire and one

Robert Curthose, Duke of Normandy

Seal of Empress Matilda

John of Gaunt

Henry VII as a young man by Jacques Le Boucq

Henry VII in middle age, by Michael Sittow

Perkin Warbeck by Jacques Le Boucq

Opposite: Lady Jane Grey attributed to Master John

Mary Tudor by Hans Eworth

servant to prove his innocence. Richard's suspicions of his uncle were continually fed by his favourites, who had good reason to fear the duke, but he had a strong advocate at court in the Princess Joan, the Black Prince's widow and the king's mother. The king publicly announced his confidence in his uncle's loyalty, issued writs to sheriffs to guard him from harm, and ordered him to return with a full complement of armed retainers. The revolt had been quelled and the duke, whom a shaken king could not afford to do without, returned to triumph over his enemies through royal favour. The terrorised haves had closed ranks behind the slogan: 'Villeins ye are and villeins ye shall remain'.

It was plain now that the duke would never become King of England. Apart from the hatred his wealth and arrogance and ill-success aroused, his elder brother Lionel had left a daughter who, with her heirs, stood between him and legal succession. Before his father's death John had attempted to eliminate them from the succession by lobbying the Good Parliament to introduce Salic law into English practice. When that failed his last hope was a nomination from the dying king; and this had not been forthcoming. So, if it could not be England, it must be Spain. In January 1382 he asked parliament for an advance of £600,000 to cover the pay of 20,000 men at arms and 2,000 archers for a six-months campaign in Portugal and Castile. The debt would be repaid within three years and the Lancastrian estates pledged as security. To achieve the goal of kingship, even his Lancastrian inheritance was to be put in jeopardy.

The peers favoured the request; the commons were cool. The duke argued the national interest in supporting Portugal against Castile and in breaking the Castilian alliance with France, but by the time the grant had been reluctantly agreed hostilities between the two Iberian powers were over. The next parliament was even cooler and favoured a peaceful settlement in Castile, but in 1386 at the age of 45 he had his way. The king himself contributed a thousand marks (borrowed from the Lombards) towards the loan, urged to do so by his favourite, the Earl of Oxford, who wanted the overweening duke as far away from England as possible.

It was fifteen years since John had married Constance and first made his claim. In seeking at last to make it good by force, he attracted an unexpected ally in the church. For Castile was a cockpit in the rivalry of the Great Schism. After the papacy returned to Rome from exile in Avignon, the French cardinals became disenchanted with Urban VI and elected a French anti-pope, Clement, back in Avignon. The religious faith of the states of Europe thereupon divided along strictly political lines: France and her allies, Castile and Scotland, believed in Clement; the emperor, England and Portugal were for Urban. In Rome John of Gaunt was seen as a Christian hero who would detach Castile from the cause of the ungodly. Urban hailed him as a Standard-Bearer of the Cross – a second Robert of Normandy – and issued bulls in his favour. The mercenary army aiding him in his dynastic enterprise was granted privileges normally accorded to crusaders. In spite of opposition within the church in England, papal indulgences were sold to finance the expedition, and crusaders and their financial backers were bribed with promises of absolution. It was as well that Wyclif was dead. On 18 February the standard of the cross was raised in St Paul's and a month later King John and Queen Constance departed in state for embarcation at Plymouth.

The expeditionary force, numbering some 10,000 men, landed safely in Corunna. From there it marched unopposed to Santiago de Compostella, the capital of the Castilian province of Galicia, where John established his headquarters. As he began issuing letters in the style of *Nos El Rey*, the real king, Enrique's son Juan, whose army had already been destroyed by the Portuguese at Aljubarrota, was begging vainly for help from Anti-pope Clement and Charles VI of France and receiving little more in response than the discouraging exhortation: 'Whom God loveth He chasteneth'. In desperation he offered John a secret deal, proposing a marriage between their children. This was a sensible solution, since even the most arrogant of Englishmen could hardly have expected to impose himself permanently on a scarcely less proud Spanish people by force of arms. But John disdained the proposal as ignoble and chose to spend the winter strengthening his position by marrying his eldest daughter, Philippa of Lancaster, to his ally the King of Portugal and extending his own territorial control over the whole of Galicia.

In March 1387 a strong English and Portuguese force marched out of Braganza to invade Castile. Nothing now seemed to stand in the way of the great pretender winning his crown and sitting on his throne after waiting so impatiently for so long. Juan was too weak to fight, but the French advised him on the correct tactics to pursue against the English: lay waste and abandon the countryside; fortify and garrison the towns. In the open during the unaccustomed heat of summer the English army was soon exposed to a fate worse than an enemy army.

The first attack came from dysentery, the second from the plague. The death roll grew so large that disbandment was the only answer. John returned to Portugal with some of the survivors; Juan gladly allowed others safe passage to Gascony. On this occasion God, it seemed, had sided with the anti-pope.

The offer of a secret treaty was still available on the same terms, and the duke had now to swallow his pride to save his face. He and Constance renounced all claim to the kingdom of Castile in exchange for 600,000 gold francs to cover the cost of the campaign, an annuity of 40,000 francs during their lifetime, and the marriage of their daughter Katharine (aged fourteen) to the Infante Enrique (aged nine). If Enrique died before the marriage was consummated Katharine was to be married to his younger brother Fernando. Only if King Juan, Katharine, Enrique and Fernando all died without heirs would the crown come to John and Constance or their heirs.

Castile was John of Gaunt's last failure. During his absence abroad Richard's misgovernment of England had roused another uncle, Thomas of Woodstock, Duke of Gloucester, to assume the role of leader of the opposition. Civil war was narrowly averted, but the lives of the king's friends and counsellors were not spared by Gloucester's Merciless Parliament which met in February 1388. The following year, when Richard regained power, he recalled John from Bordeaux and greeted him as a deliverer, exchanging a heartfelt kiss of peace. Suddenly the unpopular duke suspected of treason had become popular as a pillar of the throne. His old enemies, the mayor and sheriffs of London and the abbot and monks of Westminster, welcomed him. Services were held in the abbey church and St Paul's cathedral in his honour. His title of duke and the county palatinate of Lancaster, held personally, were made heritable by his male heirs. On parliament's petitioning he was created Duke of Aquitaine for life.

Charged with the responsibility for making a settlement with France, the most formidable knight in the world of chivalry became transformed into the most eminent of European diplomats. As the familiar of crowned heads (one a nephew and two of them sons-in-law), of French dukes, Flemish and Gascon counts and Scottish earls, in place of war he jousted and talked peace. As chief guest at a state banquet in Amiens he was seated on the King of France's right hand and served by the dukes of Orleans and Bourbon. In England he was able to impose some semblance of order on the prevailing anarchy without reviving suspicion. Even the quest for heiresses was over.

When Constance died he felt free to marry Katharine, his mistress for the past 24 years. No one rebuked him for it, and pope and king readily agreed to legitimate their children. In 1396 he sealed an *entente cordiale* with the marriage of the King of England to the King of France's daughter.

His last and best years were spent playing the part of moderator and loyalist, guarding the king from Gloucester on the one side and unworthy favourites on the other. Still loaded with honours and estates but still uncrowned, he died in Leicester castle in February 1399 in his 59th year: 'words, life and all, old Lancaster hath spent'.[7] Without his advice and protection Richard was incapable of keeping his crown. It was snatched from his head by John's son before the year was out.

John of Gaunt's obituaries make varied reading: 'one of the most honourable specimens of the character of an old English baron which the history of this island is able to exhibit';[8] 'of deservedly pious memory';[9] 'known throughout the whole realm of England as a great fornicator';[10] 'an amiable nonentity'.[11] What is indisputable is that his virtues were courage, honour and generosity, and his vice was pride. He had the will and the power, but not the shrewdness or good fortune, to make himself a king.

4

Yorkists, Lancastrians and Henry Tudor

USURPATION breeds pretenders. For this reason the fifteenth and sixteenth centuries were vintage years for claimants to the throne of England.

With John of Gaunt dead and Henry Bolingbroke, his son and heir, in exile, Richard II decided to seize the duchy of Lancaster. It was a spiteful and foolish act which brought swift and fatal retribution. Bolingbroke returned to claim his rightful inheritance and took with it the crown which his father had never worn. 'The Crown sought to grasp Lancaster; instead Lancaster grasped the Crown.'[1] Richard was forced to abdicate, imprisoned in Pontefract castle and never seen alive again.

Before his death he was impersonated by a clerk. The deposed king's supporters were said to have resorted to this deception in an attempt on the life of the usurping Henry: 'We must go after him at Windsor and raise the country on the way. We will dress Magdalen as a king and have him ride with us, giving out that he is King Richard who has been set free. Everyone who sees him or hears about him will believe it . . .'[2] But, although some were deceived, most were not. Henry was forewarned and the attempt failed. The improbably named Magdalen is one of those scarcely known pretenders who were mere look-alikes and, whatever the outcome of their imposture, would never have been allowed to wear the crown in earnest.

While asserting his lawful rights in the matter of the duchy,

65

C. HOUSE OF YORK AND THE TUDOR CLAIM

This simplified genealogical tree omits John of Gaunt's first two marriages, which are included in Table B.

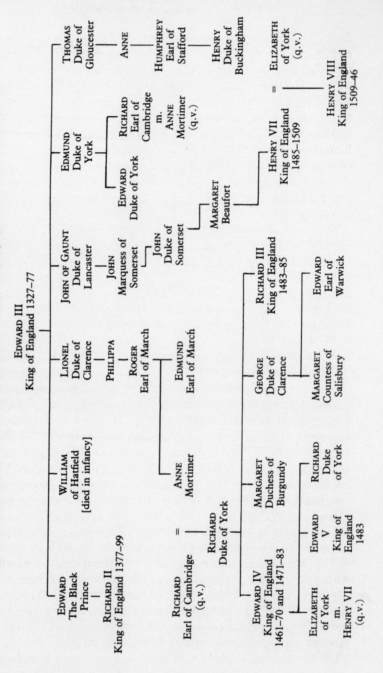

Bolingbroke had shown no respect for the lawful rights of others in the matter of the crown. In deposing and murdering his anointed sovereign lord he committed a mortal sin and the crime of high treason, whatever the provocation. And once the childless Richard was dead his true successor was the eight-year-old Edmund Mortimer, fifth Earl of March, on whose father Roger the succession had been formally settled by Act of Parliament. Through force of arms Bolingbroke was duly recognised and crowned as King Henry IV, but civil war was the ultimate consequence of his usurpation. Throughout the succeeding century no King of England was to enjoy an undisputed title to the crown. A self-effacing or openly defiant pretender was ever present, waiting for the wheel of fortune to turn.

Edmund was kept in confinement during Henry IV's lifetime, but released by Henry V. In 1415 a plot by his brother-in-law, Richard, Earl of Cambridge, to put him on the throne was betrayed by Edmund himself and Cambridge executed. During Henry V's wars in France Edmund served him faithfully as captain, admiral and king's lieutenant in Normandy. After Henry's death he was appointed Lieutenant of Ireland, where he died of the plague.

Thus after initial unrest (in 1403 at Shrewsbury Henry IV had narrowly won what nearly proved to be his Bosworth) the Lancastrian kings ruled unchallenged for three generations, until misgovernment, financial mismanagement, national humiliation at defeat in the Hundred Years War and Henry VI's feeble-mindedness opened the way for a rival claimant despite the passing of half a century. Edmund had firmly rejected the role of pretender, but his nephew and heir, Richard, third Duke of York (son of the beheaded Earl of Cambridge), was of a different mind. He advanced his claim with the assertion that 'though right for a time rest and be put to silence, yet it rotteth not nor shall not perish'.[3] In blunter terms, the heirs of Henry Bolingbroke had no more right to the crown than the heirs of any common thief to property he had stolen. A confusion of kings, usurpers and pretenders was the outcome of this declaration.

The bitter argument between York and Lancaster was essentially a dispute about the priority of heirs general over heirs male – the argument which had been lost by Lancaster in 1376 when the members of the Good Parliament rejected John of Gaunt's plea for the introduction of the Salic law, which barred female succession. Both families were direct descendants of Edward III. The Lancastrian kings were descended in the male line from John, the fourth son, and the third Duke of York in the male line from Edmund, the fifth son. But the superiority of York's claim was as heir general to Lionel, the third son, through his daughter Philippa, her son Roger, fourth Earl of March and his daughter, Anne Mortimer, who was the duke's mother. In France it was pragmatic use of the Salic law to bar the succession of Edward III of England (in the right of his mother, Isabella) which had turned the English kings into perpetual claimants to the French throne. Ironically, the most determined of these royal pretenders was Bolingbroke's son, Henry V, although setting aside the Salic law to make him King of France would logically have entailed an admission that he had no right to be King of England.

The Duke of York paid for his temerity with his head, which was cut off after a skirmish at Wakefield and hoisted above the Micklegate at York, adorned with a paper crown: fitting mockery for a failed pretender. But the death of the duke did not kill Yorkist rights. It merely transferred them into stronger, less fumbling hands. His eldest son had the courage, will and strength to realise the claim. The eighteen-year-old Edward, Earl of March, a six-foot-four-inch Plantagenet who was to fight six closely contested battles and win them all, avenged his father's death with bloody victories at Mortimer's Cross and Towton and was crowned as Edward IV. Henry VI was still alive, so for ten years (1461 to 1471) England enjoyed the doubtful privilege of more than one crowned and anointed king. Until 1470 Edward ruled while Henry was relegated to the role of fugitive pretender. Then for six months, by courtesy of Warwick the Kingmaker, the roles were reversed, until Edward returned from exile to win decisive victories at Barnet and Tewkesbury. In the fighting at Tewkesbury Henry's only son and heir was killed, and afterwards Henry himself died, probably put to death, in the Tower of London.

The royal house of Lancaster had ceased to exist, and surviving Lancastrians unreconciled to Yorkist rule were forced to back a rank outsider, the pretender Henry Tudor. Born in Pembroke castle on 28 January 1457, he was the son of Edmund Tudor, the eldest of three brothers who were the children of a misalliance. Young widows of rank were often susceptible to the charms of good-looking stewards or pages in their households. One such was Catherine of Valois, daughter of Charles VI of France and widow of Henry V. In retirement as queen dowager she took into her bed a personable young Welsh squire, and five children had been born to them before the royal council became aware of the liaison. Their union may well have been a valid marriage under canon law, but it would never have been authorised by the council and was considered politically scandalous. Either for this or for some other, unknown reason Catherine was ordered into Bermondsey abbey and Owen ap Meredith, later calling himself ap Tudor (the Welsh for Theodore), found himself in Newgate gaol.

These were Henry Tudor's paternal grandparents. His Lancastrian blood came through his mother, Lady Margaret Beaufort, who was aged thirteen and already a widow when he was born. Her father had been John, Earl and later Duke of Somerset, a grandson of John of Gaunt and Katharine Swynford. The children of that union had been born out of wedlock and their subsequent legitimation in 1397 was qualified by their half-brother Henry IV, ten years later, with the words *excepta dignitate regali*. An argument was mounted, nevertheless, that this statute of 1407 expressly disqualifying the Beauforts and their descendants from any right to the crown was a royal pronouncement without the force of law.

Henry was thus a mongrel of doubtful breeding. He was half English, a quarter French and Bavarian and, despite his Celtic upbringing, only a quarter Welsh. The royal blood of England and France flowed in his veins, but in each case through unions barely the right side of the blanket. His Welsh forebears had little connection with the famous Cadwallader whose red dragon he flaunted. They were an Anglesey family who had come down in the world since an ancestor served as steward to Llewellyn the Great (whose blood flowed, not in Tudor veins, but in those of the Yorkist kings, Edward IV and Richard III, through the marriage of Ralph Mortimer to Llewellyn's daughter, Gwladys the Dark).

Henry's father, Edmund, was, however, acknowledged by Henry VI as a half-brother; his legitimacy was endorsed by parliament; and he was dignified with the title of Earl of Richmond. After his death as a prisoner of war in his mid-twenties his posthumous son was brought up at Pembroke, under the guardianship first of the Lancastrian earl, his uncle Jasper Tudor, then of the man who became the Yorkist earl, William Herbert. Although the honour of Richmond had been declared forfeit to the crown after the Lancastrian defeat in 1461, the young Henry was still a valuable prize to Herbert, the leading Welsh Yorkist, who paid the crown £1000 for his wardship and intended to marry him to his eldest daughter. Henry's mother soon re-married, so his boyhood was spent as a member of the Herbert family in

Pembroke and Raglan, far removed from worldly events and royal expectations.

Warwick the Kingmaker's rebellion against Edward IV turned the wheel of fortune in Lancaster's favour. Herbert, loyal to the White Rose, lost a skirmish against Warwick near Banbury and was beheaded. During Henry VI's brief readeption in 1470/71 Henry Tudor, aged thirteen, set foot in England for the first time, being taken to London to meet the king. But then the wheel turned again. Edward IV returned from exile to bring the Lancastrian dynasty to a final, violent end – and clear the path to the throne for the boy from Pembroke.

It was Jasper Tudor who first realised that his elder brother's son was the best prospect for the Lancastrian cause left alive after the carnage of Tewkesbury. On learning the news at Chepstow, he hurried his nephew to Pembroke, where they were besieged. Escaping, they begged a ship off the mayor of Tenby and sailed for France. Henry had suddenly become a refugee in a forlorn cause. As a pretender to the throne for the next fourteen years his chances appeared slim indeed – much slighter than those of his predecessors, Robert and Matilda, who had strong claims and a following large enough to attempt to enforce them. Henry's unpredictable success was the result of a series of unlikely accidents shrewdly exploited.

Evading pursuit in the aftermath of catastrophe was lucky enough. Just as providential was a storm in the Channel which forced a change of course and led to landfall in Brittany, the last of the independent French duchies. Duke Francis's life was devoted to the maintenance of Breton independence, which Louis XI, the spider King of France, was weaving plots to bring to an end. The attitude of England, the other neighbouring power, was crucial. The duke needed the English alliance to preserve his duchy; the king needed English complicity or weakness to seize it. The leverage to be exerted through possession of a pretender to the English crown would have been welcome to either party. The obvious Tudor destination was France, which had launched the failed Lancastrian expedition to oust the Yorkists, who were allies of its enemy, Burgundy. But Louis was later to come to terms with Edward, and there is little doubt that if the Lancastrian pretender had been in French hands at the time of the Treaty of Picquiny he would have been handed over as part of the price of peace.

In Brittany Henry kicked his heels for thirteen discouraging years in honourable custody. Like other refugee pretenders in the middle ages, he was both guest and prisoner, a diplomatic pawn living in comfort and safety but without liberty. Still known by his forfeited title of Earl of Richmond (which Edward had given to his brother George, Duke of Clarence), he was moved from castle to castle, always treated with respect but often separated from his uncle and not permitted his own entourage and servants in case they should organise an escape.

King Edward offered the duke money for the return of the fugitives, but this was declined because their detention was reckoned to be more valuable, although the duke, not seeking to give offence, readily promised that they would be securely guarded. After Picquiny Edward tried again. He bound himself to treat Henry well and make a worthy marriage for him, possibly with one of his own daughters. Agreement was reached and Henry taken to St Malo to be shipped to England. There he took fright and pretended to be too ill to travel, while urgent representations were made to the duke that Edward's true intentions were very different. Probably his fears were ill-founded: Edward was firmly enthroned and pursuing a policy of reconciliation. But the duke was induced to change his mind and Henry remained in Brittany until Edward's premature death transformed his situation.

The king was survived by his queen (Elizabeth Woodville), two sons and five daughters. The boys, Edward, Prince of Wales and Richard, Duke of York, were aged twelve and nine. Edward was proclaimed king as Edward V, but his father had willed a protectorship until he came of age to the boy's uncle, Richard, Duke of Gloucester. Gloucester lived in Yorkshire and news of his brother's death in London was quickly followed by reports that the queen and her relations were intent on ignoring the protectorship and seizing power for themselves. Forewarned, Gloucester intercepted the boy king on his journey from Ludlow to London under a Woodville escort. They entered the capital together and for nearly two months the business of the government was transacted in the name of King Edward V 'by the advice of our dearest uncle, the Duke of Gloucester, Protector of this our realm during our young age, and of the lords of our council'.[4] Preparations were made for the coronation, but in the event it was his dearest uncle who was crowned, not the young Edward.

The assumption of the crown by Richard was occasioned by the discovery of a plot against his life 'by the queen, her blood, adherents and affinity'.[5] This must have led him and his advisers to believe that unless he took the crown himself he and they could never be secure from Woodville vengeance when Edward came of age. The fate of two previous dukes of Gloucester who had been Protectors (to Richard II and Henry VI) were ominous precedents. At the end of their period of office both had been murdered. Richard of Gloucester's period as a pretender lasted from a Sunday to the following Thursday. His claim was made public in a sermon on 22 June 1483 and he ascended the throne on the 26th, 'for he saw he could not live unless he were king; there was no safety but in sovereignty'.[6] From the date of his accession his deposed nephew became the new Yorkist pretender.

Richard III, as he became, took the crown with the assent of an assembly of lords and commons and the backing of the city of London. His coronation was among the best attended of any in the middle ages and his title to the crown was later confirmed in an Act of Parliament. Edward IV's children were declared to be illegitimate because he was troth-plight to the daughter of the Earl of Shrewsbury before his marriage to Elizabeth Woodville, which was therefore invalid under canon law. The pre-contract was vouched for by the Bishop of Bath and Wells. If the story is true, Richard's claim was better than his nephew's. If untrue, it served as a convenient fiction in securing the succession for the person widely regarded as most suitable. At a time when strong rule was required to end lawlessness and prevent a renewed outbreak of civil war Richard stood pre-eminent as a man of high reputation and proven ability as both soldier and administrator. The reign of an untried boy king under his unpopular mother's influence was not an inviting prospect.

When Richard was crowned the young Edward and his brother were still lodged in the Tower of London, where kings traditionally resided before their coronation. What happened to them subsequently is the most hotly debated of historical mysteries. Speculation is unending, but their fate remains unknown to this day. Their disappearance while under his protection and in his power has led naturally to the supposition that their uncle disposed of them, as Henry IV and Edward IV were presumed to have disposed of their predecessors on the throne. But these are not true parallels because Richard had no need to kill his nephews to take the crown and they were still alive when he was crowned. The sanctity of the medieval monarch derived from his coronation, most particularly from the anointing with holy oil. The murdered kings – Edward II, Richard

II and Henry VI – all enjoyed this semi-divine status in the eyes of their subjects, but not the uncrowned, unanointed Edward V. It was Richard III who was crowned and anointed, and the princes while alive remained more of a threat to the pretensions of Henry Tudor, who could hardly have expected to succeed to the throne without their death.

For Henry, Yorkist dissension was another act of God. By his successful coup Richard had humbled the Woodville faction and antagonised Edwardian loyalists. New hope stirred Lancastrian survivors in England. Eyes began to turn towards Brittany, where the duke seized the opportunity to complain that he would be obliged to yield to pressure from France and hand Henry over to the French king unless Richard sent him a large contingent of archers to help protect the duchy. Richard, needing all available archers at home, found the price too high, but Louis' death in August brought a temporary respite for the duke, and his hostage stayed in Brittany.

In England the misnamed Buckingham rebellion broke out in October. Motives were mixed. Richard was (and remains) the only King of England to have come to power at the head of northerners. In the south his followers were feared and resented. Many of Edward IV's household and other officials displaced by them became disaffected. One stated objective of the rebels was to rescue the princes; another to avenge their death. Henry, second Duke of Buckingham, nominal leader of the revolt, was a descendant, through the female line, of Edward III's youngest son and had pretensions of his own. He had done more than any man to put Richard on the throne and now turned against him. It is possible that he had had the princes murdered and Richard had not thanked him for it. Under the influence of Bishop Morton, one of the conspirators against Richard's life, he publicly announced his conversion to Henry's cause and invited him to sail for England. It is a reasonable supposition, however, that Buckingham was aiming for the crown himself and intended Henry as his next victim after Richard.

Fanning the flames of insurrection from London was Henry's redoubtable mother, Lady Margaret Beaufort, now married to her fourth husband, Lord Stanley, who still held the post of Richard's chamberlain despite suspicion of involvement in the plot against him. Throughout Richard's two-year reign Lady Margaret took full advantage of her husband's position to devote herself to lobbying for her son, forging alliances for him with Buckingham and Edward IV's widow, and supplying him with an invaluable flow of money and intelligence. Richard's forbearance towards her when her activities became known was remarkably foolhardy. Although herself the real Lancastrian heir (yet allowing the claim to pass through her to her son, as Matilda had eventually been persuaded to do for an earlier Henry), she was left at liberty, subject only to restraint by her barely loyal husband.

Richard's treatment of Lady Margaret and Queen Elizabeth Woodville belies his reputation as a blood-thirsty tyrant. The only female political victim to suffer death in Plantagenet times was Joan of Arc. It was the Tudors who were to introduce the killing of women into English political life, and the practice was to die with them – but not before it had proved fatal to two female pretenders.

Encouraged by Buckingham's invitation to his captive and in expectation of favours to follow, Duke Francis gave Henry his blessing and ten thousand gold crowns. A fleet of fifteen ships with several thousand men aboard set sail in mid-October 1483, only to be scattered by a storm. This proved to be another intervention by providence on Henry's behalf, for in England the ill-organised revolt had fizzled out without even a fight. The bad weather had prevented Buckingham's army from Wales crossing the Severn, and if Henry's expedition had landed it would have been doomed. As it was, Henry's own ship reached the English coast alone. But without the support of the rest of the fleet he refused to be inveigled ashore by a small guard on the coast who pretended to be fellow rebels but were, in fact, the king's men. Throughout his career, as pretender and king, Henry's suspicious nature served him well.

The collapse of the rebellion cost Buckingham his head, but it was the making of Henry. More fugitive rebels found asylum in Brittany, and suddenly he was surrounded by men of stature and experience. The new exiles included three bishops – John Morton of Ely (who took refuge in Flanders), Lionel Woodville of Salisbury and Peter Courtenay of Exeter, as well as the Marquess of Dorset (another Woodville) and the future Earl of Devon (another Courtenay). Henry now had a court at Vannes and on Christmas day his adherents gathered in Rennes cathedral to swear homage to him, while he in return promised to unite the rival red and white roses by marrying Edward IV's eldest daughter.

Events in 1484 continued to run in his favour. Richard made no move to deprive him of the proposed union with Elizabeth of York by marrying her to someone else. Henry's mother was operating an efficient and well-funded network of messengers and spies, so that he enjoyed what nearly all medieval pretenders so notably lacked: accurate and up-to-date information. In April Edward of Middleham, the recently created Prince of Wales, who was Richard's only legitimate child, died, leaving the king without a direct heir.

But the best of Henry's good luck came in June when he escaped extradition to England by a hair's breadth. Anne of Beaujeu, the strong-minded Regent of France, had reimposed the threat to absorb Brittany, and the duke and his treasurer, Peter Landois, were desperate for allies. Landois' own position was also under threat from dissident Bretons and while the duke was ill he decided to act on a secret agreement made with Richard for the supply of a thousand archers in exchange for handing over the pretender.

Wind of the agreement reached Morton in Flanders and he contrived to warn Henry in the nick of time through one of Lady Margaret's secret agents. Riding out from Vannes with only a handful of retainers on the pretext of paying a visit in the neighbourhood, Henry stopped in a wood to change his clothes and disguise himself as a servant. He then galloped for the French border, which he crossed a bare hour ahead of troops sent in pursuit by Landois. The duke, on his recovery, was said to be outraged by his minister's behaviour. More probably he was making the best of a botched job and appeasing France when he allowed Henry's followers, some three hundred in number, to join him. In France they received an enthusiastic welcome as bargaining counters in the age-old game against England.

At this juncture another escape heightened Henry's credibility as a pretender. The de Veres were among the most illustrious of Lancastrian loyalists. John, thirteenth Earl of Oxford, had commanded the left wing of the army defeated at Barnet. Afterwards, as a privateer, he had seized St Michael's Mount before being captured and spending eleven years imprisoned in the castle at Hammes in the English pale of Calais. He made his getaway by suborning the garrison commander, Sir James Blount, and they rode away together to join the English exiles in Paris.

Henry was now in a position to adopt the style of royalty and, although wholly dependent on the good will of England's traditional enemy, to allow himself the airs of a real king. Letters, 'given under our signet', were signed 'H.' or 'H.R.' The French court under the boy king Charles VIII was quick to admit his claim but slow to back it with tangible aid. He was to be kept on tenterhooks for twelve months.

In addition to the enmity between the two kingdoms running from Norman and Angevin times up to France's recent support for Lancaster against York, the current King of England was personally unpopular in France. Almost alone among the English, Richard, then Duke of Gloucester, had refused to be party to the Treaty of Picquiny, not concealing his disgust when his brother Edward IV allowed himself to be bought off by Louis XI instead of fighting. After his accession the French chancellor, in a general attack on the English as a nation of regicides, had publicly accused him of murdering his nephews. Nevertheless, French diplomacy was hard-headed and there would have been no compunction in making a deal with an enemy of France had it suited France's purpose.

The most pressing motive in succouring Henry was to avoid English intervention in Brittany, but there were wider benefits in prospect. According to a proclamation by Richard, 'one Henry Tydder', in usurping 'the name and title of royal estate', 'whereunto he hath no manner [of] interest, right or colour, as every man well knoweth', had covenanted to surrender to 'the ancient enemy' the English claim to 'the crown and realm of France, together with the duchies of Normandy, Anjou and Maine, Gascony and Guienne' and the 'castles and towns of Calais, Guisnes and Hammes with the marches appertaining to the same'.[7]

All this seems likely, for the French were in a position to impose extortionate terms. But they were to be disappointed. Some commercial concessions were obtained as a result of Henry's usurpation, but not the prize of Calais, and Henry even came to adopt the by now traditional English claim to the sovereignty of France. Even the benefit to be gained in Brittany proved a miscalculation, for in July 1485, while the invasion force was mustering, the Anglophile Landois was ejected from office, and France and Brittany signed a treaty two days after Henry had landed in Wales. From that moment his success or failure could have little effect on French interests, and it is difficult to avoid the conclusion that a further delay of two or three weeks would have aborted the expedition and left him to end his days as miserably as a Jacobite.

He sailed from Harfleur on 1 August at the head of some 400 English exiles, a small number of Breton and Scots mercenaries and a French army of 4000 men supplied by the Marshal of France, Philippe de Crèvecoeur, including 1500 veterans discharged from a military base near Rouen. They were favoured by a 'soft, southern wind' and the fact that an army under Lord Lovel was waiting for them at the wrong Milford. He was on guard in Hampshire when they landed unopposed near Dale in Milford Haven on the south-west tip of Wales.

Neither the Welsh nor the English flocked to join his standard, as later Tudor chroniclers liked to suggest. But by hugging the coastal route north of Cardigan he managed to march through Wales without encountering any armed opposition. To avoid being nipped in the bud was one success; to reach Shrewsbury and Stanley country in safety was another. The intentions of the Stanley brothers were crucial to his do-or-die attempt on the crown. Lord Stanley was his step-father and Sir William had already been proclaimed a traitor by the king. Their power lay in the north-west, in Lancashire and Cheshire. Henry met them secretly at Atherstone on 18 August. By then he had been joined by about 800 Welshmen under Rhys ap Thomas, 400 Englishmen under Gilbert Talbot, uncle of the young Earl of Shrewsbury, and a few other dissidents, the most important of whom was Sir John Savage. But that was hardly enough. Not a single peer had defected from Richard, and without the Stanleys Henry was lost.

News of the landing on 7 August had reached the king in Nottingham four days later. He at once advanced to Leicester, confident and probably relieved that this troublesome pretender had at last ventured within reach. On the evening of Sunday, 21 August 1485 he occupied the high ground of Ambion Hill in open moorland to the south of Market Bosworth in Leicestershire. There he was strategically well placed to intercept Henry on his route along Watling Street towards London, and early the following morning their armies were engaged in one of the most momentous and worst documented battles in English history.

Estimates of the numbers involved vary and all are unreliable. Richard, underestimating Henry, had moved before his army was fully mustered (the contingent from York arrived too late), but even so it must greatly have outnumbered Henry's. In the event, however, neither the contingent under the Earl of Northumberland, who lurked in the rear, nor that of Lord Stanley, who hovered on the wing, took part in the fighting. Those who did fight – Richard's van under the Duke of Norfolk and Henry's under the Earl of Oxford – were probably roughly equal in number, and the most likely explanation for Richard's defeat is the superiority of the seasoned French troops. These, rarely mentioned by English chroniclers and historians, included gunners as well as infantry, and French artillery at that period was accounted the best in Europe. When the king's leading troops charged downhill to scatter the foreigners and rebels, the opposition proved unexpectedly professional and fierce. In the hand-to-hand fighting honours were even until the death of Norfolk demoralised his men.

Unlike Sir William (later executed as a traitor by Henry), Lord Stanley was a trimmer. He had not lined his men up with the rebel army, as his stepson had implored and expected: he was waiting to come in on the winning side. So was Northumberland. When they saw how the fighting was going both commanders refused Richard's orders to join battle. Throughout the Wars of the Roses the nobility had been steadfast in the pursuit of self-interest, some shamelessly switching allegiance from rose to rose according to where the advantage was perceived. Tudor claims that Richard was deserted for being a monstrous tyrant were propaganda. Stanley and Northumberland betrayed their king at Bosworth because they reckoned to do better with Henry. Cautiously they had not shown their hands in advance, but chose treachery in the middle of the battle. Had Norfolk's initial advance overwhelmed the enemy as intended, their loyalty to Richard would no doubt have been demonstrated in a valiant contribution to a victory already won.

When their treachery became apparent the king had two choices: he could flee the field and re-group his forces to fight another day or he could pluck triumph out of disaster by killing the pretender with his own hand. A man of courage and chivalry, he chose to gather his household knights around him and make a cavalry charge across the bare heath, defiantly exposing himself to attack by Stanley troops massed on his flank. He may have calculated that Lord Stanley would dither until it was all over and, if so, he may have calculated correctly. But Sir William, already publicly branded a traitor, had nothing to lose. The king had time to axe down Sir William Brandon, Henry's principal standard-bearer, who must have been close to Henry himself, before the Stanley men recovered from their surprise and fell on him and his small band. Cut down and unhorsed like Stephen at Lincoln, he died 'fighting manfully in the thickest press of his enemies'.[8]

The death of the king signalled the end of the battle. It had lasted little more than an hour and there is no contemporary evidence that Henry had taken any part in the fighting. He was a politician, not a soldier. He had led the perilous adventure, but others had won the crown for him and he showed gratitude to his uncle Jasper by making him a duke and to the French by creating their commander, Philibert de Chandée, Earl of Bath – a significantly high honour for a foreigner. Lord Stanley's reward for delayed treachery was the earldom of Derby. Legend records that Richard's crown (probably a gold coronet worn round his helmet) was retrieved from a thorn bush and placed round Henry's head on what is still known as Crown Hill. The rule of the Plantagenets, who had worn the crown since the Empress Matilda's son had succeeded King Stephen nearly 350 years before, was thus brought to an abrupt conclusion. The Tudor pretender had succeeded in the face of apparently unsurmountable odds and his triumph must have been greeted less with joy or sorrow than with astonishment throughout the country.

The problem of legitimacy was solved without fuss by a simple enactment that 'the inheritance of the crowns of the realms of England and of France . . . be, rest, remain, and abide in the most royal person of our now sovereign lord King Harry VII and in the heirs of his body lawfully come, perpetually . . .'[9] In other words, he was king because no one was in a position to argue. In assuming the guise of one sent from Heaven to rescue the realm from a usurper, he realised the unfulfilled ambition of every pretender. The dreams of others became nightmares, but his came true.

5

Lambert Simnel, Ireland's King

LESS than two hours of fighting by his supporters had transformed the Tudor pretender into King Henry VII. God, he declared, had given him the crown in battle. That apart, he had the worst claim of any English king since William of Normandy. When Richard III lay dead there were, it has been estimated, 29 people still alive with a better claim than Henry's. Yet he even anticipated the divine will by dating his reign from the day before the battle at Bosworth so that the crowned and anointed king and all who had kept their oaths of fealty and fought for him could be, and were, attainted for committing high treason against a man who at the time had been himself a traitor condemned under an Act of Attainder.

In the dubious circumstances of his accession all the new king's considerable political guile and single-minded dedication to self-interest were to prove necessary to retain what he had won. Awaiting a papal dispensation, he was slow to bolster the legitimacy of his rule by honouring his promise to marry Edward IV's eldest daughter, Elizabeth of York, and, determined to be recognised in his own right, even slower to consent to her being crowned as queen (a ceremony which he himself chose not to attend).

The crown became Henry's in August 1485 and the first armed rebellion by the defeated Yorkists erupted at Easter the following year. Francis, Viscount Lovel, who had been King Richard's close friend and chamberlain, broke out of sanctuary at Colchester with the brothers Humphrey and Thomas Stafford to raise a force which would take the usurper by surprise in Yorkshire. Henry narrowly escaped assassination while at worship on 23 April, the feast day of England's patron saint, St George. It was a dangerous incident, but he rose to the challenge and proved – as he was to continue to prove – too quick and resourceful for his enemies. While hastily mobilising an army, he proclaimed a general pardon for any rebel who submitted immediately. The rising collapsed, Lovel was driven into hiding, and the Staffords sought another sanctuary, this time in the abbey at Abingdon, from which they were forcibly removed. The policy which was to become Henry's formula for survival – a carefully calculated blend of harshness and leniency – was again applied. Humphrey, the elder brother, suffered brutal torture and execution; Thomas, the younger, was pardoned.

The rebels' purpose had been to restore the house of York to the throne, but whom did they seek to crown? Although persistently rumoured to be still alive, Edward IV's sons, the princes in the Tower, were missing, generally presumed dead. In their absence the leading pretender was their cousin, Edward, Earl of Warwick, son of the executed and attainted George, Duke of Clarence. His father's attainder had disinherited the young Edward and barred him from any claim to the throne. Otherwise, as the son of an elder brother, he would even have stood between his uncle, Richard of Gloucester, and the crown. But attainders were political acts readily reversible on a change of regime, so Richard's kindly treatment of this nephew, who was scarcely less of a threat to him than the bastardised princes, is often cited as an indication of his innocence in the mystery surrounding their disappearance and a clue to their possible survival.

To Henry, Clarence's young son posed a greater threat. One of the first acts of the victor of Bosworth was to despatch a posse of men to Sheriff Hutton in Yorkshire to secure the person of Warwick, along with those of Elizabeth of York and her sisters, who were living in a royal nursery in the castle. Edward, aged ten, was taken to the Tower of London, where he was kept a close prisoner for the remaining fourteen years of his life, until judicially murdered by Henry on a trumped-up charge of high treason.

Incarceration and ill treatment may have sent the boy simpleminded – according to one chronicler he was kept so ignorant of the world that he could not tell a goose from a capon – but as an undoubted, legitimate Plantagenet, descended from no fewer than three of Edward III's sons, he was the obvious figurehead for Yorkist disaffection. After the death of Richard III's only son he had even been briefly considered as heir to the throne and, although his father's titles and estates were forfeit, the title inherited through his mother was one to stir men's hearts and memories. Warwick was the premier earldom of England, made famous throughout Europe by his grandfather, the kingmaker. In the young Edward, if they could rescue him, those determined to restore Yorkist rule would have a leader whose birth and blood would win wide acceptance for him as the rightful king.

In Ireland in January of 1487 the standard of rebellion was raised in his name. A young priest called Richard Simons had arrived there with a 'comely youth and well favoured'[1] said to be Warwick. Unlike the previous year's, this threat was to gather strength beyond Henry's immediate grasp. Bitter experience had taught Lovel that a general uprising in England could not be expected and there could be no appeal against the verdict of Bosworth without foreign aid. The French had put Henry on the throne; Irish, Flemish and Germans had to be enlisted to remove him.

From his refuge on the Lancashire coast Lovel had sailed secretly to Flanders, where the Yorkist cause was being stoutly maintained by Edward IV's and Richard III's sister Margaret, widow of Charles the Bold (or Rash) and now the dowager Duchess of Burgundy. In March he was joined there by John de la Pole, Earl of Lincoln who, in the words of his subsequent attainder, 'traitorously departed' from England with many other 'false traitors'.[2]

Lincoln was a more formidable adversary than the imprisoned Warwick. Then in his mid twenties, he was the eldest son of the eldest sister of the Yorkist kings: Elizabeth, Duchess of Suffolk. Under Richard III he had served as President of the Council of the North and as the king's Lieutenant in Ireland. In May 1485, superseding Warwick (presumably on grounds of age), he had been formally designated heir to the throne. After fighting for Richard at Bosworth he had become a beneficiary of Henry's leniency, for the de la Poles may well have been thought too powerful a family to drive into opposition, at least until Henry had a surer hold on the crown. Lincoln was even appointed a member of the privy council: partly perhaps so that Henry could keep a vigilant eye on him – but, as it proved, not vigilant enough.

Once in Flanders, Lincoln was recognised by both sides as the real leader of the false Warwick's rebellion, but he paid lip service to the comely youth's pretensions and advanced no claim of his own. His aunt Margaret's court at Tournai became the headquarters of the campaign, and she took upon herself the post of paymaster, hiring a company of German mercenaries under the command of a captain of renown named Martin Schwartz. The invasion was to be launched from Ireland where there was a strong attachment to the house of York and fighting men could be recruited in large numbers.

Oxford men have been prominent in the affairs of England for eight centuries, and the Warwick who had made his appearance in Ireland hailed from that seat of learning beside the Thames. But Lambert Simnel was town, not gown: the son of an Oxford tradesman variously described as a joiner, carpenter, organ-builder, baker or shoemaker. He was the same age as Warwick and had been well coached in princely behaviour by the 'subtil' Simons. At first, in view of reports that at least one of Edward IV's sons had survived, he was groomed to impersonate the younger prince, Richard, Duke of York. But then came the rumour that Warwick had been murdered in the Tower and a switch in imposture seemed opportune. If the tale was true, Henry would be unable to produce Warwick and either be branded as his murderer or exposed to the danger of Simnel's claim being credited. If it was untrue, at least Warwick's supporters would be reassured that he was not dead and all the more ready to fight in his cause.

To prove Simnel 'a vain shadow'[3] Henry responded to the imposture by parading the real Warwick through the streets of London and allowing him into St Paul's cathedral to join the congregation for a high mass. A free pardon was offered to all who would abandon the rebellion. The Irish, however, preferred to believe that they had the real earl and it was Henry's who was the impostor. Nor were they impressed by the offer of pardon from a man they regarded as a usurper. In England their pretender might be denounced as a low-born dissembler, but in Ireland he was acclaimed as the rightful heir to the kingdom of England and lordship of Ireland in succession to Richard III.

Ireland and the house of York had been drawn together more than fifty years before when, on the death of his uncle Edmund Mortimer, the duke who was King Richard's father had inherited the Mortimer, Lacy and De Burgo titles and estates to become Earl of Ulster and Lord of Connaught and Trim and thus pre-eminent among the Anglo-Irish barons. After his defeat by the Lancastrians at Ludford in

1459 it was to Ireland that he fled and when he returned to England to claim the crown it was with a large Irish following. In April 1460, as Lieutenant of Ireland, he had held a parliament at Drogheda at which it was enacted that Ireland was to be bound only by laws passed by her own parliament and by the decisions of her own courts – the first dawning of Irish independence since the papal Bull of 1155 which had instructed the Irish people to accept and obey King Henry II of England as their liege lord.

This declaration was the bedrock of Yorkist loyalty in Ireland. The duke, in John Stow's words, 'won such favour among that people as could never be separated from him and his lineage'.[4] To the Anglo-Irish he was 'one of our own'. In the Wars of the Roses they fought fiercely for York, headed by the Fitzgeralds, the leading Irish-Norman family, who held the earldoms of Kildare and Desmond. In 1477 the eighth Earl of Kildare, known as the Great Earl, was appointed Deputy Lieutenant and began his long reign as uncrowned King of Ireland. To him and his affinity the Tudor victory at Bosworth spelled disaster.

Henry's preoccupation with English affairs offered a respite. Any hasty attempt to remove Kildare from office and power would have meant a war which the new king was too insecure to contemplate. But should he retain the crown he would be bound to assert his rights in Ireland in time, or so the Irish lords believed. The arrival of Simons and his protégé gave Kildare the opportunity to make a pre-emptive strike of his own. They both swore to him that the boy was indeed Warwick, the Duke of York's grandson, the son of the Duke of Clarence who had been born in Dublin and had lived there when, like his father, he had held the office of Lieutenant. Both personally and politically Simnel was irresistible. He 'could reckon up his pedigree so readilie'[5] and answer all their questions about life at Edward IV's court. And was he not vouched for by his cousin Lincoln and his aunt, the dowager Duchess of Burgundy?

The imposture of Lambert Simnel later became apparent to all, and historians enjoying the benefit of hindsight have therefore judged that Kildare and his associates must have been aware that the boy's claims were spurious. But this is by no means certain: the Deputy was too adroit to stake his life on a palpable fraud. It of course suited his ends to acknowledge Simnel as Warwick, but no more than it suited Henry's to call the boy a tradesman's son. Accurate information was hard to come by in the fifteenth century.

Once committed, the Great Earl was not given to half measures. He had been in correspondence with the Yorkist exiles in Flanders and when Lincoln arrived in Dublin with an army of English loyalists and German mercenaries Kildare proceeded to have the boy crowned in Christ Church cathedral by the Archbishop of Dublin. Thus Simnel became King Edward VI, wearing a crown borrowed from a statue of the Blessed Virgin Mary.

After the ceremony the new king was carried in triumph through the crowded streets on the shoulders of the mayor to his coronation feast in the castle. The Deputy appointed himself his tutor and protector and summoned a parliament to give formal recognition to their new sovereign lord. All Ireland 'yielded obedience',[6] except for the pro-Tudor Butler family (earls of Ormonde), the city of Waterford (which they controlled) and some bishops who were mindful of a Bull with which Pope Innocent VII had armed King Henry the previous year. This required them to excommunicate all who rebelled against the king, and Kildare was duly excommunicated, although doubtless not unduly concerned. Excommunications, like attainders, were political tools: temporary measures subject to re-negotiation when the wheel of fortune turned.

The army from Flanders had reached Ireland on 5 May 1487, the coronation took place on the 24th, and on 4 June the expeditionary force sailed for England, reinforced by a large but ill-armed Irish contingent led by Sir Thomas Fitzgerald, the Deputy's brother, who resigned the chancellorship of Ireland for the occasion.

Lincoln's escape to Flanders and the gathering at Margaret of Burgundy's court had led Henry to believe that the invasion would come from that quarter. Troops were assembled to guard the east coast and watch was 'diligently kept' there 'that none other might escape or give them succour'.[7] Henry himself travelled to Norwich. Then on 8 May, learning that the destination of Lincoln's army was Ireland, he moved to the midlands, where he made Kenilworth his headquarters and issued a general summons to arms.

Earlier he had taken the precaution of stripping his mother-in-law, Elizabeth Woodville, of all her possessions, including even her widow's jointure, and immuring her in Bermondsey abbey where she led 'a wretched and a miserable life'[8] until her death there, penniless, five years later. The former queen was an inveterate conspirator and Henry's action at this date raises the suspicion that she may have been plotting with his enemies in the belief that one or other of her sons by

King Edward was still alive. A son by her previous marriage, Thomas, Marquess of Dorset, was imprisoned in the Tower at the same time, and Henry was still delaying the coronation of her daughter as queen. Henry may well have had in mind the treasonable actions by his own mother, Margaret Beaufort, committed on his behalf before Bosworth. Who could know what similar sympathies and furtive assistance the Yorkist invaders might be attracting in high places? (Two years later the Abbot of Abingdon, head of one of the most important abbeys in England, was to be arraigned with others for traitorously conspiring to destroy the king and bring aid to the Earl of Lincoln.)

Conveyed across the Irish Sea by 'a great navie', Simnel, Lincoln and Lovel with 'a great multitude of strangers'[9] made landfall near Broughton in Furness at the head of the Duddon channel in a remote part of the Lancashire coast. There they were joined by Sir Thomas Broughton, who had concealed Lovel after his abortive rising with the Staffords, and marched across the Pennines into Yorkshire where they were counting on local support and took care to avoid 'spoiling or hurting' the inhabitants and their livestock and crops. From Masham messengers were sent to York, only to return with a message from the mayor that rebels would be denied entry to the city.

This was an unexpected rebuff, for the north was believed to be as staunchly Yorkist as Ireland. The Duke of York had married a Nevill, and the Nevills were a northern family as powerful as the Percys. During the last eleven years of Edward IV's reign Richard, Duke of Gloucester had been lord of the north and won wide popularity for firm and fair administration as his brother's viceroy. After Edward's death it was with the backing of northerners that he took the crown, and during his reign they received substantial rewards from his patronage.

After Richard's death the memory of him in the north remained so strong that, in Francis Bacon's words, 'it lies like lees in the bottom of men's hearts and if the vessel was but stirred it would come up'.[10] That part of the country never became fully reconciled to the Tudor usurpation. Less than two years after the invasion from Ireland a visit by Henry's tax collectors was to succeed where Simnel and Lincoln had failed. It turned the restlessness of the north into a 'great mutiny', and 'the meaner sort' took their revenge on the Earl of Northumberland, who had betrayed Richard at Bosworth, by killing him and his servants in his own house. An army had to be sent to put down disturbances in York and Durham. Later, the north was to march against Henry VIII in the Pilgrimage of Grace and northern earls to lead a revolt against Elizabeth I. But in 1487, when the suspicions Henry VII harboured about Yorkist sympathisers in the south were more justifiable in the north, the one real opportunity to make amends for the débâcle of Bosworth was let slip.

In the Act of Attainder against Lincoln the meagreness of his English adherence is pitifully revealed. Apart from Broughton only one other knight is named (Sir Henry Bodrugan), together with eight squires, six gentlemen and fourteen yeomen. Nevertheless, 'many other ill-disposed persons and traitors'[11] brought the total number of rebels to 8000, if the Act is to be believed. By the time a similar Act was passed against Lovel, after an unaccountable delay of seven years, the number had, by a strange discrepancy, been reduced to 5000. Presumably it was thought important at the time to exaggerate the danger which had been overcome and politic later to minimise the scale of disaffection. Not much is revealed by these figures except the unreliability of contemporary records.

Lincoln's first objective had been to avoid an early encounter. He needed time to rally Yorkist England. But England as a whole was neither Yorkist, nor Lancastrian, nor Tudor; it was profoundly apathetic. After his disappointment in Yorkshire there was no course open except to engage the enemy before his men lost heart. He struck south to Southwell and from there, on 15 June, crossed the Trent by a ford near Fiskerton.

Henry meanwhile had brought his army northwards to Nottingham and on to Radcliffe-on-Trent, preparatory to moving up Fosse Way, the old Roman road, to deny Newark to the rebels. His army was probably not dissimilar to Lincoln's in size (about 6,000) but far better equipped and under the command of two experienced generals: the Earl of Oxford (of Bosworth fame) and the king's uncle, Jasper Tudor, now Duke of Bedford. The young Earl of Shrewsbury led a band of retainers, as did Lord Strange, son and heir to the Lord Stanley of Bosworth infamy.

It was an impressive array of Lancastrian strength but as a muster of the nobility of England at the summons of their sovereign lord in his hour of need its numbers compared unfavourably with those who had obeyed King Richard's call to arms before Bosworth. Some were presumably tardy or reluctant or downright disobedient in failing to aid a usurping king, or it may be that, mindful of the treachery on the former occasion, Henry had not summoned men of doubtful loyalty.

The final, decisive engagement in the Wars of the Roses took place near East Stoke, a village beside the Trent in Nottinghamshire (not at Stoke-on-Trent in Staffordshire, as often stated). It was fought on 16 June 1487 on open ground between Fosse Way and a loop of the river some half mile to the south of the village. Lincoln took up his position on an escarpment with his flank across the road barring Henry's passage. As with Richard at Bosworth, he had secured the advantage of relatively high ground. As with Henry at Bosworth, his best troops were foreigners.

Martin Schwartz's Germans bore the brunt of Henry's main attack, as the French had borne Richard's. The royal vanguard, under Oxford's command, was repulsed with heavy casualties and the second of Henry's three 'battles', or divisions, had to be sent to its rescue. Early reports reaching London spread news of Henry's defeat, but the fighting continued for three hours and in the end the tide turned. Estimates of the number of Germans vary from 1,500 to 2,000

Lambert Simnel as a royal turnspit

and probably the English rebels numbered no more. Together they were unable to sustain the action and carry the day. They fought with swords, spears, bows and some hand guns, but probably without any artillery support to counter Henry's cannon.

The bulk of the rebel force was composed of 'a great multitude of beggarly Irishmen, almost all naked and unarmed'.[12] What weapons they had were darts. They fought courageously, but could offer no real resistance to well-armed troops and were 'stricken down and slain like dull and brute beasts'.[13] Their wholesale slaughter demoralised the rest of the army, and the battle became a rout. The line of escape to the river ran through a narrow ravine where the fleeing were trapped and butchered. The gully is known to this day as Red Gutter. Of those who succeeded in reaching the river many were drowned in the panic of crossing.

Lincoln, Schwartz, Fitzgerald and Broughton were all killed. Lovel vanished mysteriously. He may have been cut down and unidentified or drowned in the Trent in flight, or he may have fled to a secret death while in hiding afterwards at his home in Minster Lovell, where in 1708 a skeleton was discovered in a sealed underground chamber. The puzzle of his fate was never solved. His retroactive attainder eight years after the battle carried the scarcely convincing explanation that in the earlier Act 'the said Francis Lovel was ignorauntly lefte out and omitted'.[14] It was also scarcely necessary, since he had already been attainted after Bosworth.

Stoke was a close-fought engagement – as crucial and narrowly won as Bosworth – and Henry, a prudent man, was never to run the risk of battle again. The vanquished were said to have lost 4,000 men and the victors 2,000. Propaganda reported that Henry's main 'battle' had turned the tables on the charging enemy so successfully that his reserves were not called into action, but the length and ferocity of the fighting makes this highly questionable. What is more than possible is that Lord Strange played the Stanley game which his father and uncle had played at Bosworth – hanging back to be sure of ending on the winning side.

After the fighting Henry retired to Lincoln to give thanks to God for a second victory. He then descended on Yorkshire in a mood of vengeance and intimidation to scour the countryside for traitors and, by executions, imprisonment and fines, to 'purge his land of all seditious seed'.[15] Some Yorkshiremen would have done better to have heeded the rebels' call to try conclusions with the king on the field of battle.

Although his army and his cause were lost, Lambert Simnel himself suffered the lightest of punishments. Since he was patently not Warwick, Henry could afford to be merciful and judged it good policy to content himself with humiliating a pleasant and well-mannered youth who had no pretensions once his real identity was established. Simons, his tutor, was sentenced to imprisonment for life. As a priest he could not be legally put to death, but his life is unlikely to have been spared for long. Simnel himself was demoted from earl-king to scullion and later promoted from scullion to falconer. He was spared to be mocked and, by his example, to discredit other pretenders. At a banquet in the king's palace at Greenwich he was employed as a cup-bearer when Henry entertained some Irish lords and wished to take the opportunity of insulting them. The Irish, he remarked, would be crowning apes next.

In time Henry grew tired of the sight of him and the pretender was dismissed from the royal service. As a servant in the household of Sir Thomas Lovell, a Tudor loyalist, he lived on until 1525, dying at the age of fifty – a remarkable record in survival for one guilty of treason in Tudor times.

The next aspirant to Henry's throne was to prove far more troublesome and suffer accordingly. For King Henry was:

Still to be haunted; still to be pursued,
Still to be frightened with false apparitions
Of pageant Majestie and new-coyned greatness.[16]

But whether the new pretender was in fact as false an apparition as Simnel, whether his majesty too was only 'pageant' and his greatness really 'new-coyned', remains a matter open to question. What is sure is that, although haunted, pursued and frightened, never again after Stoke did Henry have to face an army which would fight a pitched battle for the restoration of the white rose, which had blossomed so splendidly and withered so abruptly.

The Oxford lad was nearly a winner. But if Schwartz had repeated at Stoke de Chandée's success at Bosworth it seems improbable that an impostor would have been re-crowned as Edward VI. Either the real Warwick would have taken his place or Lincoln become a second King John. Or might Edward IV's younger son have emerged from hiding in Flanders to lay claim to the vacant throne?

6

Prince Perkin

TOWARDS the close of the fifteenth century Henry Tudor's right to the throne of the Plantagenets was contested by one said to be Piers Osbeck, otherwise Perkin or Peterkin Warbeck, but also known amongst other of his contemporaries as the Duke of York, Prince Richard of England and King Richard IV. For six years England's political and diplomatic relations with her neighbours were entangled in a web of intrigues on behalf of this son of a Flemish boatman (as his enemies declared him to be). Most of the states of western Europe became involved in the dispute over his identity: Scotland and Ireland, France and Spain, Venice and Milan, the Imperial territories of Germany and Austria, the Netherlands above all, and even the Papacy.

Charles VIII of France, James IV of Scotland, Maximilian, King of the Romans (and later Emperor), the King of Denmark and the Duke of Saxony were some of the sovereign rulers who formally recognised this handsome, well-spoken young man as one of the missing sons of Edward IV of England. From his first appearance at Cork in 1491 to his surrender at Beaulieu abbey in 1497 he was seen to behave with much of the charm, grace and ease of a born Plantagenet. Not until his execution in 1499, fourteen years after Bosworth and twelve after Stoke, was the victor of those triumphs firmly established on the English throne.

Like Simnel, Warbeck was taken to Ireland to 'move, inveigle and provoke the rude and rustical Irish nation (being more of nature inclined to rebellion than to reasonable order)'.[1] Ireland was 'soil where the mushrooms and upstart weeds (that spring up in a night) did chiefly prosper',[2] and after Stoke it was a 'ticklish and unsettled state'.[3] The Earl of Kildare, who had lost both a king and a brother, found himself in a precarious situation but remained, even so, too powerful to be deprived of the deputyship. With extraordinary *sang froid* he was still, two months after the battle, making grants in the name of King Edward VI, who by that time was less than royally engaged turning spits in King Henry's kitchen. The loss of the battle, the death of Lincoln in the fighting and Simnel's confession had mortally exposed Kildare but, as he coolly judged, Henry's weakness and temperament were his salvation. The Tudor was not a fighting king like the Plantagenets: he chose to rely instead on his considerable political and diplomatic skills.

In the vexing matter of Ireland he was wise to be a realist and come to terms with the man who had crowned a pretender to his throne. Had he led an army across the Irish Sea, Ireland might have emerged from the ensuing conflict with a King Gerald in place of a Lord Henry, and who could have predicted what might have occurred in England once his back was turned? The fate which overcame Richard II in such circumstances would not have been forgotten. As for Kildare, he was a master of the time-honoured Irish ploy of humbly acknowledging faults and craving pardon while going on doing precisely what he wanted to do, irrespective of royal wishes and commands. For his part Henry knew all about crafty rebels from first-hand experience. He had no difficulty in recognising another expert practitioner of the machiavellian arts. They were well matched adversaries, and both knew that, whatever the future might hold, for the moment Kildare held the trump cards. He alone could protect the English Pale and keep the whole island as peaceful as it was ever likely to be. He alone, by allying himself with his disgruntled Desmond cousins and through his connections among the rebellious O'Neills and O'Connells in the north, could head a rising which would destroy the English lordship over Ireland, perhaps for ever.

So in the aftermath of Stoke Henry punished the English rebels, but not the Irish who were the main culprits. After an exchange of conciliatory letters Kildare received his pardon provided he behaved himself in future; which he had no intention of doing. In the following year Henry sought to exert his authority by sending a mission headed by Sir Richard Edgecombe and backed by 500 men. These were insufficient to secure Kildare's submission. After an inauspiciously stormy passage Edgecombe was met with snubs and insults. The Deputy, he was told, was away on a pilgrimage and would not be back in Dublin for four or five days. He was forced to cool his heels for nine until Kildare arrived – at the head of 200 horsemen – and even then the Deputy did not deign to wait on the king's representative: the king's representative was required to wait on him. The delegation sent to fetch him was headed by the bishop who had preached the sermon at Simnel's coronation.

Negotiations were prolonged. Edgecombe's brief was to obtain the agreement of Kildare and his council (the other Anglo-Irish 'Lords of Ireland') to a bond which would entail forfeiture of their estates if they broke their oaths of fealty to the king. But the lords were adamant in refusing to swear to anything which would jeopardise ownership of their estates. If Edgecombe persisted in this demand, they threatened, they would 'become Irish every one of them'.[4] In the end he had to be content with an oath of allegiance sworn on the sacrament, and this was solemnly taken by all of them on 21 July 1488 after weeks of argument. In the true tradition of feudal barons, Kildare and his fellow lords preferred to risk their immortal souls rather than their precious estates. And before the next pretender landed in Ireland Kildare had defied Henry again. When ordered to England, even the offer of a pardon and safe-conduct did not induce him to obey.

Perkin Warbeck's arrival in Cork in November 1491 was hardly for the purpose of acting as a male model for a Breton silk merchant, as improbably alleged in the confession published while he was in Henry's hands. He came with a group of Yorkist exiles to a port controlled by the dissident Earl of Desmond. Once ashore he wrote to Desmond and Kildare soliciting support. Desmond gave it openly. Kildare did not, but may have done so covertly. Later, he protested that he 'never lay with him, ne aided, comforted, ne supported him with goods, ne in none other manner wise',[5] but he could not escape the charge that he knew of Warbeck's presence and pretensions and Desmond's treachery and made no move against them.

Strenuous efforts were made by Henry and his agents in the courts of Europe to discredit this fresh claimant to his throne. He was reported to have been born in Tournai, the son of Jehan Werbecque, variously reported as a boatman, canal pilot, 'controller' or customs official. After spending some time in Antwerp he had sailed from

Middelburg for Portugal in the company of Sir Edward Brampton's wife. In Lisbon he had spent a year in the service of a one-eyed knight named Peter Vacz de Cogna. 'And then,' in the words of the subsequent confession, 'because I desired to see other countries I took licence of him, and then I put myself in service with a Breton called Pregent Meno, the which brought me with him into Ireland'.[6]

In Cork, wearing the silk clothes of his master, he looked so handsome and princely that the Irish at once took him for Clarence's son, as they had Simnel. This he denied, and when they said that in that case he must be King Richard's bastard son he denied that too, only to be told that 'I should take it upon me boldly'.[7] They were willing to assist him in order to be revenged on the King of England, 'and so against my will made me to learn English'.[8] Only when they learned that King Richard's bastard son (John, former captain of Calais) was in King Henry's hands was it finally decided that he should become neither Edward nor John but Richard, Duke of York.

The confession to this effect was made after the pretender's capture, and printed copies were distributed all over England. Thus, although full of circumstantial detail, it was no more than official propaganda – what Henry wanted people to believe – and as such must be viewed with suspicion. Implausible in parts, it is unsupported by any independent contemporary evidence. Acknowledgement of imposture had been made a condition of full pardon for the alleged author, so that his life depended upon putting his name to it. On the other hand, modern research has revealed the pretender's supposed father and mother as real people who did indeed have a son known as Pierre or its diminutive Pierrechon (Peter or Peterkin), born in 1474. (The younger of the princes in the Tower had been born in 1473.)

The mention of Lady Brampton's name explains the Portuguese connection, but otherwise serves only to heighten the mystery. Her husband, Sir Edward, was a Portuguese Jew who had begun life humbly as the son of a Lisbon blacksmith, name unknown. Born in about 1440 he came to England in 1468 and adopted the name of Duarte Brandao, which became transliterated into Edward Brandon and then (possibly because the Brandons were a Lancastrian family) into Edward Brampton. Since the expulsion of the Jews in 1290 a charitable *domus conversorum* in Chancery Lane, London had housed those willing to become Christians. On their conversion, according to custom, the king of the day became their godfather and they usually took his name. In this home for impoverished apostates Brandon appears to have lived for several years on a subsistence allowance of a penny ha'penny a day.

When in due course he was received into the Christian church and became a godchild of Edward IV the king took a personal interest in him. In 1472, presumably because of seafaring experience, he was given a command at sea and did well enough to be granted letters of denization, which made him an English subject. The following year he was at sea again and it was he who forced the surrender of the Earl of Oxford after he had captured St Michael's Mount. In this enterprise he shared the command of four ships and 600 men and is said to have brought about the capitulation by bribing the Genoese who manned the enemy's ships and suborning the garrison with false information that the king had agreed to grant a general pardon.

Brampton may have had fewer scruples than his sovereign lord, but in some ways they were two of a kind. Both were swashbuckling adventurers and in this bold brash Jew Edward found a man after his own heart. In 1475 he was in the king's company on his expedition to France. In 1480 he was granted manors in Northamptonshire and married a rich English widow. In 1481 he commanded a ship in Lord Howard's assault on Scottish shipping in the Firth of Forth. In 1482 he was appointed Captain, Keeper and Governor of Guernsey.

When Edward died Brampton continued in the service and favour of his successor, Richard III. In 1483 he led the attack on Sir Edward Woodville's rebel fleet in the Channel, again inducing Genoese mercenaries to desert. In return for his services he received the first knighthood ever bestowed on a converted Jew, becoming a Knight of the Body to King Richard, and enjoyed further grants from the crown. Some were mercantile, for his military exploits were complemented by equally dashing commercial activity. By 1481 he had been in a position to lend the treasury £700, in exchange for which he was allowed to export wool through the straits of Gibraltar free of duty. In 1484 he was granted an annuity of £100 a year for twenty years 'in consideration of services to be rendered by him according to certain indentures'.[9] In all, in the Calendar of Patent Rolls for the reigns of Edward IV, Edward V and Richard III no fewer than seven grants of various kinds are recorded, some involving lands and large sums of money for unspecified reasons.

Nor were Brampton's enterprises confined to England. Through Edward IV he made the acquaintance of the Duke of Burgundy and was permitted to open a trading establishment in Bruges. Through the duke he met the exiled King of Portugal, Alfonso V, to whom he later lent money which enabled the king to return home. As a result Brampton went back to Portugal a royal favourite, was renaturalised as a Portuguese subject (while retaining his English citizenship) and opened a new branch of his import-export business in Lisbon.

Brampton did not fight at Bosworth. Presumably he was absent on duty as Governor of Guernsey or away trading and therefore not available to alter the course of history by bribing the Stanleys and Northumberland. When the result of the battle became known he sailed to Lisbon, where he was appointed a member of the council of the new king, Joao II, made an aristocratic second marriage, and was honoured as a famous English knight (bragging untruthfully that he was a Knight of the Garter).

Even at a distance of five hundred years response to acquaintance with the details of Brampton's career can only be wide-eyed wonder. It is a fair supposition that here if anywhere is the man who could have revealed the truth about the princes in the Tower and the identity of Perkin Warbeck – the man who might indeed have been employed to dispose of the princes in the Tower, whether through a cruel death or a dare-devil rescue. If the princes were to be smuggled abroad out of Henry's grasp, what better qualified candidate for the job? If a fraud was to be perpetrated to regain the throne for the house of York, what more promising impresario?

Whatever the truth, the Brampton connection with Warbeck is significant. The boy came from a home in Tournai, the city of the Yorkist dowager duchess, who was still a power in the land of Flanders where Brampton traded in and out of Bruges. The boy's alleged father was Flemish, but his alleged mother (named as Katharine de Faro) was Portuguese. It was in the company of Brampton's wife (and therefore probably of Brampton himself) that he was taken from Flanders to Portugal, where he is known to have met Yorkist exiles, notably Anthony de la Forse, son of Richard's ambassador to Castile. It is clear that the groundwork for his claim to the throne of England had been in preparation for years before he surfaced in Cork. If it was genuine, Simnel had presumably been employed to test the ground and seize an opportune occasion while Warbeck was still too young. In that case, if Stoke had been won, Simnel, Warwick and Lincoln might all have stood aside and the boy from Tournai been brought over to be enthroned.

But while Warbeck was still in Lisbon, Brampton – ever an

opportunist – deserted. In 1489 he hospitably entertained a delegation from the English king and, no doubt for sound business reasons, decided to make his peace with Henry. Four years after Bosworth a general pardon and restitution of all his lands and possessions were granted to Edward Brampton, Knight, of Portugal and London, 'merchant *alias* gentleman'.[10] Two years later, on a visit to England, Brampton's son was knighted at Winchester. Henry, another opportunist, had skilfully neutralised a dangerous member of the opposition. Did he buy Brampton's silence and refusal to authenticate Warbeck? If Brampton had not turned his coat, could he have provided such authentication, and if he had would it have been genuine? Leaving all such questions unanswered, Brampton prospered until 1508 when he died with honour in Lisbon and was buried under a tombstone proudly incised with the false 'KG'.

In Ireland, then, Warbeck was in other hands. The Breton merchant, Pregent (Pierre Jean) Meno, was also a man of strange parts: he later became a naturalised Irishman and captain of Carrickfergus. But John Taylor, an English exile, was identified by the Venetian ambassador in England as the man who 'devised Perkin's expedition to Ireland when the latter first declared himself the son of King Edward'.[11] Another leading Yorkist in his retinue was Stephen Frion, who had been Henry VII's French-language secretary before changing ends and taking service with the French king. Margaret of Burgundy was also involved, and so was the King of Scots. The previous year a herald from Ireland had been paid £18 by James IV and sent on to the dowager duchess in Flanders. The conspiracy against Henry was designed as an encirclement.

Probably the landing at Cork had been at the invitation of the Earl of Desmond, who was in open rebellion in Munster and would have taken command of the expedition. But an English army followed on Warbeck's heels, led jointly by an Englishman, Thomas Garth, an associate of Cardinal Morton, and an Irishman, James Ormonde. With Kildare lying doggo and no prospect of success without his help, Warbeck and his small band did not risk another Stoke but sailed for France. The enterprise had failed, but at least the Yorkist standard had been raised once more, to Henry's alarm and the delight of his many enemies.

The King of France could always make good use of a pretender to the English crown, as Henry well knew. Charles VIII recognised Perkin as Prince Richard, housed him in the castle at Amboise and gave him a guard of honour under the captaincy of Lord Monypenny, a Scottish peer in the French service. There a court of a hundred Englishmen, led by Sir George Nevill, paid him homage, but this semblance of majesty was to be short-lived. A pretender under foreign protection is always expendable, and when the Treaty of Etaples was concluded (in November 1492) it contained a provision that this one should be handed over to the English king. The French king's honour, however, would not permit such a flagrant act of betrayal; nor would his still lively interest in Perkin as a pawn. Before the ink on the treaty was dry in Paris a word of warning reached Amboise and Prince Richard was hustled out of France by night.

In Flanders his supposed Aunt Margaret received him with open arms and another guard of honour: thirty retainers dressed in the Yorkist colours of murrey and blue. She named him the White Rose of England and the nobility of Flanders paid him full reverence. To the Tudor chroniclers Margaret of Burgundy, the only surviving Yorkist with the resources and determination to mount a counter-attack, was the original inspiration of the Warbeck imposture, a 'diabolical duchess'[12] behaving 'like a viper that is ready to burst with superfluity of poison'.[13] Childless herself, she grew pregnant with impostors:

> In her age
> (Great Sir, observe the Wonder) she grows fruitful
> Who in her strength of youth was always barren,
> Nor are her births as other mothers' are –
> At nine or ten months' end. She has been with child
> Eight or seven years at least; whose twins being born
> (A prodigy in Nature) even the youngest
> Is fifteen years of age at his first entrance.[14]

After her ill success with Simnel and Lincoln the duchess acted 'like a dog reverting to her old vomit'. 'For her purpose she espied a certain young man of visage beautiful, of countenance demure, of wit subtle, crafty and pregnant, called Perkin Warbeck'. She 'him with such diligence instructed both of the secrets and common affairs of the realm of England, and of the lineage, descent and order of the house of York, that he like a good scholar not forgetting his lesson could tell all that was taught him promptly without any difficulty or sign of any subornation: and besides he kept such a princely countenance, and so counterfeit a majesty royal, that all men in manner did firmly believe that he was extracted of the noble house and family of the dukes of York.'[15]

With the aid of Maximilian, King of the Romans, and his son, the boy Archduke Philip, Duke of Burgundy, an invasion of England was prepared. Englishmen disillusioned with Henry's rule escaped across the Channel to join the conspiracy; others plotted secretly in England. The pretender's claim was 'received for an infallible verity and most sure truth, and that not only of the common people, but also of diverse noble and worshipful men of no small estimation which swore and affirmed it to be true'.[16] One Englishman in Flanders wrote back to his fellow conspirators in London that 'he knew him to be King Edward's son by his face and other lineaments of his body'.[17] Leaders of the plot included Lord Fitzwalter, Sir Simon Mountford and Sir Robert Ratcliffe. Even Henry's own chamberlain, Sir William Stanley, the man whose treachery had brought him the crown at Bosworth, was named. Warbeck's supporters among the clergy included the Dean of St Paul's, the Dean of York and the Grand Prior of the Order of St John of Jerusalem. All England was reported to be divided by sedition.

1493 was the year of greatest peril to the Tudor king. A lesser man might have succumbed, but Henry kept his wits about him. On a single day he concluded a peace treaty with France at Calais and his envoys at Coldstream agreed a truce with Scotland. Later the truce too became a treaty, whereby Henry bought off James for a thousand marks. To Flanders he sent two of his ablest ambassadors (Sir Edward Poynings and Dr William Warham, later Archbishop of Canterbury) to assure the Archduke's council that Prince Richard had been murdered in the Tower, 'as many men living can testify',[18] but they were coldly received, so he made ready for hostilities. Ships of war were ordered to be victualled and 'new coppered' and their crews 'waged' on the east coast. Contingents of the army were ordered to stand at the alert fully equipped and be ready to move at a day's notice.

Meanwhile spies too had been sent to Flanders (partly to entice exiles home); also an agent provocateur, Sir Robert Clifford, to discover details of the plot and the names of the conspirators in England. When Clifford returned home he was arrested (to disguise his role) and then disclosed all he knew in exchange for a pardon and £500. The leaders were arrested and put to death, including Sir William Stanley, who was brought to the block on Clifford's evidence of a remark that 'he would never fight nor bear armour against the young man if he knew of a truth that he was the undoubted son of King Edward the Fourth'.[19] This slender evidence suggests that Henry was cleverly using the occasion to rid himself of a trouble-maker (Sir William was discontented at being denied the earldom of Chester for his services at Bosworth) and make some easy money (Sir William was the richest commoner in the realm and all his possessions were declared forfeit).

After the failure of his embassy Henry's next move was to apply economic sanctions against Flanders, whose prosperity was heavily dependent on trade with England. Flemish goods were banned; English cloth merchants were forbidden to export to Antwerp and other Flemish ports and ordered to use Calais instead. This embargo was met with counter-measures and both countries suffered for nearly three years until Henry gained his point. Under the terms of the Intercursus Magnus, which restored peace and trade and was signed in London in February 1496, each country bound itself not to aid the other's enemies. Specifically, the archduke was forced to agree to stop the dowager duchess harbouring English rebels, and if she disobeyed all her goods and estates were to be confiscated.

In combatting the threat to his crown and realm so energetically, Henry enjoyed the benefit of some circumstances beyond his control. Since the time of the Hundred Years War when France and England were the leading European powers, England had shrunk in signi-ficance through the loss of her French territories: her population of four million compared with France's twelve; her annual income was no more than £150,000 compared with France's £800,000. The new protagonists were France and Spain, and they turned their backs on England in their squabble over who should have Italy. Neither side was interested in England except as an ally against the other, and both were concerned not to drive Henry into the other camp. It was a situation tailor-made for the diplomacy in which he excelled. Ferdinand of Aragon ruthlessly used the threat of support for pre-tenders to try to bring him to heel, but in order not to offend him Spain, alone among the major European powers, never gave open recognition to Warbeck's pretensions – even though it may be de-duced from study of the Spanish archives that his claim was believed to be genuine. Elaborate ciphers were used for communication with ambassadors abroad, and the name of the pretender was to be found in the section reserved for persons of royal blood. He was code number 907: between Margaret of Burgundy and the King of Naples.

But the genuineness of the pretender was not the real issue at stake. What use could be made of him was the main consideration of all parties, and when the crunch came there was little enthusiasm in Europe for a change in the status quo in England with all its unforeseeable consequences. Flanders, the major trading partner, stood to gain most, and in December 1494 a formal agreement was reached between the Burgundian council and the pretender's advisers. 'With regard to the Duke of York,' wrote the archduke's father, now Emperor Maximilian, 'we entertain great hopes that after obtaining the kingdom of England he will soon attack the King of France; and to this effect have we received every promise and certainty from the duke aforesaid.'[20]

The following summer, when the long-awaited invasion sailed at last, it became apparent that the Emperor's hopes were greater than the means provided for their fulfilment. A small number of ships carried an army composed largely of thieves and vagabonds. Their only prospect of success lay in a rapturous welcome, but when a hundred or two disembarked on the Kent coast near Deal they were attacked by the local population and killed or captured. The fleet sailed on, leaving them to their fate: an ignoble fiasco for a leader who claimed Plantagenet blood.

In Ireland, at least, friends were still to be found and the pretender was once more well received in Munster by the Earl of Desmond, who took advantage of this unexpected reinforcement to besiege loyalist Waterford. But, although attacked from land and sea, the city resisted desperately for eleven days until a relief force arrived from Dublin. Three of Warbeck's ships were captured in the fighting.

Ireland may have 'remained corrupted and swelled again in every place with the overblown reports and rumours of Perkin's royalty, to which every traitorous ear lay open,'[21] but the country was divided and leaderless. In February the Great Earl of Kildare had at last been brought to account for 'his great and manifold treasons':[22] attainted by a Drogheda parliament, tricked into Dublin, arrested, shipped to England and thrown into prison in the Tower. Without him there was no organised resistance strong enough to face an English army. The majority might favour Warbeck's cause, but the Pale and the towns (except for Cork) were loyal strongholds of the English ascendancy. As the English saw it: 'In Ireland there are two kinds of men, one soft, gentle, civil and courteous . . . The other kind is clean contrary from this, for they be wild, rustical, foolish, fierce.'[23]

It was the rustical and fierce who kept the pretender's guttering hopes alight during his five months in Ireland. With Desmond at his side he was entertained and escorted through Connaught and Donegal by local chiefs. The leading rebel in the north was Hugh Roe O'Donnell, who had just concluded a formal alliance with the Scottish king, and it was to Scotland that the hapless Warbeck was at last despatched in safety. There his fortunes took a turn for the better.

James IV's father had supported Henry Tudor's invasion of England (in retaliation for Yorkist backing of his dissident brother, the Duke of Albany), but the rebels who had killed James III in 1488 had become the councillors of his son. Thereafter the Scottish court soon became involved in anti-Tudor correspondence with Margaret of Burgundy, while Henry in revenge sent arms to Scottish rebels. So in Stirling on 20 November 1495 the pretender was greeted with royal honours as Prince Richard of England. Arras had been specially brought from Edinburgh for his reception, and the king summoned the nobility of Scotland to meet him. In June a Scottish embassy to the imperial court at Worms had agreed with Maximilian on an alliance against England: the price was the return of Berwick, taken for England by Richard III thirteen years earlier.

James IV had an open and generous nature and, on close acquaintance, became convinced that the youth from Flanders was indeed the missing Duke of York. Both in their early twenties, they were of an age for friendship. The pretender was granted a personal allowance of £1,200 a year from the Treasury through a special subsidy, and his large English and Irish retinue were liberally provided for by a levy on the Scottish burghs. The genuineness of his claim was publicly recognised by his marriage to the king's cousin, Lady Catherine Gordon, a grand-daughter of James I. A Burgundian agent, Roderic de Lalain, was supplied with a ship to exchange intelligence with the dowager duchess and bring reinforcements from Flanders. He returned with arms and a company of six score German soldiers.

Henry's agents in Flanders, Ireland and now Scotland kept him well informed of developments. James Ramsay, formerly Lord Bothwell, and James, Earl of Buchan (James IV's great-uncle) were both secretly in his service as paid spies. Buchan promised to kidnap 'the duke of Zork' one night, and from Bothwell Henry even learned the terms of the secret agreement whereby, in the event of a successful invasion, James would be paid 50,000 marks to cover the cost and Berwick would be surrendered to him.

When Maximilian made marital overtures to James, proposing to bestow on him his daughter Margaret of Savoy, Henry countered by offering his own daughter Margaret, but James wanted neither of them. He was already happy with a Margaret of his own: his mistress Margaret Drummond. Then a flattering embassy from Spain offered inducements, which included an Infanta, if he would abandon his Prince Richard, conclude a long truce with England and join the nations leagued against France. This offer was spoiled by the interception of King Ferdinand's brief to his ambassadors, which revealed that Henry was the instigator, and James refused the bait. Through the possession of Prince Richard his friendship was much in demand, proving yet again that a plausible pretender in the right hands can become a valuable asset.

Their invasion of England in September 1496 was another damp squib. Accompanied by the king and a hopelessly inadequate mixed force of about 1,400 men, the pretender crossed the border as Duke of York and, once on English soil for the first time, proclaimed himself King Richard IV. The inhabitants of Northumberland, however, recognised only another murderous raid by Scottish intruders and 'neither gentleman nor man of worth'[24] extended a hand to help him. In what became known as the raid of Ellem two unimportant towers were captured and the surrounding countryside laid waste. The butchery of his subjects and devastation of his kingdom sickened King Richard IV and after an advance of four miles he turned back, followed by a disappointed King James.

There was now no choice for the itinerant claimant but to move on again. Tempting offers for the acquisition of his person were available from England, France and Spain. The French ambassador bid as high as 100,000 crowns, but in a dishonourable age James was a man of principle. Confronted by a large English army under the Earl of Surrey and a peace proposal from Henry's ambassador, the Bishop of Durham, which stipulated the surrender of Warbeck, he accepted a Spanish compromise that the pretender should no longer be succoured, harboured or maintained by him and agreed to dismiss him, but with dignity. A Spanish ship was hired to take the now unwanted King Richard and his wife and entourage away. It was handsomely provisioned and escorted through dangerous waters by the brothers Andrew and Robert Barton, naval captains with a reputation for piracy against the English.

On arrival in Stirling little more than eighteen months earlier the pretender is reported to have opened his address to the Scottish court with touching words: 'High and Mighty King, your Grace, and these your Nobles here present, may be pleased benignly to bow your ears to hear the tragedy of a young man that by right ought to hold in his hand the ball of a kingdom, but by fortune is made himself a ball, tossed from misery to misery and from place to place.'[25] His brief period as royalty was over when he sailed from Ayr on 6 July 1497 in the good ship *Cuckoo* for yet another tossing. For where next could he go for a princely reception and royal recognition?

Henry's relentless diplomacy was progressively isolating his rival. Unpopular at home – 'rather feared than loved'[26] – the king was pursuing a policy of offending nobody abroad, especially the King of France, from whom he received what he prized most after his throne: money. The Emperor Maximilian 'considered it his duty not to abandon the Duke [of York], nor to fail affording him all just and fitting favour',[27] but he was coming under increasing pressure from fellow members of the confederacy against France. Ambassadors from Spain, Venice, Milan and Naples all begged him not to antagonise Henry by continuing to comfort his enemies. If the person known throughout Europe as the Duke of York stood in the way of England joining the Holy League, then it must be conceded that he was Perkin Warbeck after all. To achieve this, Henry eventually agreed to what was in effect associate membership of the league. Minimising the offence to France, he joined subject to the proviso that he would not be obliged to fight.

In these circumstances Ireland remained the pretender's least unpromising destination, but here also Henry's pragmatism had taken effect. So far from being hanged, drawn and quartered for his flagrant acts of high treason, the Earl of Kildare was back in office as Lord Deputy. When king and earl had met in London each recognised qualities of his own in the other. Both men were shrewd, untrustworthy, unprincipled and totally committed to self-interest. On trial for his life the earl blustered and jested, pleading stupidity and a poor memory. When told that he might choose an advocate to speak for him he instantly chose Henry. When accused of burning down Cashel cathedral he replied that he never would have done such a thing had he not been told that the archbishop was inside; at which sally Henry and his council burst into laughter. 'He is as you see,' his accuser told the king: 'For all Ireland cannot rule yonder gentleman.' 'No?' replied Henry. 'Then he is meet to rule all Ireland.'[28]

The trial was over. Kildare's attainder was reversed and a pardon issued to the Earl of Desmond and all except two of Warbeck's Irish supporters. The Great Earl became even greater, being given one of Henry's cousins to marry and, with this new wife on his arm, returning to Dublin in triumph to rule Ireland for another seventeen years. Henry took the precaution of keeping his and Desmond's sons and heirs in London as hostages for their fathers' good behaviour.

In dealing with the ticklish state of Ireland Henry had acted with exemplary wisdom. Warbeck's third excursion there was doomed to failure before he sailed. On landing he received no support from Kildare, nor from the earl's relations and friends, nor even from Desmond and O'Donnell. The Yorkist cause no longer suited the purposes of the Irish and Anglo-Irish lords. After more than a decade of bickering they had reached an accommodation with the Tudor usurper and secured the continuation of their treasured near-independence on acceptable terms. Kildare was the key. His desertion of the Yorkist movement was decisive. Once power was returned to him, with appropriate safeguards, Henry's Irish problem was solved.

The loss of Ireland was a mortal blow to Warbeck's cause. In this crisis he was in desperate need of sound advice, but his small circle of counsellors included, not men of the world, but tradesmen without experience of politics or war. John Heron was a bankrupt mercer, Richard Skelton a tailor and John Astley a scrivener. Under the guidance of these 'lewd captains'[29] the decision was taken to venture all on another invasion of England, this time unaided.

Earlier in the year the burden of taxation had brought Cornwall into open defiance of the crown, much as it had Yorkshire eight years earlier. Incensed at being forced to pay for the protection of the Scottish border, a large number of Cornishmen had taken to the road in a protest march on London. They had reached Blackheath before being attacked and dispersed by the king's forces. Two thousand were said to have been killed, and their leader, Lord Audley, was beheaded.

Devon and Somerset were also rife with disaffection and, counting on a general rising in the west country, the pretender landed at Whitesands Bay on 7 September 1497. For a second time he proclaimed himself King Richard IV. To back his claim he had only three small ships and 300 men, and even the short passage from southern Ireland had not been uneventful. The Spanish vessel in which he was travelling was boarded by a search party from an English man-of-war and he was forced to hide in the bows, where he lay undiscovered and unbetrayed despite the promise of a reward.

In Cornwall, though, he was less fortunate, attracting only an unarmed rabble, 'naked men and rascal'[30] for the most part. With this force, no more an army of soldiers than the ill-armed Irish at Stoke, he launched two assaults on Exeter. Both were unsuccessful, and the mob moved on, dispirited, towards Taunton. 'No one of the nobility or better sort'[31] rallied to his cause, and even the poor and needy began to lose hope and desert him.

But on the approach of a royal army it was he who deserted them, stealing away in the middle of the night to take sanctuary at Beaulieu in Hampshire. Once again he showed little stomach for a fight and was derided for his cowardice. He may have left his followers because he believed they were about to leave him (Henry had again adopted a policy of offering deserters a pardon) or it may have been the tenderness of heart displayed in Northumberland that decided him not to lead a naked mob to slaughter.

At Beaulieu abbey he gave himself up on a promise of 'pardon of life' and 'comfort of liberty, yea, honourable maintenance'.[32] Brought back to Taunton to make his submission to the king in person, he publicly confessed himself a fraud. Henry 'found him superficially instructed, of a natural wit, of reasonable qualities, well-languaged, and [of] indifferent apprehension, but far from that highness of spirit or heroic disposition to deserve the character of a prince or lay claim to a diadem.'[33]

In England few appear to have believed any longer that Warbeck was really the missing Duke of York, but some may have been cowed into silence. The Venetian ambassador in London reported to the doge that he had 35,000 followers and that Henry had sent his wife and eldest son to a castle on the coast for fear of another pretender winning another Bosworth. But generally the invasion was seen for what it was: a futile act of desperation. Curiosity was the main reaction. On his journey to London in custody crowds flocked to catch a glimpse of the pretender 'as he were a monster'.[34]

On his arrival in town keepers were appointed 'to attend on him, which should not (the breadth of a nail) go from his person, to the intent that he might neither convey himself out of the land, nor fly anywhither'.[35] Warbeck made an escape despite this heavy guard; which raises the suspicion that Henry contrived it to arm himself with an excuse to renege on the liberty and honourable maintenance he had unfaithfully promised. Reported to have been making for the coast, the fugitive got no further than the priory at Shene on the Thames (in the opposite direction to the sea), where the prior surrendered him in exchange for an assurance that his life would be spared.

His punishment was severe. He was put in the stocks at Westminster, taken out to be taunted in the streets of London as a spectacle, put to the rack to extract a further confession and thrown into a windowless cell in the Tower 'where he sees neither sun nor moon'.[36] On first setting eyes on the 'monster' the Venetian ambassador had reported: 'He is a well favoured young man, 23 years old, and his wife a very handsome woman; the king treats them well, but did not allow them to sleep together.'[37] The Milanese ambassador had reported that the young man was bearing his misfortune bravely. But when the Spanish ambassador was allowed to meet him in August 1498 during the period of his incarceration in the Tower he found him 'so much changed that I, and all other persons here, believe that his life will be very short. He must pay for what he has done.'[38]

Henry's change in attitude towards the treatment of his prisoner can be attributed to only one cause. Despite the propaganda of confessions and public humiliation, the powers of Europe were still not convinced that they had backed a false duke. Whereas Simnel had faded from insignificance into harmless oblivion, Warbeck had not, and the problem of Warwick was also outstanding. To achieve permanent recognition and respectability Henry had set his heart on a dynastic marriage with Spain for his eldest son, but Ferdinand and Isabella would not permit the marriage between Prince Arthur and their daughter, Katharine of Aragon, to be consummated while a legitimate Yorkist heir existed as a living reproach and threat to the Tudor usurpation. Warwick's 'very name and title,' they believed, 'was not only formidable to other nations, but superstitious to the wavering and unconstant English.'[39] So much so, that false Warwicks continued to spring up. An Augustinian friar in Suffolk coached a poor scholar called Ralph Wulford in the part. The friar was sentenced to life imprisonment and Wulford hanged.

The fate of Warbeck and Warwick was settled in a manner typical of Henry. It was announced that a plot had been uncovered in the Tower to kill the lieutenant and free the two prisoners. A jury found that Warwick had conspired to seize the Tower, escape overseas and proclaim himself king – or else that he intended to free Warbeck and make him king. The simple-minded Warwick was arraigned before the Earl of Oxford, Constable of England, found guilty of treason and beheaded on Tower Hill in a flagrant act of unprovoked and cold-blooded murder.

Warbeck's suffering was more grievous. He was drawn on a hurdle through London to Tyburn, hanged on the gallows and cut down to be disembowelled, castrated and dismembered while still alive. His body was severed into quarters and his head cut off and stuck on a pole on London bridge.

The execution of the two youths was recognised at the time as brutal slaughter, and the superstitious noted that it was followed by a great plague (in which the number of dead in London was estimated at 30,000) and by Henry's favourite palace at Shene being burned to the ground. But the Tudor claim to the throne was at last undisputed. In January 1500 the Spanish ambassador was able to report: 'England has never been so tranquil and obedient as at present. There have always been pretenders to the crown of England; but now that Perkin and the son of the Duke of Clarence have been executed, there does not remain a drop of doubtful royal blood, the only royal blood being the true blood of the king, the queen and, above all, the Prince of Wales.'[40]

'Uneasy lies the head that wears a crown,' especially a usurper's. But after a decade and a half of insecurity Henry had emerged victorious over all other pretenders.

Was Perkin Warbeck Richard, Duke of York? Proof of the death of Edward IV's sons would have been incontrovertible evidence of an impersonation, but Henry remained unable (or unwilling) to produce that proof either during Warbeck's lifetime, when it was so compellingly demanded, or afterwards when the implausible tale circulated to satisfy the Spanish royal family merely served to acknowledge that the mystery was insoluble (or the real solution known and not to be revealed). The more the traditional account of the princes' end as recounted by More and Shakespeare becomes discredited, the greater the temptation to take seriously the possibility of a resurrection in the guise of a pretender.

There are several persuasive pointers towards the validity of Warbeck's claim. For a Flemish boy of humble stock to assume a princely persona and carry off an imposture clever enough to deceive men like James IV of Scotland, the Emperor Maximilian and the Earl of Kildare would be an accomplishment of some magnitude. Even among records hostile to him, it is nowhere suggested that Warbeck spoke English like a foreigner – let alone one who had learned no English until the age of seventeen. His surviving signature has been judged to be a bold, characteristically English autograph. In appearance he bore some, possibly a strong, resemblance to Edward IV, and while he could have been coached in the protocol and personalities of the English court by Brampton and others (though less probably by Margaret of Burgundy, who had left England in 1467 and returned only for one short visit) there is no record of his committing a howler or a solecism. He is said not to have recognised the lords surrounding Henry at Taunton, but this would not be surprising and no revealing confrontation appears to have been arranged with someone whom the boy duke must have known intimately, such as his eldest sister Elizabeth, King Henry's queen. The silence of the records on such a likely event might even suggest a meeting which had not gone according to plan.

The scantiness of the evidence that this pretender was really Prince Richard is not much less than the scantiness of the evidence that he was really the son of Jehan Werbecque of Tournai. Every pronouncement made by Henry and by the pretender himself when in Henry's hands is necessarily suspect. What, for example, can one make of the public confession in which he solemnly declares that his name is Piers Osbeck, followed a few days later, when also under duress, by his signing a letter to his supposed mother 'votre humble fils Pierrequin Werbecque'?[41] Is it plausible that the name 'Osbeck', appearing in an important document copied and circulated throughout the kingdom, is nothing more than a scribe's error?

When Warbeck ceased to be of value to him the French king offered to oblige Henry with evidence that he was a barber's son and to send the boy's parents to England to prove it. The Spanish king and queen, also anxious to oblige Henry and not allow him to be beholden to their enemy, denounced the French evidence as fraudulent but made a counter-offer to send one Ruy de Sosa, who had been Portuguese ambassador at King Edward's court and would swear to Warbeck not being the Duke of York. The worthlessness of such witnesses was tacitly admitted by Henry himself when he spurned both offers.

What does not seem in doubt is that the pretender was brought up in the Warbeck household in Tournai, either as a real son or as a foster-child. The theory that he was a bastard son of Edward IV by Jehan Werbecque's wife does not bear close examination. Edward's second period of exile in Flanders ended early in 1471, and Perkin was not born until 1474. According to the municipal records in Tournai he was one of two legitimate children of Jehan Werbecque, who also acknowledged two bastards. If the Perkin known to history was Prince Richard disguised, then the real Perkin must have died in childhood and his identity been assumed by the prince.

Another explanation of Warbeck's striking likeness to a Plantagenet is the malicious rumour, reported by the Emperor Maximilian, that the pretender was the son of Margaret of Burgundy by a favourite cleric, the Bishop of Cambrai. But in 1474 the dowager duchess was not living in seclusion like Henry V's widow when giving birth to illicit Tudors. Her husband was still alive and a son born to her at that time would have been hailed as the much prayed-for heir to the Burgundian dukedom.

But despite the favourable indications Warbeck's pretensions ring hollow. Not only did his claim lack the supporting evidence of anyone coming forward to vouch for his escape from England to Flanders, but he himself gave no satisfactory or detailed account of the escape and his subsequent adventures. One version of what he told James IV runs as follows: 'Our uncle [Richard III] was not the tutor and preserver of our stock and lineage, but the confounder and destroyer of our blood and progeny. For that tyrant, blinded and gutted with the cupidity of ruling and sovereignty, commanded Edward my brother and me to be slain and despatched out of this mortal life. Whereupon that person to whom the weighty and cruel charge was committed and given to oppress and destroy us poor innocent infants and guiltless babes, the more he abhorred this heinous and butcherly offence the more he feared to commit it. And so wavering in mind and dubious what to do, at the length, willing in part to satiate the bloody thrust of the unnatural tyrant and in part to abstain from so facinorous and detestable homicide, destroyed my brother and preserved me . . . And farther, to the intent that my life might be in a surety, he appointed one to convey me into some strange country, where when I was furthest off and had most need of comfort he forsook me suddenly (I think he was so appointed to do) . . . So that I . . . forgot almost myself and knew not well what I was, but after long wandering from country to country and from city to city . . . I came to my own aunt the lady Margaret living in Flanders.'[42]

In another account of this speech to the Scottish king he hinted at good reasons for reticence. 'For the manner of my escape it is fit it should pass in silence or (at least) in a more secret relation: for that it may concern some alive and the memory of some that are dead.'[43]

These speeches are the fabrications of Tudor and later chroniclers following the official Tudor line. Thus Richard III, not Henry Tudor, is the villain with murderous intent. In the absence of any independent Scottish record there is no reason to accept their accuracy. On the other hand, the two pieces of surviving evidence uncorrupted by Tudor propaganda are no more informative. The proclamation issued in July 1497 by 'Richard by the grace of God King of England and of France, Lord of Ireland, Prince of Wales' declares only that 'we in our tender age escaped by God's great might out of the Tower of London and were secretly conveyed over the sea to divers other countries, there remaining certain years as unknown.'[44]

Perhaps no fuller recitation would be thought appropriate in a proclamation, but a letter to Queen Isabella of Spain soliciting support might well be expected to contain sufficient circumstantial detail and naming of names to carry conviction and establish credentials. But the plea for help which has survived in the Spanish archives tells the same vague and unlikely story (although without any mention of the Tudor bugbear, wicked uncle Richard). The pretender writes (in 1493) that when his elder brother was 'miserably put to death and I myself, then nearly nine years of age [the actual age of the younger prince was ten in August 1483], was also delivered to a certain lord to be killed, it pleased the Divine Clemency that that lord, having compassion on my innocence, preserved me alive and in safety; first, however, causing me to swear on the holy sacrament that to no one should I disclose my name, origin or family until a certain number of years had passed. He sent me therefore abroad, with two persons, who should watch over and take charge of me.'[45]

Shortly after Richard III's coronation rebels were arrested for plotting to start fires in different parts of London to distract attention while the princes were stolen from the Tower, and there is a slender possibility that the death of Edward V and smuggling abroad of his brother Richard resulted from some such attempt to obtain possession of them by Edwardian loyalists or a Woodville faction in 1483, or from an attempt by Yorkists to remove them from Henry Tudor's reach after Bosworth in 1485. But Warbeck's account, however corrupted, does not bear the stamp of truth. An assassin rough and cruel enough to kill one young prince but too nervous or kind-hearted to kill a second (who is so ill-guarded that the assassin can contrive his escape) belongs, like other accounts of the boys' fate, to the realm of fiction.

Although history has condemned this pretender as a fraud, many have continued to accept the truth of his claim. 'It is not singular that I should entertain a belief that Perkin was, in reality, the lost Duke of York,' Mary Wollstonecraft Shelley wrote in 1830: 'Whether my hero was or was not an impostor, he was believed to be the true man by his contemporaries. The partial pages of Bacon, of Hall and Holinshed and others of that date are replete with proofs of this fact.'[46] What is also true, but less of a clue in helping to solve the mystery, is that everyone at the time whose interest it was to recognise him as genuine believed him to be Prince Richard and everyone whose interest it was to dispute this claim denounced him as an impersonator.

The likelihood that Perkin's career was founded on falsehood does not detract from its importance. Who he was mattered less than who he was believed to be. He came nearer than any real heir to York to toppling the Tudor king: 'the push' he gave to Henry's 'sovereignty did throughly try his sitting, being of force enough to have cast an ordinary rider out of saddle'.[47] But impostors are jokers in the pack. They can be fatal to real pretenders. As Simnel had brought down Lincoln, so Warbeck gave the kiss of death to Warwick: 'this winding ivy of a Plantagenet' did 'kill the true tree itself'.[48]

Warbeck's autograph: 'Your friend Richard of England'

7
Queen Jane

PRETENDING dynasties are hydra-headed. No sooner was Perkin dead than the White Rose of York and England flowered again in the person of Lincoln's younger brother, Edmund, Earl of Suffolk. After Lincoln's death at Stoke he was the eldest surviving son of the second Duke of Suffolk and Richard III's and Edward IV's eldest sister. Forced to surrender the dukedom when his father died, he had to be content with the lesser title of earl. In 1501 he fled abroad with a younger brother or nephew, Richard, to raise opposition to Henry. At Calais he met Sir James Tyrell, who was executed on suspicion of conspiring with him (not for murdering the princes in the Tower, as widely but wrongly supposed). The emperor allowed him to live unmolested at Aix-la-Chapelle but was otherwise chary of offending Henry, and the pretender, impoverished, was soon reduced to begging for food and clothing from the Archduke Philip.

Worse was to follow. In January 1506 the archduke encountered a violent storm in the Channel while sailing to Spain with his wife Joanna, the heiress of Castile. His fleet was scattered and his own ship driven ashore at Weymouth. This was a stroke of good fortune of a kind which Henry was adept at exploiting. The distinguished visitors were hospitably entertained, but there was no question of their being permitted to resume their journey until a promise to hand over the Yorkist pretender had been extracted. 'King Philip of Castile had been urged so strongly by the King of England that he had decided to deliver up Suffolk into his hands. He had not done so, however, until the King of England had given him a solemn promise in writing, sealed with his own seal, that Suffolk should receive a full pardon for all his past offences and not be exposed to persecution during the whole of the remainder of his life.'[1] But a promise from Henry, however solemn and sealed, was not worth the paper it was written on. Brought back to England by force, Edmund spent seven years a prisoner in the Tower and was then beheaded by Henry's son. His younger brother William, who had been arrested earlier, was kept there in captivity for 38 years out of 'suspicion and jealousy' because he was 'near of blood'.[2]

Killing Edmund and holding William did not quell the activities of the de la Poles. Richard, the new White Rose, became the most dangerous of them. At first in Hungary, where the king granted him a pension, and then in France, where he entered the service of Louis XII and Francis I, he was recognised as the rightful King of England. Like the Stuart Duke of Berwick, he won fame as a general in the French army and on at least two occasions also anticipated the Stuart pretenders by making preparations for an invasion of England via Scotland. Henry VIII and Wolsey plotted his assassination, but after a long run as exiled leader of the opposition he was killed on the battlefield during the French defeat by the emperor Charles V at Pavia in 1525.

Plantagenet descendants remaining within Henry VIII's grasp received short shrift. His victims included Buckingham's son (then heir presumptive to the crown) and grandson, Clarence's daughter and grandson, and Edward IV's grandson Henry, Marquess of Exeter (another heir presumptive). All were judicially murdered without compunction on trumped-up charges of treason, and this butchery put an end to dynastic competition for the English crown. In the post-Reformation era inaugurated by Henry VIII's quarrel with the pope religion, not family, became the dominant issue. The struggle for the succession developed into a tug-of-war between rival faiths. Under the new rules the first loser was Lady Jane Grey (Protestant), the second Mary Queen of Scots (Catholic).

Henry VIII's breach with Rome was not motivated by spiritual considerations. The occasion was his wish for a divorce from Katharine of Aragon, who could not produce a male heir. The underlying cause was a financial crisis which focussed covetous eyes on the wealth of the church, in particular the religious houses, which were believed to own a third of England. Self-aggrandisement too was not without appeal, and Henry must have enjoyed displacing the pope as Supreme Head of the Church in England and abolishing purgatory by Act of Parliament. Yet his own religious beliefs were conservative. On one day, to demonstrate his impartiality between Papist and Protestant extremists, he had three men hanged for denying the royal supremacy and another three burned for heresy. Henry was a Henrician, which in a broad religious context meant Catholic, but not Roman Catholic. No heretic by his own reckoning, he died a devout Catholic.

His will set out his wishes for the succession and he endeavoured to command posthumous obedience to it through an Act of Parliament. This was the opening chapter in the tragedy of Protestant Jane, the nine-day queen. Like the Lancastrians and the Yorkists before them, the Tudors were already running out of male heirs. Hitherto no woman had sat on the throne of England: Matilda alone had asserted a right to it. But if Henry's only son, Edward, were to die without a male heir, there would be no men within sight of the crown, thanks to Henry's policy of extermination.

First in the succession after Edward (according to the terms of the royal will) stood Princess Mary, the Catholic daughter of Katharine of Aragon whom Henry himself, not recognising the validity of the marriage, had declared illegitimate. Next came Princess Elizabeth, the Protestant daughter whom all Catholic Europe, not recognising the divorce, regarded as illegitimate. After her came the Grey family: first Jane's mother, then herself, then her two younger sisters. Thus as a child Jane stood fifth in line. Both for this reason and as a likely bride for her cousin Edward, she was brought up as a princess who might one day become a queen. Unlike Mary's and Elizabeth's, her claim to the throne was not overshadowed by doubtful legitimacy.

It came through her mother Frances, Marchioness of Dorset and Duchess of Suffolk, who was the elder daughter of Henry VIII's sister Mary. The younger daughter Eleanor, Countess of Cumberland, and her daughter Lady Margaret Clifford completed the queue of eight female successors eligible under Henry's will. Specifically excluded, on the grounds that they were foreigners, were the descendants of his other sister, Margaret, Queen of Scotland. These were also female: Mary, the infant Queen of Scots (another candidate for wife to Edward) and Lady Margaret Douglas, Countess of Lennox.

Edward VI and Lady Jane Grey were born in the same month

D. THE TUDOR SUCCESSION

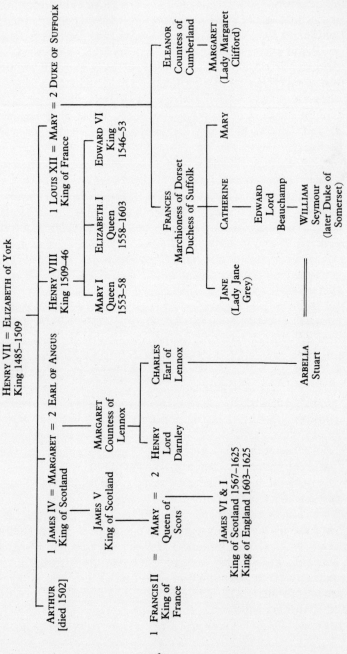

HENRY VII = ELIZABETH of York
King 1485–1509

1 JAMES IV = MARGARET = 2 EARL OF ANGUS

HENRY VIII
King 1509–46

1 LOUIS XII = MARY = 2 DUKE OF SUFFOLK
King of France

JAMES V
King of Scotland

MARGARET
Countess of
Lennox

MARY I
Queen
1553–58

ELIZABETH I
Queen
1558–1603

EDWARD VI
King
1546–53

FRANCES
Marchioness of Dorset
Duchess of Suffolk

ELEANOR
Countess of
Cumberland

1 FRANCIS II = MARY = 2
King of
France

Queen of
Scots

HENRY
Lord Darnley

CHARLES
Earl of
Lennox

JANE
(Lady Jane
Grey)

CATHERINE

MARY

MARGARET
(Lady Margaret
Clifford)

JAMES VI & I
King of Scotland 1567–1625
King of England 1603–1625

EDWARD
Lord
Beauchamp

ARBELLA
Stuart

WILLIAM
Seymour
(later Duke of
Somerset)

(October 1537) and died within a few months of each other, Edward shortly before his sixteenth birthday, Jane shortly after hers. Educated in the new learning of the Renaissance and the new faith of the Reformation, they were both doomed to become Protestant puppets, although each developed a strong character and held determined views.

It is not known why Henry chose a leading exponent of the new thinking to be his son's tutor, but it was a decision which profoundly affected English history. John Cheke held a chair of Greek at Cambridge. He was an inspiring lecturer and a prominent member of the Protestant party at university and court. Among his pupils and disciples were Roger Ascham, who became tutor to Elizabeth I and Lady Jane, and William Cecil, who became his brother-in-law and Elizabeth's chief minister. Like everyone else, Henry may have been dazzled by Cheke's brilliance; certainly the young Edward was captivated. The prince was treated by his tutor as a companion in scholarship. Cheke's method of teaching was a joint adventure by master and pupil in the exploration and discovery of knowledge. His was the main influence on Edward from the age of seven to fourteen.

What religious instruction did he, and Jane under similar influences, receive? Transubstantiation was one fundamental issue dividing Christianity. Orthodoxy asserted that in the eucharist consecration miraculously transformed the bread and wine into the body and blood of Christ. This doctrine of the Real Presence had been challenged in England by Wyclif in John of Gaunt's time. To Protestants of the mid-sixteenth century like Cheke it was an object of derision:

> Not with our teeth His flesh to tear,
> Nor take blood for our drink;
> Too great absurdity it were
> So grossly for to think.[3]

But the element in Protestantism most enthusiastically embraced by Edward and Jane personally was its emphasis on direct communication with God, in revolt against the authoritarianism of Rome which insisted on the word of the divine Creator reaching the faithful through the filter of an ecclesiastical hierarchy. When Cheke fell ill and his doctors said there was no hope of recovery, Edward told them they were wrong: 'This morning I begged his life in my prayers and obtained it.'[4] And his message proved correct, for Cheke recovered. When Jane was offered the crown as Edward's heir she prayed to God for guidance and blamed herself afterwards for accepting it despite receiving no clear response.

Thus when his father died in the Catholic faith Edward was already a Protestant in Protestant hands: not only his tutor's, but those of Archbishop Cranmer and of his uncle Edward Seymour, who became Duke of Somerset and Protector of his realm. In an unprecedented coronation ceremony Cranmer announced that he was not acting as an agent of the Bishop of Rome but as a messenger from their Saviour, Jesus Christ. He crowned and anointed the young Edward as Defender of the Faith and Supreme Head of the Church as well as king and told him he was now 'God's Vice-Regent and Christ's Vicar within your own dominions'.[5] These were the titles which Edward attempted in vain to pass on to his like-minded cousin and which would have become hers if her reign had lasted one week longer.

Bradgate, Jane's birthplace and family home, lies five miles to the north of Leicester. Today its deer park, sloping steeply down to a winding stream, is thick with bracken and dotted with oaks, much as in her day. But the house, owned by the Greys until the twentieth century, is a ruin. The great hall, in which two hundred could dine in state, was levelled to the ground by a fire in the eighteenth century. Jane's father, Henry Grey, a surprisingly weak-willed man for one descended from Queen Elizabeth Woodville, was said to be poor but, since he employed a staff of three hundred at Bradgate, this must be taken to mean that he lived above his income.

The roost was ruled by her mother – daughter of a queen of France (Mary Tudor), grand-daughter of Henry VII and great-grand-daughter of Edward IV – a large masculine lady who bore an unnerving resemblance to her fearsome cousin, Henry VIII. Neither parent appears to have felt much affection for their eldest daughter, who preferred Plato to hunting and her tutor's company to theirs. But they valued her as a means of rising still higher in the world.

Jane was a small, neatly built girl, sandy-haired, fair-skinned and freckled, extremely clever and fanatically religious. She loved music and her education included lessons in dancing and playing the lute, harp and cithern as well as needlework and foreign languages. She read the Bible assiduously and had begun studying the classics by the age of three. After Henry's death she moved into the more congenial household of his widow, Queen Katharine Parr, another Protestant intellectual, with whom she lived in Chelsea and Whitehall. There she met Cranmer and Coverdale and other luminaries of the reformed church. From the queen dowager – and the new king himself – she won the praise and admiration which she had had to do without at home.

It was a life too good to last. Queen Katharine, re-married, died in childbirth. Jane, not yet eleven, attended her funeral as chief mourner and then returned to her parents. Finding her a spoiled child, precocious and scornful of their opinions and way of life, they welcomed an overture from the queen's widower, Thomas Seymour, brother to the Protector and uncle to the king. Seymour offered to become Jane's guardian and arrange for her marriage to the king, baiting his proposal with hard cash. In effect he bought her from her parents for his own ends, and these involved a scheme to overthrow his brother which miscarried and cost him his life. Jane's parents hurried her back to Leicestershire to distance themselves from the consequences. The first attempt to make her a queen had failed and she was kept in seclusion at Bradgate for another three years.

John Dudley, Earl of Warwick, later Duke of Northumberland, succeeded where Thomas Seymour had failed. The son of one of Henry VII's most notorious extortioners, he was tall, handsome and charming, one of those natural leaders of men who seem able to do anything better than anyone else, be it fighting or arguing, administration or management, tilting or tennis. He defeated the French at Boulogne, the Scots at Pinkie, the rebel Kett in Norfolk, and Protector Somerset in dark recesses off the corridors of power. The rule of 'the good duke' was over and Dudley became absolute master of king and country. His aspirations brought Jane to the scaffold.

Despite a pallid complexion (much admired at the time) the king had enjoyed a healthy childhood, but in April 1552 a severe attack of measles left him sickly and brought the problem of the succession into the centre of the political arena. Dudley was determined to emulate his powerful predecessor and become Warwick the Queenmaker. As a fervent Protestant he detested, and was as heartily detested by, Princess Mary (John Knox was his chaplain and, although a foreigner, his nominee for the see of Rochester). Princess Elizabeth, who stood next in line, was a Protestant, as intelligent as Jane and five years older. But she was much more astute in the ways of the world and would never dance to anyone else's tune. Her relationship with Dudley was one of mutual distrust. Elizabeth might have been his choice nonetheless, had his personable son Robert been available to marry her. Robert was to become her favourite when queen, but in 1552 he already had a wife in Amy Robsart.

The king's own preference for Jane may have been decisive, for he had to be persuaded to nominate his successor in a bequest of the realm which would supersede his father's. They were two of a kind: lonely, serious-minded, humourless children; religious zealots of the Lutheran persuasion. As a passionate believer in divine revelation of the Truth, she would be the ideal guardian of the Protestant revolution, protector of the infant reformed church against Marian backsliding or Elizabethan compromise.

Fortunately for Dudley's ambitions, one of his five sons was still a bachelor, at hand to marry Jane and be a consort king. Jane's mother was induced to waive her rights, as Margaret Beaufort had done for Henry Tudor, and the marriage between Lady Jane Grey and Lord Guilford Dudley took place with due pomp and splendour on 25 May 1553. It was an unhappy day for the bride, who had refused the groom with some vehemence and had to be bullied into compliance by her parents. The grounds for her refusal were both principled and personal. Since she had once been contracted to marry the Duke of Somerset's eldest son (before the Protector's fall) she did not believe herself free in the eyes of God to marry anyone else. That apart, she loathed the sight of the oafish Guilford, who shared neither her intellectual tastes nor her religious enthusiasm.

Edward was now terminally ill and known to be so, dying of the tuberculosis or consumption which had killed his illegitimate half-brother, the Duke of Richmond, at the age of eighteen. He had reigned for six and a half years but never been allowed to rule. Somerset, his first Protector, had even adopted the use of the royal 'we'. Dudley, his successer, now Duke of Northumberland, was also king in all but name. He controlled the council and the army and corresponded with the King of France and the emperor on equal terms. The dying king was powerless, but in the matter of the succession had no wish to resist. Northumberland had little difficulty in persuading him that he could 'expect revenge at God's dreadful tribunal'[6] if he allowed Mary to become queen, or in obtaining his signature to a 'King's Devise' bequeathing the kingdom to Jane and her heirs male (who would be Dudleys).

Without parliamentary endorsement this devise had no constitutional validity. The law officers of the crown, when summoned, pronounced it to be illegal and treasonous. But in the face of savage threats by Northumberland and a valueless promise from the king that he would call a parliament to ratify it, they agreed to draft and sign the necessary deed if granted a formal pardon. This deed was then signed by all members of the council and other lords and officials at Northumberland's insistence, until it bore more than a hundred signatures added with various degrees of reluctance. Even then the Queenmaker was not satisfied, and councillors were forced to put their names to an additional written undertaking that they would always support Lady Jane as queen 'to the uttermost of their power' and 'never at any time during their lives would swerve from it'.[7]

Of all this the outside world, including Jane herself, knew nothing. When on 3 July, three days before Edward died, the Duchess of Northumberland told her she would be queen Jane did not believe her. On 7 July the Lord Mayor of London and the city fathers were informed of the king's death in confidence and made to swear loyalty to Jane. Mary and Elizabeth were then summoned to their brother's deathbed on the pretext of hearing his last commands. Mary at once set out from her home in Hertfordshire but turned back at Hoddesdon when warned that the king was already dead: without that warning she might have ended her days as a pretender. The wily Elizabeth responded to the summons with a doctor's certificate regretting that she was too ill to travel.

Retreating to the safety of Framlingham castle in Suffolk, Mary wrote to the council expressing surprise that she had not been notified of Edward's death, nor of their allegiance to her. She was proclaimed queen in Norwich, while in Chelsea Jane was ill in bed and had received no message from the council. On 9 July it agreed to notify her of her accession and proclaim her as queen. She was taken up the Thames by boat to Northumberland's palace at Sion and there told of the late king's wishes and the council's decision. Taking their cue from Northumberland, as President of the Council, the assembled company fell on their knees before her in homage. At this she swooned and, when she recovered, burst into tears.

When Jane could speak it was to inform them that Mary was the rightful queen and she was therefore unable to accept their offer of the crown; at which Northumberland lost his temper with her. His anger was terrifying, but she stood firm and declined to re-consider her decision. When her parents and husband rounded on her she took refuge in prayer, seeking God's guidance. None was forthcoming, except the thought that God would not wish her to disobey her parents. Without an unequivocal 'no' from Above the pressure on a fifteen-year-old, however strong-minded, was in the end too great to withstand. With misgivings all too well-justified – for at that moment Jane signed her own death warrant – she bowed to the will of the most powerful in the land with the proper but ineffectual proviso 'if what has been given to me is lawfully mine'.[8]

Lady Jane was now Queen Jane. Her 'just and right title in the imperial crown of this realm'[9] was proclaimed and contrasted with the 'feigned and untrue claim of the Lady Mary, bastard daughter to our great-uncle, Henry the Eighth of famous memory'.[10] A procession of gilded state barges brought her ceremonially to the Tower, where a salute of cannons greeted her, but no acclamation: the public was as astonished and bewildered as the new queen herself. A belated reply to Mary's letter, signed by every member of the council, reinforced the proclamation. It asserted that Jane had succeeded in accordance with the 'ancient good laws of this realm' and 'our late sovereign lord's letters patent, signed with his own hand and sealed with the Great Seal of England'.[11] Mary was reminded of her parents' divorce and her own illegitimacy and ordered to be 'quiet and obedient'[12] in submission to her sovereign lady, Queen Jane.

The luxury of the state apartments in the Tower of London did nothing to alleviate the misery of the new sovereign lady. Another family quarrel had broken out, this time over her adamant refusal to have her husband crowned as king. A dukedom was as far as she would go, and she would not be budged. Guilford and his parents and her own were all in a rage at her incorrigible obstinacy, and ordering material for her coronation robes and inspecting jewellery which had belonged to Henry VIII's assortment of wives offered little consolation to a bluestocking with a taste for ancient Greek philosophy and biblical commentaries.

Outside, events were moving in Mary's favour. Two of the Dudley brothers had failed to capture her and the earls of Derby and Oxford and other magnates were gathering an army round her. Northumberland was much hated, and his personal enemies and political opponents hastened to Mary's side, dismayed at his coup and the prospect of a royal Dudley dynasty. Many families had suffered at the hands of 'King Guilford's' grandfather, Henry Tudor's tax-gatherer, whom Henry VIII had won popularity by executing.

The religious aspect of the succession was at this juncture a secondary consideration. Popery had rarely been welcome in England and Mary's Catholic supporters alone would never have carried the day. But – fatally for Jane – the new doctrines of Calvinist Europe were still the preserve of an elite minority. They flourished under Edward VI and Somerset's protectorship, but had no deep roots in a country which has always been, not passionately but sentimentally, attached to old customs and traditional observances. Mary's promise of tolerance (not to 'compel or constrain other men's consciences')[13] was enough to overcome Protestant forebodings.

The council quickly became aware that it was out of step with the mood of the country, but in London Northumberland still held the reins of power. The most urgent necessity was the despatch of an army to East Anglia before support for Mary grew out of hand, but who should lead it? Northumberland nominated Jane's father, the Duke of Suffolk, but in terms of leadership and military prowess Northumberland himself was the obvious choice. His reluctance to go and leave a vacuum in the centre of power is understandable. Once his heavy hand was removed, could the council be trusted to stay true to its new allegiance?

The dilemma is thought to have been resolved by Jane herself. Well aware of her father's incapacity, she urged Northumberland to lead the army in person, and on 14 July he rode out of London at the head of a large force of infantry, supported by cavalry, artillery and four of his sons. Contemporary estimates of more than 30,000 probably exaggerate the numbers, but even so they should have been ample enough to extinguish all prospect of Mary's succession. Unfortunately for Jane, the troops were ill-disciplined and not committed to her – or, as it was generally seen, Northumberland's – cause. During the two-day march to Cambridge so many deserted that the duke had to send back to London for reinforcements. These the council was loth to supply because London would then be unprotected if, as was half suspected, the Lord President were to find it expedient himself to desert Jane for Mary.

The new queen's fate was decided on 17 July when Northumberland, after advancing to Bury St Edmunds, returned to Cambridge to await reinforcements before fighting. He mistrusted the loyalty of his army and his nerve had failed. In London the next day the council, anticipating his collapse and alarmed by reports of the approach of a Marian army under Lord Paget, quitted the Tower and met in Baynards Castle, where they took little time in forming the unanimous view that Mary was the rightful queen after all and Northumberland a traitor.

A messenger was sent to the Tower to inform the Duke of Suffolk that his daughter was no longer queen, but no one chose to tell Jane herself that her reign had ended. While her father hastened to add his signature to the council's new proclamation recognising Queen Mary, she sat alone in the council chamber under the canopy of state awaiting the men who had sworn unswerving allegiance to her. When the news did reach her it came as a relief and she begged, unavailingly, to be allowed to go home. Suffolk himself made a speedy departure, but his daughter had to stay behind as a prisoner to help him make his peace with the new sovereign lady, whom he personally proclaimed as queen on Tower Hill. In Cambridge, before he was arrested, Northumberland also disowned the queen he had created. In the market square he tore down her proclamation with his own hand and cried 'Long Live Queen Mary'.

Protestant support in the south-east of England had been decisive in ousting a Protestant queen for a bigoted Catholic. When she entered the city thirteen tumultuous days after her brother's death, Protestant London greeted Mary with cheering and dancing in the streets, but before long the citizens were to rue the loss of the other queen, whom they had welcomed in silent disbelief. The new faith had been tolerant: when Edward was on the throne not a single Catholic suffered martyrdom. During Mary's shorter reign 283 of her Protestant subjects were burned as heretics. The queen was not personally cruel like her father, only cruel as a matter of religious principle. At first Spanish influence was blamed, but towards the end the Spanish were so concerned at the discontent aroused by her persecutions that they were vainly advising restraint. It is one of history's ironies that in creating so many martyrs and such revulsion she ensured, perhaps even more effectively than a long reign by Queen Jane would have done, that England would spend the next 400 years as a Protestant country.

Mary's first inclination was towards reconciliation and mercy. Northumberland was executed, recanting on the scaffold ('I die in the true Catholic Faith'),[14] but four of his sons, Jane's parents and the remainder of the turncoat council were spared, in response to a humble plea to 'pardon and remit our former infirmities'.[15] Jane herself and her views the new queen despised but, in spite of the urging of the Imperial ambassador, she saw no reason to take revenge on an innocent girl. 'Her conscience, she said, would not permit her to have her put to death.'[16]

Jane's court and subjects had shrunk to four: a lady in waiting (Lady Throckmorton), two female servants and a page. Removed from the state apartments to the gentleman-gaoler's lodgings, she studied and wrote with little but her faith to sustain her while others argued over her fate. The debate concluded with a decision to try her for treason. The verdict would not be in doubt, but it was understood that Mary had promised a pardon and her life would be spared.

The trial at Guildhall was a brief formality. The blade of the axe was turned towards her as the judge pronounced sentence. The usual penalty for treason was designed for male traitors. Pretenders such as Perkin Warbeck were subjected to this gruesome dismemberment, although members of the nobility like Northumberland were customarily granted the privilege of being beheaded instead. Jane was sentenced to the most severe penalty prescribed for women, that for witchcraft as inflicted on Joan of Arc: burning at the stake. She received the judgment with icy calm, but it was said that the look on her face so haunted the judge that he later died insane: 'in his raving cried continually to have the Lady Jane taken away from him, and so ended his life'.[17]

In strict confinement after the trial she fell ill. Her husband had also been condemned but was separately imprisoned and her isolation was total. Even her mother had deserted her, and no one came forward bold enough to plead for her at court. The promised pardon was unaccountably delayed, and with each day that passed Mary made more enemies and her victim attracted more sympathy.

Londoners were angered by the celebration of mass (a criminal offence) in St Paul's cathedral, and a divided England was united in outrage at the announcement that the queen intended to marry Philip of Spain and make a foreign king sovereign lord of England. Unpopularity did not deter Mary, and her obstinacy over the Spanish marriage was Jane's undoing. With the country in a mood of dangerous discontent it would have been folly to set a rival queen at liberty, particularly when Jane's father and uncles took the lead in threatening Mary with deposition unless she abandoned the marriage project. They were arrested after the surrender of Sir Thomas Wyatt, who had led an army of Protestant rebels into the city of London.

The beneficiary of the rebellion was to have been Elizabeth, not Jane. It was planned that she should marry a Protestant whom Mary had rejected. Edward Courtenay, only son of the Marquess of Exeter executed by Henry VIII, was 'the last sprig of the White Rose'. He had been imprisoned for fifteen years, mostly in solitary confinement, until released by Mary. Although his days and nights since had been spent in brothels and general dissipation, making up for lost time, he was cast in the role of Elizabeth's king to save England from the bondage of Spain. He and Elizabeth were arrested, but escaped execution. The queen had been merciful, but too much mercy would be seen as weakness. The opportunity was taken to dispose of the ex-queen and her would-be king, already condemned and still unpardoned. Within a few days Mary had been persuaded to end what her chief advisers, Bishop Gardiner and the Imperial ambassador, denounced as a foolish policy of clemency. Even so, Jane had the offer of a pardon if she would renounce the new faith and embrace the old. Most girls on the threshold of life would have been tempted, but Jane held the unshakeable belief that only her own faith would lead her into the kingdom of Heaven. Her steadfastness put to shame the apostasy of Northumberland and the unprincipled manoeuvrings of the men who had manipulated her.

The tussle over her soul continued to the end, for Mary was no less steadfast. She sent her own confessor (Dr Feckenham, later Dean of St Paul's and Abbot of Westminster) to instruct the heretic in the error of her beliefs. Jane listened, argued and was not convinced.

On the morning of 12 February 1554, granted the last mercy of a swift death by the axe, she dressed in black and watched while her husband was led to the public scaffold on Tower Hill. The sight of his headless corpse being carried back almost broke her will, but she recovered her composure in time for her last walk towards the headsman waiting within the precincts on Tower Green. She read her prayer book as she went. The Lieutenant of the Tower walked by her side in case she faltered, but her speech from the scaffold was clear and to the point: 'My offence . . . was only in consent to the devices of others . . . it was never of my seeking.'[18] When blindfolded she lost her bearings and had to be guided to the block. Before kneeling she gave her prayer book to the lieutenant as a keepsake. In it she had written: 'The preacher saith, There is a time to be born and a time to die, and the day of our death is better than the day of our birth'.[19]

This was Queen Jane's last message to herself and posterity. Thus 'this gentle young lady, endued with singular gifts both of learning and knowledge, as patient and mild as any lamb came to the place of her execution'.[20] The preacher she referred to was Ecclesiastes, who wrote in the same passage: 'A good name is better than precious ointment'. Among pretenders Jane's name deserves to stand pre-eminent. She was not ambitious or self-seeking, but quietly determined to do her duty according to God's word. She died for her faith in 'holy tranquillity'.

8

The Queen of Scots

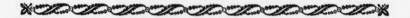

ON ANOTHER February morning, 33 years later, the balance was redressed when a Catholic queen was beheaded on the warrant of a Protestant queen. On a scaffold erected overnight in the great hall of the castle of Fotheringhay, the former Yorkist stronghold in Northamptonshire, Mary Stuart made her exit from life with a courage and dignity as unfaltering as Jane Grey's. Some 300 solemn officials and gaping villagers witnessed her end. After so much sorrow she would die gladly for her church, she told them, spurning the ministrations of the Protestant Dean of Peterborough. Her wish and purpose was to live on as an enduring witness to England's persecution of the Catholic faith. 'In my end is my beginning' was her chosen motto, reminiscent of Jane's.

'Never did any human creature meet death more bravely; yet, in the midst of the admiration and pity which cannot be refused her, it is not to be forgotten that she was leaving the world with a lie upon her lips [that she had never imagined, sought or consented to Elizabeth I's death]. She was a bad woman, disguised in the livery of a martyr.'[1] Such is the severe verdict of one distinguished historian, and it illustrates the controversy – whether she was an innocent victim or a scarlet woman guilty of adultery and murder – which has raged over the reputation of this queen with almost as much ferocity as the long-running Great Debate over the character of Richard III.

'Mary, Queen of Scots, after she came under her great and manifold troubles, has been represented to the world in very different colours; and some writers have not only disagreed in the most material circumstances, but have even flatly contradicted and opposed each other with very great warmth and bitterness.'[2] These words were written in 1727, and the optimism of their conclusion, 'Truth will at length prevail',[3] has yet to be justified.

Mary became Queen of Scotland at the age of six days, when her father, James V, turned his face to the wall in Falkland palace and died of shame and despair after the disgrace of his rout by the English at Solway Moss. The infant sovereign was at once plunged into the troubled waters of two whirlpools: the rivalry between France and England to dominate Scottish affairs and Europe's religious conflict between the old and new faiths.

At the age of five, after the further disaster at Pinkie, she was sent to France to be brought up out of the reach of the English enemy and perpetuate the Franco-Scottish alliance through marriage to the Dauphin. She became Queen of France at sixteen, but at eighteen, following the death of her husband, returned to her homeland to reign in her own right. Auburn-haired, pale-skinned, sweet-faced and nearly six foot tall, she was striking in appearance – although not, as the romantically inclined have to suppose, beautiful. All Scotland should have welcomed her, but her inheritance was an almost ungovernable land divided amongst proud and insubordinate nobles who had managed well enough without a sovereign.

During her absence, moreover, Scotland had followed the example of England in abolishing papal authority and forbidding celebration of the mass. She was the Catholic ruler of what had become a Protestant and Presbyterian realm. It was as well that she was no Mary Tudor, set on imposing her faith on others, but religious tolerance and moderation were not enough. Ahead lay two calamitous marriages and a reign of only five and a half years, leading to 20 years of almost unbroken captivity followed by execution at the age of 44.

Despite her dramatic appearance on the stage of English history Mary barely qualifies as a genuine pretender. When Mary Tudor died Elizabeth I's succession was undisputed. In the eyes of many, including the King of France, she was illegitimate and Mary Stuart the rightful queen, but Mary herself never asserted a right to the English crown superior to Elizabeth's. Her never-ending objective was recognition, not as the rightful queen, but as the rightful heir. Throughout her life the charges against her as a pretender related to the assertions of others, notably the pope, and to the challenge made in her name in Paris during her teens, when it was on the orders of the French king that she quartered the arms of England, flaunted them in the French court and allowed herself to be styled Queen of Scotland, England and Ireland.

It is true that she refused to ratify the Treaty of Edinburgh in which her claim to the English crown was formally renounced, but that was because, in exchange for ratification, she was seeking formal acknowledgement of her reversionary title. As the grand-daughter of Henry VII's elder daughter, Margaret Tudor, she stood next in line in the English succession if Henry VIII's exclusion of foreigners was deemed to have lapsed. Elizabeth, however, had no desire or incentive to nominate a successor, to, as she put it, 'set a winding sheet before my eyes'.[4] Mary received the same treatment as other heirs presumptive: alternate doses of chilly suspicion and fiery rage.

In England the most presuming was Catherine Grey, Jane's younger sister, who incurred the royal wrath for a secret dynastic marriage to the Earl of Hertford, the Seymour heir of Protector Somerset. By the time it was discovered she was already pregnant, and when the couple were imprisoned in the Tower they had the temerity to produce a second son surreptitiously. Such was the affront to the virgin queen that the marriage was declared invalid (the priest and witnesses not daring to make themselves known) and Hertford was fined £15,000 for seducing a virgin of the blood royal. Their children, stigmatised as bastards, were disqualified from the succession and Catherine was to die the queen's prisoner.

Earlier though, when in 1562 Elizabeth nearly died of smallpox, Catherine might have become queen in preference to the Catholic Mary. Her only Protestant competitor would have been the unaspiring Earl of Huntingdon (great-grandson of the attainted Clarence's daughter, Margaret, Countess of Salisbury), a Plantagenet sprig of beheaded traitors who had somehow himself escaped the Tudor axe. On her recovery Elizabeth was urged to marry and produce an heir of her own, but the queue of suitors was dismissed one by one and it became apparent that the very notion of a husband was unattractive to a woman well satisfied with the possession of power at her own command and the exercise of unshared authority.

The more feminine Mary, on the other hand, strongly felt the need of a consort and made the mistake of falling in love unwisely twice. Her second marriage was the subject of intense negotiation with

Elizabeth, whom she was anxious not to offend. To deflect her from a Spanish alliance with Philip II's son Elizabeth even proffered her own favourite, Northumberland's son, Robert Dudley, whom she elevated to the earldom of Leicester to heighten his appeal. No one, then or since, has known quite how to interpret this example of Elizabethan subtlety, but Mary's ambassador rejected the offer diplomatically. The suitor she chose instead could not have been more calculated to annoy the English queen whom it was her policy to appease.

Among the many enterprising ladies playing for high stakes in high places during the sixteenth century Margaret, Countess of Lennox deserves more attention than she has received. As the daughter of Margaret Tudor by a second marriage, she was cousin to both queens. Her husband, moreover, was a Stuart, descended from James II, so their eldest son and heir, Henry Stuart, Lord Darnley, had a claim to the succession in both realms. In the matter of religion the family nicely hedged its bets, the countess being a Catholic and the earl a Protestant. As Scottish residents in England their nationality too was ambiguous, and Henry, the heir to a Scottish earldom, was English-born.

As a youth he had been packed off by a scheming mother to ogle Mary in Orleans. In February 1564, still only 18, he was granted leave by an incautious Elizabeth to travel to Scotland. There he fell ill in Stirling and won the Scots queen's heart while she nursed him back to health. The 'long lad' was fair-haired and baby-faced, not only handsome but even taller than herself. This young god, who was amenable to attending kirk with Presbyterians and marrying according to Catholic rites, would have been the ideal husband for Mary if only he had not been both brainless and vicious: a vain, ill-natured nincompoop.

Passionately in love, the queen hastened to marry him and make him her King Henry. Elizabeth retaliated by dispatching the scheming mother to the Tower of London. In England the marriage was seen as a challenging step by Mary towards the English throne. In Scotland a stupid Anglicised Lennox king met with disgust, not least from the rival Hamiltons. Soon Mary herself became disillusioned. Darnley's participation in the murder of his wife's secretary, Riccio, in her presence while she was six-months pregnant was unforgivable, and when the king's body was found strangled after a gunpowder explosion outside Edinburgh at Kirk o' Field the queen was widely suspected of complicity in his murder. She displayed no grief, nor any inclination to bring the murderers to justice. When the chief suspect was put on trial he was acquitted for want of evidence (another case of intimidated witnesses). He was James Hepburn, Earl of Bothwell, Lieutenant of the Borders and hereditary Great Admiral of Scotland, a hairy burly man of violence who proceeded to abduct the not un-willing queen, divorce his countess in indecent haste and, only three months after Darnley's death, make Mary his wife. Neither the queen nor her reputation could be expected to survive such a scandal.

The nobles rose, held her in the island fortress of Lochleven and forced her to sign a deed of abdication in favour of her infant son. He was crowned as James VI and the government passed into the hands of her illegitimate Protestant half-brother, James Stuart, Earl of Moray. Moray was in a similar situation to Robert of Gloucester, but there the resemblance ends. When Mary escaped from Lochleven the regent's army defeated hers at Langside. She fled across Solway Firth in a fishing boat to Cumberland to solicit aid from a fellow queen against rebellious subjects. Her trust was calamitously misplaced, for she was never again to enjoy sovereignty or even freedom.

To the English government her arrival was an acute embarrass-ment. William Cecil, Elizabeth's chief minister, wrote a memoran-dum for his royal mistress outlining the implications of detaining the unwanted guest, returning her to Scotland or forwarding her to France. There were dangers in every option. Despite categorical denials of any pretensions, Mary was too close to the English throne not to be distrusted as a competitor. Elizabeth therefore decided to treat her cousin as a suspected criminal until her innocence of Darnley's murder had been proved. She refused to meet Mary or allow her to be brought to London, and the Scottish regent was invited to submit evidence of her guilt. The adoption of this moral posture scarcely concealed Elizabeth's violation of every rule of hospitality and every code of justice and honour in subjecting Mary to two trials (although she was not bound by the laws of England), to life-long imprisonment (although found not guilty of Darnley's murder) and, finally, to execution.

The first trial took the form of an investigation in which both Mary and Moray (as a rebel) were defendants. The case rested on the authenticity or otherwise of the so-called Casket Letters which Moray produced as evidence of Mary's complicity with Bothwell in Darnley's death. Both defendants were acquitted, but while Moray returned to

Scotland with a present of £5000 the unfortunate Mary was not released. Held in various castles in the midlands, she became willy-nilly the focus of every conspiracy against Elizabeth. The Duke of Norfolk planned to marry her and was executed for treason. The earls of Northumberland and Westmorland led a rising of Catholics in the north.

In May 1570 a papal bull excommunicated Elizabeth and released her Catholic subjects from any obligation of loyalty to her. In Catholic eyes Mary was the true Queen of England, and a plot for an invasion by Spanish troops from Flanders to put her on the throne was uncovered. The English parliament passed an Act barring her from the succession, and her execution was demanded. 'So long as that devilish woman lives, neither Her Majesty must make account to continue in quiet possession of her crown, nor her faithful servants assure themselves of safety of their lives,'[5] wrote Sir Francis Walsingham to Lord Burghley early in 1572. Such was the strength of anti-Catholic feeling that it was hard for Elizabeth to resist, particularly after the French massacre of Huguenots on St Bartholomew's Day, but she could not yet be brought to face responsibility for the cold-blooded murder of another queen.

It was no more than a long reprieve. For a further fifteen years events moved inexorably towards Mary's destruction. With the murder of heretic rulers openly approved by the pope and Catholic prelates and princes, her death knell was sounded. The Protestant William of Orange (William the Silent) was assassinated, and the Throgmorton and Babington plots were only two among a number of attempts on the life of Elizabeth. One conspirator, Dr Parry, was urged by the pope's own secretary to put his 'holy and honourable purposes into effect'.[6] Self-protection, if not revenge, was the inevitable response.

The crucial and still debated questions arising from Mary's second and final trial were to what extent she was an accomplice in these plots and to what extent the evidence against her was fabricated by Walsingham, who employed *agents provocateurs* and other agents in intercepting and copying Mary's correspondence. She had made a will bequeathing her rights to the English crown to Philip II unless her son became a Catholic and was without doubt privy to plans for a Spanish invasion of England. But at the trial she strongly denied any involvement in plots against Elizabeth's life or any wish to usurp her throne. If the pope referred to her as Queen of England, that was not her doing or responsibility. All she ever sought was recognition as Elizabeth's heir.

As a sovereign and foreigner, Mary also challenged the competence of the court to try her, but she was no longer recognised as queen in Scotland and had been resident in England, however unwillingly, for eighteen years. The verdict of guilty was a foregone conclusion, and both houses of parliament were unanimous in petitioning for the death sentence. Its proclamation was greeted with joy in London, but it took Elizabeth two months to sign the death warrant and have it taken to the Lord Chancellor for the Great Seal. Concern, not for Mary, but for herself and the odium she would incur was the cause of her reluctance.

Years before, she had failed to persuade two of Moray's successors as regent (Mar and Morton) to take Mary back to Scotland for execution: their price had been too high. Now she ordered Walsingham to write to Mary's gaoler, Sir Amyas Paulet, urging him to take steps to shorten his captive's life, but Sir Amyas, a hard-faced Puritan, would not oblige. 'God forbid,' he replied, 'that I should make so fond a shipwreck of my conscience, or leave so great a blot to my poor posterity, to shed blood without law or warrant'.[7] William Davison, the queen's second secretary, accordingly carried the warrant to Cecil (by then Lord Burleigh), the privy council took the decision to execute it without further delay, and the headsman was despatched to Fotheringhay.

When news of the execution reached London there were week-long festivities, including bonfires and banqueting and psalm-singing in the streets, while the queen protested furiously that she had not authorised it. Burleigh was in disgrace, and Davison was fined £10,000 (later remitted) and sent to the Tower for eighteen months (on full pay). This hypocritical charade even extended to the queen wearing mourning and ordering a delayed state funeral for Mary in Peterborough cathedral. To Mary's son in Scotland she wrote a letter of consolation regretting 'this lamentable accident' which had occurred, she assured him, contrary to her wishes. In a rare display of filial piety James refused to receive her envoy.

The balance sheet between Elizabeth and Mary is still a battleground. Her accusers were probably right in charging Mary with guilty foreknowledge of the plot to kill Darnley, and despite her denials she must have realised that the conspiracies of Antony Babington and others, of which she was made aware and which she encouraged in secret correspondence, were aimed at Elizabeth's life.

Yet her own overriding and unremitting purpose throughout years of unjust captivity was the wholly proper one of recovering her freedom and a crown surrendered under duress. In conformity with the established practice of Tudor government, Elizabeth and her advisers acted solely on grounds of political expediency, and on those grounds she had irresistible cause to eliminate an alternative queen. Even her simulated grief after the event was politically inspired; although Catholic Europe was neither deceived nor appeased. From her father and grandfather she had learned that those who wish to keep their crowns should not confuse morals and politics, and although the judicial murder of Mary added impetus to the planned Spanish assault on England, it may also have contributed to the triumph over the Armada, which sailed the following year.

With Mary dead, Philip II had become the Catholic candidate and pretender, but English Catholics did not favour a Spanish king, especially one who was the former consort of the unlamented Mary Tudor. Her death therefore effectively settled the succession on her Protestant son, James VI, who was kept fretting for sixteen years waiting for Elizabeth to die. When the great prize of England at last fell into his lap he had his mother's body reburied in a magnificent tomb to vie with the Tudors where they lay at rest in Henry VII's chapel in Westminster Abbey.

James VI's accession as James I was smoothly managed by the ministers of the English crown. His nearest competitor was the only child to emerge from another piece of ambitious match-making by Darnley's mother, the indefatigable Countess of Lennox, and this too had earned her a spell in the Tower under the cloud of Elizabeth's severe displeasure. Without the queen's permission she had married her only other son, Charles Stuart (who was to become Earl of Lennox), to Elizabeth Cavendish, the daughter of another formidable virago, Bess of Hardwick. These were the parents of Arbella Stuart who, if she had been a boy, might well have been crowned in preference to any foreign king.

Since, after James, she stood next in line of succession, Elizabeth could not bear the sight of her. She was banned from court and kept in Derbyshire in the custody of her grandmother Bess. When her other grandmother died James, as her grandson, took all the Lennox estates in Scotland while Elizabeth with less excuse seized the properties in England. They also united to make sure that Arbella did not marry without their consent, and preferably not at all. She was neither beautiful nor clever, but her blood royal, as they well knew, would be a temptation to any man.

On Elizabeth's death Arbella spiritedly refused to act as chief mourner at the funeral of a woman who would not have her within sight when alive. James graciously permitted her to come to court, where he could keep an eye on her. In her mid-thirties she grew restless and decided to make a marriage without his consent, since it would not be granted. Her chosen groom was 22-year-old William Seymour, eldest son of the elder of the two bastardised children of Catherine Grey and therefore himself of the blood royal. As soon as James learned of the marriage they were hurriedly separated: William sent to the Tower of London and Arbella ordered into house arrest with the Bishop of Durham in the far north.

At East Barnet on the way to Durham she feigned illness and escaped disguised as a man to keep a rendezvous with William at Blackwall, where they intended to board a boat and sail for Calais. But William's escape from ill-guarded custody in the Tower was delayed and they never met. He reached Ostend, but she had stayed too long waiting for him. The alarm was raised. In a naval chase she was intercepted in the Channel and brought back to take his place in the Tower, where she died 'after a long and chronic sickness'.[8] As the years passed, she had lost the will to live, and seems to have starved herself to death. Her brain was reported to be 'cracked'.

A successful escape would have made Arbella a pretender to be reckoned with, for there can be little doubt that support would have been forthcoming for a claim to England as good as James's. Had she produced a son, a whole new dynasty of pretenders might have been born. But, thanks to William's poor time-keeping, her almost un-noticed death in 1615 brought the golden age of pretenders to a close on a note of anti-climax. She was of Stuart and Tudor blood and her body rightly found a place of honour in the vault of Mary Queen of Scots' tomb, where it has lain scarcely noticed ever since.

9

King Monmouth

THE STUART monarchs of Scotland and England were little loved in either kingdom. Mary Queen of Scots' son was shrewd enough to keep the two crowns despite his strange ways and his apprehension that his brilliant eldest son, Prince Henry, would see him buried before he was dead. Henry, however, predeceased his father, and it was his younger brother who, as Charles I, provoked his subjects to rebellion and was brought to the scaffold.

After Oliver Cromwell's death a resumption of Stuart rule was preferred to the run-down Commonwealth, and in Charles II's footsteps, following his return from exile, came his favourite but illegitimate son, later to be known and acclaimed as 'The Protestant Duke'.

In Macaulay's words, 'the great mass of the people abhorred Popery and adored Monmouth'.[1] 'King Monmouth' was the spiritual heir to Queen Jane, and he gathered the popular support which she, an unknown, had never enjoyed. On his quasi-royal progress through the west country in the summer of 1680 he was mobbed like a twentieth-century pop star. From Longleat to Exeter crowds lined the roads to cheer and, if possible, touch him. An escort of 5000 horsemen accompanied him to Chard. In a ceremonial parade of honour 900 youths in white uniforms marched before him into Exeter. At every stop he dined in state while the public filed through the room to catch a glimpse of their idol eating.

Bonnie Prince Charlie belongs to Scottish romance: Monmouth is his English counterpart – the most romantic of England's pretenders. He too was a handsome Prince Charming, brave and sincere, brighter in charisma than intellect. Ending on the scaffold like Queen Jane, he remained as steadfast in his faith: 'I die a Protestant of the Church of England'.[2] After death he became the subject of extravagant lament:

> Come, Mortals, come, now set yourselves to weep,
> Is not your Glorious Monmouth gone to sleep?
>
> Created Things, come set yourselves to mourn
> Since lovely Monmouth from the World is torn.[3]

In the west of England his second coming was long expected 'when the harvest was over'. It was said that he had five look-alikes and one of those had been executed in his place. An unnamed great lady who knew him is reported to have had his coffin opened and to have exclaimed: 'Tis not he!' when she looked inside. Today there is a shrine to his memory at the border seat of his descendant, the Duke of Buccleugh and Queensberry. The Monmouth Room at Bowhill contains his cradle, his saddle and the shirt he wore for his execution as well as portraits and other mementoes for visitors to wonder at.

Yet this hero was liable to be weak and irresolute, his courage sometimes melted into cowardice, and his enemies were not too wide of the mark in dubbing him The Booby Duke. Although Dryden recorded

> His motions all accompanied with grace;
> And Paradise was open'd in his face,[4]

he also recorded how the young duke's vanity was so tickled by royal favour and popular adulation that he was 'made drunk with honour and debauched with praise'.[5] The harshest of verdicts has come from a biographer of his rival and inveterate foe, James II: 'Of Monmouth it is safe to say that no man who appeared so attractive to his contemporaries figures in history as so worthless and contemptible'.[6]

Whatever the measure of truth in this judgment, he was certainly as unfortunate a choice for leader of the Protestant party as Queen Jane had been. In each case, within a few years of their own failure, their cause triumphed in the more capable hands of better claimants – Elizabeth I and William and Mary. In a moment of exasperation

Monmouth's normally doting father once described him as a 'block-head' and, although he was not quite that, his political naivety was certainly an attraction to those 'crafty knaves' among the Whig politicians who recruited him for their figurehead. William of Orange was far too astute to become the tool of other men, but Monmouth's pride and vanity, like Jane's youth, made him an easy prey.

Born in Rotterdam on 9 April 1649, during the period of his father's exile, the future Duke of Monmouth was the eldest son of the future King Charles II. His father was aged nineteen and his mother eighteen. They were not man and wife, nor even partners in more than a fleeting liaison. Lucy Walter was the daughter of English gentlefolk who had settled in Pembrokeshire. She had run away from home to become the mistress of a parliamentarian colonel in London, who had passed her on to his royalist brother in The Hague, who finding her 'already spent' had passed her on to the heir to the throne. She then passed through various other male hands, living precariously and constantly pestering Charles for an annuity. Clarendon disparaged her as a 'Welchwoman of no good fame'. Other enemies of her son denounced her more bluntly as 'a common whore'. John Evelyn, the diarist, shared a carriage with her in Paris in the year of Monmouth's birth and reported that she was 'a browne, beautiful, bold, but insipid creature'.[7]

Despite the generous spread of Lucy's favours Charles acknowledged paternity. He grandly made her a grant of £1500 a year, but this did not satisfy her because there were no funds to pay it. When she grew too much of a nuisance in The Hague he gave her ready money and pearls on condition that she returned to London. There she was arrested on suspicion of being a spy, imprisoned in the Tower with her child and then shipped back to Holland.

When the boy was nine his father made two attempts to kidnap him from his mother. The second was successful. He was taken to Paris and put in the care of Lord Crofts, a gentleman of the bedchamber, who passed him off as a relative under the name of James Crofts. Since he was unable to read or count up to twenty, special attention was paid to his education, but without much result. Although he was later to be installed as Chancellor of the University of Cambridge, his surviving letters are evidence of no more than semi-literacy.

His mother died in 1658 shortly after she lost the struggle to keep him. On her deathbed she is said to have left to her confessor a black box containing documentary evidence of her marriage to Charles. The existence of this Black Box, legitimising Monmouth, was to become an article of faith among the extreme Protestant party bent on excluding Charles's younger brother, James, Duke of York (later James II) from the succession after his open conversion to Roman Catholicism. The marriage certificate which it contained was even rumoured to have survived until 1879 when it was destroyed by Monmouth's descendant, the then Duke of Buccleugh, with the comment: 'That might cause a lot of trouble'. Which indeed it might have, since it would have given him a claim to the throne superior to that of Queen Victoria. There seems little doubt, however, that the black box and its alleged contents are wholly fictitious and properly belong to the realm of legend.

Charles appears to have taken little interest in 'young Jemmie' until two years after his return to England on the restoration of the monarchy. In August 1662 the boy, aged thirteen, was brought over from Paris by his grandmother, Queen Henrietta Maria, and the king was enchanted by his good looks and high spirits. He had no legitimate children and this 'most pretty spark',[8] the eldest of his bastards, found a ready place in his affections. 'Young Jemmie' was so doted upon, fondled and kissed in public and extravagantly indulged in every way that rumours soon began to circulate that, if he was not the offspring of secret wedlock, he would soon be legitimised and acknowledged as the lawful heir.

Such encouragement led the boy who had been dragged up in poverty to display the royal arms of England and France with no bar sinister and even to touch for the king's evil. In grants he was formally styled the king's 'beloved son' instead of the customary 'natural son'. It is hardly surprising that such a change of circumstances and prospects should have gone to his head and enticed him into advancing a claim to the crown despite the disability which had restrained a worthier man in Robert of Gloucester. But his backers could point to Henry Tudor's accession in spite of a claim flawed with illegitimacy and to the precedent of William the Bastard who became William I. All the same, when the crunch came, no one of rank in church or state, whatever his politics or religion, was willing to see the son of Lucy Walter anointed and enthroned. It would have been 'offensive to the pride of the nobles and to the moral feeling of the middle class'.[9]

The closest parallel to Monmouth as pretender is another claimant of doubtful birth in the Netherlands: Perkin Warbeck. Both were married into the Scottish nobility. Both invaded the west country with inadequate forces. Both were welcomed by the populace and shunned by the gentry. Both chose to desert rather than die with their men and fled to the New Forest in vain bids to escape. Both were captured, humiliated and executed. It was Nell Gwynne, with her sharp cockney wit, who first bestowed on Monmouth the apt but ominous nickname of Prince Perkin.

The Scottish heiress whom Charles selected for his son was Anne, aged twelve but already Countess of Buccleugh in her own right. The bridegroom, aged fourteen, had been created Duke of Monmouth and Earl of Doncaster. On his wedding day he took her family name and titles and became James Scott, Duke of Buccleugh and Earl of Dalkeith too. There were other titles and honours as well, most notably the Garter, and the young Monmouth received formal recognition as the fourth person in the realm, taking precedence over everyone except the king, the Duke of York and Prince Rupert of the Rhine. At nineteen, as Captain of the Life Guards, he became commander of the king's bodyguard. He was made a member of the Privy Council, High Chamberlain and Master of the Horse. He was given money and houses and jewellery and £6000 a year to add to his wife's £10,000.

His life was devoted to pleasure. He enjoyed hunting and preferred mistresses to his wife, who was reserved and intellectual. In sport and athletics he was a champion, winning cups as a jockey and prizes for races on foot even when handicapped by running in boots against competitors wearing shoes. In 1665 Pepys recorded in his diary: 'The Duke of Monmouth is the most skittish, leaping gallant that ever I saw, always in action vaulting or leaping or clambering'.[10]

There was a dark side to this horseplay and high jinks by a pampered coffee-house blade. In the following year Pepys was complaining that the duke was vicious and idle, given to 'whoring' and 'roguing'. Two examples of the roguing were inexcusably unsavoury. He employed men to slit the nose of a member of parliament who had slighted his father in a speech in the House of Commons, and the victim (Sir John Coventry) was left for dead on a London street. On another occasion he himself killed an innocent beadle in cold blood, running him through with his sword in a brothel brawl. Protection from prosecution secured by his father's intervention hints at other brutal excesses perpetrated by a callous rake. The king is on record as granting a 'gracious pardon unto my dear son James, Duke of Monmouth, of all Murders, Homicides and Felonyes whatever at any time before the 28th day of February last past, committed either by himself alone or together with any other person or persons'.[11]

His military exploits were more honourable. A first taste of action came with the navy against the Dutch. Then, on an embassy to France, he so charmed Louis XIV that the French king offered him a commission in the French army. In tune with his father's wavering foreign policy he successively led English contingents in the French army against the Dutch and in the Dutch army against the French. Praised for his daring by Louis and Marshal Turenne, he became famous for an act of heroism at the siege of Maastricht in 1673. Five years later, in command of an expedition against the French in Flanders (and after much petitioning), he was appointed Captain-General of his father's land forces – commander-in-chief of the first standing army in English history.

In this capacity he was quickly tested. In 1679 a rebellion of Covenanters broke out in the Scottish lowlands. The Archbishop of St Andrews, Primate of Scotland, was murdered and 20,000 men were reported to be in arms. It was a crisis which needed and received all the Captain-General's renowned energy. At the head of a punitive force he reached Edinburgh in three days and quelled the rising on the next day by defeating a rebel army of 4000 at Bothwell Bridge (on the Clyde near Hamilton). Three hundred of them were killed in the fighting, but he forbade a massacre of fugitives and the 1000 prisoners taken were pardoned and allowed to disperse to their homes. Like Robert of Normandy, Monmouth was not a bloodthirsty warrior and his clemency, long remembered, was immortalised by Sir Walter Scott:

> The hardy peasant, by oppression driven
> To battle, deem'd his cause the cause of Heaven;
> Unskilled in arms, with useless courage stood,
> While gentle Monmouth grieved to shed his blood.[12]

The victor returned to London in triumph, the darling of the city, greeted with bells and bonfires and acclaimed as a national hero worthy to be set beside another of his name – Harry of Monmouth, the victor of Agincourt. It was the high point of his life. Only six years later the royal army would crush another rebel force, and the former Captain-General would then be among the rebels.

Politically the turning point in Monmouth's life had come earlier. In 1670 Charles II, a covert Catholic, concluded the secret Treaty of

Dover with Louis XIV, who allowed him a handsome annuity in return for aiding Catholic France against Protestant Holland (or at least for refraining from aiding Holland against France). In or about the same year the king's brother and heir presumptive, James, Duke of York became a convert to Rome. Soon, unlike the king, he was making no secret of the fact and in 1673 he married a pious Catholic princess (Mary of Modena). With no likelihood of Charles's barren queen (Catherine of Braganza) producing an heir, a Protestant country faced the prospect of a Catholic ruler – the first since the reviled Mary Tudor, vividly commemorated in Foxe's *Book of Martyrs*.

In the seventeenth century men took their politics from their religion. As Lord Admiral, the Duke of York had won popularity for victories over the Dutch fleet at Lowestoft and Southwold Bay, but his conversion clouded his career. A Protestant party gathered round Monmouth in a bid to deprive him of the succession. Uncle and nephew became rivals for the king's favour and Charles's subtle grace swung like a pendulum between them: he would neither desert the principle of legitimacy for which the house of Stuart stood nor abandon the indulgence shown to his beloved son. Dryden's casting of Monmouth as Absalom and Charles as David in his *Absalom and Achitophel* was accurate:

> What e'er he did was done with so much ease
> In him alone 'twas natural to please.
>
> With secret joy, indulgent David view'd
> His youthful image in the son renewed.[13]

Achitophel, the villain of the piece, was Anthony Ashley Cooper, Earl of Shaftesbury, who led the opposition to York's succession and was for ever demanding that the king legitimise his son. Using Monmouth to further his own ambitions he was:

> In friendship false, implacable of hate,
> Resolv'd to ruin or to rule the state.[14]

In character York and Monmouth were not unalike. York too was brave and handsome and sincere, obstinate about his religion but otherwise indecisive and weak-willed. He was jealous of the younger man – there was rivalry over mistresses – and they came to detest each other heartily. When York became James II and Monmouth a rebel, this personal hatred precluded any consideration of mercy and brought Monmouth inevitably to the block. He had, after all, publicly denounced his uncle as 'a mortal and bloody enemy'.

In the contest for the succession those who had been cavaliers in the civil war generally supported York. They had become the court party and were soon to be known as the Tories. They stood loyally for King and Church in fervent opposition to the republicans and 'sectaries' of the Cromwellian interregnum. Their church was Anglican, a monument to English compromise and distaste for fanatical extremes, and they hated Protestant nonconformists no less than Roman Catholics. York's conversion posed a dilemma. Not to deviate from their principles they must back the legitimate heir but somehow protect the realm from recapture by Rome. It was these men who brought York to the throne, opposing Monmouth both before and during his rebellion. But later, when their king attacked their church and the opposition called in a Protestant to turn him off the throne, they stood aside in divided loyalty and allowed William of Orange a usurpation unopposed.

Those who preferred Monmouth to York were largely those who had preferred Cromwell to Charles I. These heirs of puritanism, who became the country party or the Whigs, were parliamentarians who believed in liberty but also in the rule of law; most would now accept a king, but one who reigned rather than ruled. Under Shaftesbury, a rich, free-thinking landowner who had deserted Charles I for Cromwell, they sought to substitute Monmouth for York even though some would have voted for a republic. Since Monmouth's qualifications for sovereignty were not impressive it is likely that his role was intended by some as a stepping stone to a republican England. Meanwhile he was their only available candidate to run in the succession stakes.

Soon after his conversion became known, a Whig-dominated parliament succeeded in driving York out of public life by means of a Test Act which excluded from office everyone who refused the Anglican communion. When Titus Oates, a persuasive liar, convinced the privy council of the existence of a Popish Plot to assassinate Charles and put York on the throne, a wave of national hysteria swept the exclusionists to a landslide victory in the general election of 1679 and an Exclusion Bill was drafted to remove York from the succession. Monmouth had taken the opportunity to purge the army of some Catholic officers, but his antiPopery was unenthusiastic and he was reluctant to offend his father. When the bill was introduced he chose to go racing. He was, after all, a member of the court party, a natural Tory who had little in common with the Whigs except antiYorkery.

Charles, distracted from his pleasures, sat on the fence waiting for the commotion to subside. He judged it prudent to send an indignantly protesting York into temporary exile, but compensated for this by repeating in public an oath which he had sworn to the privy council affirming that he had never married Monmouth's mother. Since his son was then at the height of his popularity those rallying under the banner 'Let Monmouth Reign' simply refused to believe the disavowal. For this they had some excuse: the king's record in truthfulness was patchy.

Adulation of Monmouth in the country at large made him irresistible to the Whigs and he was tempted into their arms in a marriage of convenience. If his uncle was to be excluded, why should he refuse the nomination? His father, committed to a policy of even-handedness, responded by depriving him of his appointment of Captain-General and ordering him too into exile. While York pined in Catholic Brussels, Monmouth made himself comfortable in Protestant Utrecht. In England ballads and broadsheets were published lamenting his banishment.

On his return to make his defiant royal progress through the west country, reception committees of gentlemen as well as the common mobs welcomed him everywhere. To win the crown he would need the gentry, but other influences prevailed. This was recognisably a revolutionary movement. In Oxford, for example, where the university stood for James as the legitimate heir, Monmouth was greeted by the townsfolk with cries of 'No bishops, no university'.

The transformation of his cherished son into an idol of the people and his flaunting of a baseless claim to the succession infuriated the king, who had contrived the defeat of two Exclusion Bills and ordered the summary dissolution of a contumacious parliament. York was granted leave to live in Scotland, although not to return to England until the hostility towards him had abated. During his absence from London a discreet visit to the English court was paid by his nephew and son-in-law, William of Orange. Charles had four more years to live, but the vultures were beginning to circle and hover.

A second royal progress two years after the first, this time in the north, led to Monmouth's arrest, but he was soon released and rashly chanced his luck with another in the south. His enemies became alarmed and the Rye House plot in 1683, in which it was alleged that both York and the king were to be assassinated, may have been more of a conspiracy to bring about the downfall of Monmouth – a Tory riposte to the Popish Plot. He was implicated by Robert West, a royalist Titus Oates. Lord Russell and Algernon Sidney were executed and Monmouth went into hiding.

His misfortune softened his father's heart – it was unthinkable that his son had plotted to kill him – and little effort was made to discover the fugitive until a secret reconciliation had been arranged. Appeasing his uncle proved more difficult. He was forced to send a grovelling letter of submission and beg the king for pardon 'by the intercession of the Duke of York whom I acknowledge to have offended and am prepared to submit myself in the humblest manner'.[15] York's intercession was highly priced. Monmouth would have to sign a written confession and give evidence against those accused of being his fellow conspirators. On these agreed terms a royal pardon was forthcoming and the two dukes were persuaded to embrace each other in the king's presence.

Once the pardon had been granted, Monmouth made a fool of York by not writing the promised confession nor giving any evidence which might help to convict any of those under suspicion. To avoid keeping his word he fled abroad and took refuge at the court of William and Mary, his Protestant cousins, in The Hague. Without the magnet of his presence the exclusionist cause lost its attraction and disintegrated. When Charles died in February 1685 York became James II unchallenged. He at once announced a policy of religious toleration and, by releasing more than 1000 imprisoned Quakers, demonstrated reassuringly that the end of religious discrimination was not designed to benefit Catholics alone.

Charles's unforeseen death came as a disaster to the prospects of his pretender son, who was not at his bedside – although at least out of James's reach. Stranded in Holland, he had lost the contest for the crown and would set foot in England at his peril for as long as his uncle reigned. James was soon demanding his extradition in chains, and there was a strong danger of his being kidnapped: a common hazard for pretenders in exile. Despite suggestions from English and Scottish expatriates, however, rebellion was not yet in his thoughts.

The pension from his father had ceased, and so (since he was living with a mistress, Lady Henrietta Wentworth) had any allowance from his wife. The means to afford the princely life to which he had grown accustomed had vanished. Ruefully he considered spending the summer at the court and expense of the King of Sweden and then retiring to Switzerland for a life of contemplation and adult education. The practical William of Orange, perhaps pointing to the crusading example of an earlier disappointed pretender, suggested enlistment in the Imperial army for service against the Turkish invaders of Hungary.

An invitation to a conference of exiles in Rotterdam reached Monmouth while still downcast and undecided. He accepted and in one of his not infrequent weak moments became convinced of his duty to rescue the realms of Great Britain from the papist James. 'Poor Monmouth', as James scornfully remarked, 'was always easy to impose upon'[16] – in this instance by men for whom he represented the best available means of a safe passage home. They were a motley assembly of old commonwealth loyalists and more recent refugees: Rye House suspects, Anabaptists, Covenanters and republicans of all shades. The only Englishman of rank among them was the callow and shifty Lord Grey, who was to become Monmouth's ineffectual second in command.

The leader of the Scottish expatriates, on the other hand, was one of the most powerful noblemen in Britain. The Earl of Argyll, head of the clan Campbell, had been sentenced to death for treason by James when king's commissioner in Scotland. He had escaped from prison and was in the process of mounting an expedition to return to Scotland, raise his highlanders and take a bloodthirsty revenge. As an ally Monmouth did not impress him favourably, it seems, but a simultaneous invasion of England suited his purpose well and agreement was reached.

The smooth and speedy co-ordination envisaged was not achieved, however. Argyll eventually landed in the Western Isles on 13 May, more than three months after Charles's death. Monmouth's sailing was delayed still further until the end of the month. Meanwhile in England the militia had been alerted and known conspirators rounded up. In Scotland lowlanders felt no sympathy for the vengeance of a highland chief and even Argyll's own clan showed little enthusiasm for his cause: instead of an army of 5000 he could raise only 500 and they went home without fighting. Monmouth's own invasion force represented the puniest of assaults on England's shores. His army numbered 82 and the Monmouth armada consisted of one elderly frigate of 240 tons plus two fishing boats, all on charter and under orders to return to Holland as soon as he had disembarked.

If his folly seems beyond belief, the alternative must be remembered: bleak obscurity in exile. The previous November he had slipped across the Channel to pay a secret visit to his father. Yet another reconciliation had taken place and arrangements were agreed for his recall to England in February. Instead, when February came, he suffered a double humiliation in the aftermath of Charles's death. William, under pressure from James and dependent for survival on his alliance with England, ordered him out of The Hague. In Brussels the viceroy of the Spanish Netherlands brusquely told him to move on, and he was forced to hide in penury in Antwerp. Thus the proposal of a coalition against the hated James found him in a receptive mood. The offer of a leading role in great events was tempting, and he was assiduously fed with false reports by hardened expatriates who mistrusted and disliked but sought to use him. They wanted a change of regime, not another king; especially a foppish bastard. But lacking a leader they could not afford to be particular and therefore inveigled him into their conspiracy. They told him what he wanted to hear and was vain enough to believe: that if he were to land in England unarmed and alone he would be able to walk to London with nothing but a switch in his hand. The west country would rise to him to a man, and so would London. In Cheshire Lord Delamere had guaranteed him 20,000 men, while Scotland would have fallen to Argyll.

Not all of this was fantasy, but Monmouth took too long to be lured into action. Haste and resolution were essential requirements, but decisiveness was not a quality he possessed and he suffered as Duke Robert had: Argyll had money to buy ships and arms, but he had none. Funds were still being laboriously collected when James summoned a parliament and brought Whig leaders of doubtful loyalty to London where they would be under his eye. With parliament sitting, the king had the means at hand to be assured of the financial and other legislation necessary to combat a rising. Monmouth's timing was crucially wrong. Even a delay of two or three years would have served him better, for in 1685 James still enjoyed a measure of good will, his heir was a Protestant, and the menace of popery was thought to be receding. On his accession he had promised to respect the Church of England, 'its principles being so firm for monarchy'.

In spite of all this, Monmouth's cause was far from hopeless when he landed at Lyme Regis on 11 June 1685 with his 82 men, four light cannons and sufficient small arms, ammunition, powder and armour to equip 1500. Behind the local militia James had a standing army variously estimated at 4000 and 8000, well trained and well equipped, but Monmouth was confident that he had only to show himself for them to come over to their former Captain-General. It was one of several optimistic assessments in which he was deceived by himself or others. Three years later this army did indeed refuse to fight for James, but that was after the birth of a Catholic heir and against William of Orange who took the precaution of arriving with a fleet of 600 vessels carrying 15,000 men.

Nevertheless, Monmouth had only to step ashore on the famous Cob at Lyme, kneel to ask for God's blessing (as Henry Tudor had at Dale) and declare 'We come to fight Papists' for a tumultuous welcome to burst out all round him. Although in Dorset, Lyme was the Channel port for Somerset, a county with a long tradition of dissent and an extensive cloth trade in the throes of economic depression. Within 24 hours of landing he had 1000 recruits under arms, within ten days 3000. The rush to enlist under the Protestant duke was so great that the clerks could not keep pace with recording their names.

Monmouth's army was a social phenomenon. The men who answered his call were pious, earnest dissenters – Baptists, Presbyterians, Republicans, Independents, even peace-loving Quakers – brought up on the Bible and the *Book of Martyrs*. To them James II was a devilish reincarnation of Bloody Mary, and they hailed Monmouth as a saviour, an English leader cast in the mould of Gustavus Adolphus, the hero of Protestant Europe. For the most part they were not ignorant, hot-headed youngsters, but religious family men; not peasants, but artisans – weavers, tailors and shoemakers, yeomen and sailors. These children of God were descendants of the New Model Army of Cromwell and Fairfax, but without military training, not yet baptised in the fire of battle, and without Cromwell or Fairfax to lead them. They were staunch, unflinching raw recruits, who were soon to learn that in war prayer is not enough and faith no substitute for cavalry.

Armed rebellion had been a recurrent feature in English history up to this time. Monmouth closed the chapter of civil warfare: his was the last popular uprising in England. It was not motivated by class hostility and envy of the rich, as the Peasants Revolt against John of

Gaunt and his kind had been. It was a revival of the spirit which had given birth to Cromwell's Commonwealth. Three years after Monmouth came the Glorious Revolution of 1688 which began the process whereby power passed from king to landed aristocracy in an evolution towards universal franchise. In contrast to France and Russia, revolution without bloodshed became the English style hereafter.

Some of Monmouth's supporters were certainly democrats with ideals of equality and social justice in the tradition of John Ball and Wat Tyler, but the objective of most was no more than the replacement of Stuart autocracy and papal interference by parliamentary rule and freedom of religious thought. Urban artisans held property to be sacred as fervently as any land-owner. Their slogan was 'Liberty and No Popery'. Their leader was a popular hero, but not a man of the people or a rabble-rouser enticing have-nots with prospects of a redistribution of the nation's land and wealth. His friends were at the Catholic king's court and in the opposing army. Nevertheless, he and his rebel army were seen as a threat to the whole order of society and not a single lord or gentleman among the former exclusionists joined them. Instead they made common cause with those who condemned him as a traitor and fought against him in the field. The Anglican establishment was more hostile to dissenting tradesmen than to Catholic gentry.

Monmouth is thus the most improbable of insurgents: a metropolitan aristocrat among country artisans, a Stuart among parliamentarians, a professional soldier at the head of undisciplined volunteers, the dissolute idol of the pious. Without benefit of foreign troops at his back or experienced officers and level-headed advisers at his side, such as those who had gained the crown for Henry Tudor, he at least enjoyed the wide support which Henry had had to do without. This alone might have dealt him a winning hand, for there were many other parts of England whose inhabitants held the same views as the men and women of Somerset. Had he raised his standard in Norwich or Chichester or Chester, Monmouth would have attracted a similar following, but without an organised movement or the magnetism of his presence they stayed at home.

At Lyme hard choices between options faced him. He held the initiative and needed to move quickly before the royal army had time to muster and move into action. On the other hand his recruits had to be trained in military disciplines and drilled in musketry. There were worrying shortages of officers and artillery which had to be made good. Most serious of all was a lack of horses and horsemen, for in the seventeenth century cavalry was the decisive arm in battle.

A strongly fortified headquarters with an arsenal was required and Exeter seemed ripe for the plucking, but it lay in the wrong direction if he was to march on London, as he must. The compromise was Bristol, the second city in the realm and on the line of march for a junction with the northern supporters who were expected to rise in Cheshire. Bristol was the key to the west, as it had once been for Matilda. Since her times it had grown into the largest sea-port in Britain, a European gateway to the discoveries of the West Indies and America, where some of the colonists were strongly attached to Monmouth's cause. It was a softer target than London, the key to the whole kingdom. That would need to await recruitment of sufficient cavalry to protect the rest of the army as it ventured across the open country of Salisbury plain and beyond.

The first opposition to be encountered came from the county militias, which had received ample warning of the invasion. The Somerset militia was out under the Duke of Somerset, the Devon militia under the Duke of Albemarle, the Wiltshire militia under the Earl of Pembroke and the Gloucestershire militia under the Duke of Beaufort. These were the Home Guard of the day, recruited from men of the same kind and with the same outlook as Monmouth's, and their commanders did not dare bring them too close to the rebels for fear of mass desertions. At Axminster they retreated to avoid an engagement, and Monmouth's burgeoning force marched unhindered and in high spirits into Taunton, the largest town in Somerset, where it was greeted with rapture and its numbers were swollen to 7000 by new recruits from town and country who far outnumbered the weapons available for them. A prosperous centre of trade in a rich agricultural vale, Taunton had a long history of stubborn opposition to the crown. In the late civil war it had been twice besieged by royalists and successfully defended by no less a parliamentarian than Robert Blake, later admiral of the Commonwealth fleet.

At Lyme Monmouth had contented himself with a declaration denouncing James for the murder of his brother Charles (a charge without foundation) and announcing a resolve to bring him to justice. Styling himself 'Captain-General of the Protestant Forces of this Kingdom', he refrained from making a claim to the crown with the words: 'doth not at present insist upon his Title'.[17] This restraint is more likely to have been caused by Argyll's insistence that he would be acceptable as a protector but not as a king than by any reluctance on his own part. The idea of a new Oliver Cromwell instead of a new King James would have appealed to many in the west country too.

In Taunton, however, some dubious advice was accepted, to the effect that if Monmouth were proclaimed king his supporters could not be treated as rebels. A proclamation was therefore issued asserting his legitimacy to clothe the rebellion in a semblance of legality. The Duke of Monmouth, not the Duke of York, was declared to be 'our lawful and rightful sovereign and king, by the name of James the Second'.[18] The earlier defiance issued at Lyme had reached London, where it was condemned by king and parliament and ceremonially burned outside the Royal Exchange by the common hangman. Since this parliament, still sitting at Westminster, had been summoned by one regarded in the west as a usurper and had attainted Somerset's king as a traitor (putting a price of £5000 on his head), it was damned in the Taunton proclamation as 'a rebellious and treasonable convention'.[19] The country was now blessed or burdened with two James the Seconds.

When the march resumed on 21 June Monmouth's period of grace was expiring. An army of three battalions of foot guards and six troops of cavalry, supported by eight pieces of artillery, had left London the previous day. Sixteen more guns were in train ready to follow, six regiments of English and Scots troops had been recalled from Holland, and commissions had been granted to ex-officers to raise auxiliary forces. Already an advance troop of horse under John Churchill, the future Duke of Marlborough, had reached the west to harry the insurgents. James had moved with more speed and determination than his nephew.

Bristol lies 60 miles from Taunton, and the prize was in sight of the rebel army within three days. Towards the south the city's defences were strong, but on the Gloucestershire side they were in poor repair. It was therefore decided to cross the Avon by Keynsham bridge six miles upstream and attack at the weakest point. After a brief recruiting stop at Bridgwater numbers had risen to 8000 foot and 1000 cavalry, but most were ill-equipped, some armed with nothing more lethal than a scythe or a pitchfork. Additionally, ten thousand 'club men' (peasants who had armed themselves with clubs to protect their homesteads and cattle) were said to be offering their services. Only lack of weapons impeded further recruitment.

The Avon was safely crossed, a royal army nowhere in sight. Bristol was a stronghold of dissenters defended mostly by friendly militia-men. All Monmouth had to do to take the city was to advance the last few miles and charge the crumbling walls. This he failed to do, and from that moment all was lost – a secure base, an arsenal, the initiative, his nerve and the propaganda victory crucial to raise his troops' morale and inspire others to rise in the Protestant cause dear to most of the country. Indecision at Keynsham cost Monmouth his last hope of the crown and doomed him and many of his followers to an unenviable fate. What could have been the reason for an error of such magnitude?

Rain is a feature of the western counties of Britain and weather may have been the determining factor. The army's camp beside the river was flooded by a torrential downpour which soaked men to the skin and reduced their shoes to pulp. Ammunition was dampened as well as bodies and spirits. In view of this and their inexperience under fire Monmouth postponed the attack so that the city could be stormed at nightfall under the cover of darkness. During the delay some prisoners were brought in who gave an exaggerated account of the size of Churchill's troop and led him to fear the proximity of the whole royal army. Faint-heartedly he concluded that unless he withdrew his men they would be trapped between two enemy forces: one in Bristol and the other to his rear.

The abandonment of Bristol left Monmouth aimless. With no news of the expected uprising in Cheshire there was nothing to be gained from heading north. Bath was royalist and impregnable. The best prospect appeared to lie in Wiltshire where there were reports of 500 horsemen waiting to join him. A faint flicker of hope rested on his lingering belief that the guards regiments which he had commanded would never fight against him. Their new commander, the Earl of Feversham, was a Frenchman, a nephew of Marshal Turenne, but endowed with none of his uncle's military genius. At the village of Philips Norton his advance guard, under Monmouth's half-brother, the Duke of Grafton, obligingly blundered into an ambush and withdrew in confusion, but Monmouth did not have enough cavalry, or enough confidence in what he had, to exploit the situation by ordering a pursuit which might have developed into a general engagement.

He had become sunk in melancholy, conscious of having frittered away days of golden opportunity. In London and throughout the country those on whose support he had counted had been seized or gone to ground. From Scotland came the news of Argyll's defeat and capture. The reinforcements expected from Wiltshire did not appear. When a proclamation by James offered pardon to all who surrendered within eight days (ringleaders excepted), many of the sodden, ill-armed and ill-shod volunteers vanished disenchanted from the rebel ranks. In desperation Monmouth concluded, like the earlier Prince Perkin in similar circumstances, that it would be best if he disappeared too. At a council of war he argued that all the officers, himself included, should desert and take refuge abroad: since it was now apparent that the only professional army in Britain had chosen to stay loyal to James, fighting a battle would be suicidal. The proposal was realistic but too ignoble even for Lord Grey who, although a base man himself, denounced it as 'so base that it could never be forgiven by the people to be so deserted'.[20]

Disaster at Sedgemoor justified Monmouth's pessimism but, according to an account by the rector of the neighbouring parish of Chedzoy, his stout-hearted weavers, colliers and ploughmen, in combat against regular troops, 'came as near to an entire victory as men could well be and miss it'.[21] The moor was a peat bog, drained by ditches, extending for some 13,000 acres between Bridgwater and the ancient county capital of Somerton. The size of the army of westerners who fought there so doggedly has been set by some historians at 5000 and by the royalist victors at 10,000. But probably it was no larger than that opposing it – about 3000, representing a resolute hard core who had not been tempted from their allegiance by promises of pardon or the odds against them.

Forced to fight against his will, Monmouth at least gave his men the benefit of his military experience and prowess, which was markedly superior to that of the royalist commander. His battle plan was well conceived. Conscious, as ever, of his weakness in cavalry and artillery, he ordered a surprise attack by night. The moon was full, but at ground level visibility was reduced by mist and the rebels' silent six-mile march was a remarkable feat. Against the ill-prepared Feversham, his drunken officers and sleeping soldiers, it would have succeeded but for two accidents.

Three rhines, or ditches, had to be crossed in the mist. The first, Black Ditch, was safely negotiated, but the causeway over Langmoor Rhine was missed and in the confusion someone fired a shot accidentally, alerting the enemy. Even more serious was the fact that Monmouth and his officers had not been made aware of the existence of the Bussex Rhine, which protected the front of the royal army. Instead of overrunning a sleeping enemy encampment, the main rebel force of infantry and cavalry under Grey were caught floundering on open ground exposed to musket fire at close range as alarms and drum-beats roused the royalists to arms.

The Somerset tradesmen and rustics stood their ground against the cavalry charges which followed. When their ammunition ran out some fought on with scythes and musket butts until forced to run for their lives. In the pursuit many who had escaped death in the heat of the battle were caught and hanged in cold blood. During the fighting 300 were killed; 1000 died in the pursuit.

More vengeance was demanded by the king. In the punitive Bloody Assizes, Judge Jeffreys condemned 1200 to death and others to transportation as indentured labourers in the West Indies, boasting when he was done that he had hanged more people than all the judges of England since the time of the Conqueror. In his memoirs James hypocritically regretted that Jeffreys had acted 'beyond the terms of moderation and mercy',[22] but the brutal judge was dispensing the king's justice and the king could have exercised his prerogative of mercy had he chosen. The sentences were to be expected. What is shocking is the absence of the customary reprieves. James's crocodile tears over the fate of Monmouth's brave followers are reminiscent of Elizabeth I's over Mary Queen of Scots. Both reflect the mixture of hatred and guilt felt by monarchs towards pretenders and rebels who fall into their hands and pay the penalty.

In the punishment inflicted upon Monmouth himself James has no scapegoat. The pretender had fled the battlefield before the fighting was over. For three days a hunted fugitive, he was discovered hiding in a ditch in the New Forest disguised in shepherd's clothing. His trembling behaviour when captured is said to have been even meaner than his garb. In a craven letter to James he assured the king of his zeal for his preservation, claimed that he had been deceived and misled by 'some horrid people',[23] and wished him a long and happy reign.

At Whitehall James granted the fallen idol a last interview; which by custom he should not have done unless he intended a pardon, for 'A king's face/Should give grace'. While Monmouth crawled on his knees begging in vain for his life, James used the occasion to rebuke him for the disgraceful lie that he had murdered his brother. Monmouth, blaming others to the end, excused himself with another lie: that he had signed the declaration without reading it. It was a final encounter from which neither party emerged with credit.

If James could have overcome his loathing and contempt, he might have realised that the exercise of mercy would not only have been more seemly in a prince professing such a deep devotion to the Christian faith; it would also have been better policy. As his observer, Lord Dartmouth, reported to him after Monmouth's execution: 'You have got rid of one enemy, but a more dangerous one remains behind.'[24] James had every justification for putting his nephew to death, but it would have been more prudent to keep him alive instead of clearing the way for William of Orange, 'that ambitious prince, exempt from the tyranny of honour and conscience'.[25] James, though, had none of the cunning of Henry Tudor, whose treatment of Lambert Simnel set an example in the punishment of discredited losers which no other winner was wise or compassionate enough to imitate.

Monmouth's life had been devoted to pleasure. He could be brave in battle and when in the public eye, but his courage was not rooted in any deep commitment or religious faith like that of Queen Jane or Mary Queen of Scots. In adversity it had deserted him lamentably, but once he knew that he must die – and before crowds on Tower Hill – he pulled himself together and made a brave exit in circumstances unusually gruesome even for a public execution. Instead of the felon's noose James had granted him the nobleman's privilege of the axe, but the blade was blunt. The headsman 'made five Chopps before he had his head off'.[26] At the second unsuccessful blow it is recorded that Monmouth turned on the block and stared his tormentor in the face. After the third the man threw down the axe in disgust and had to be goaded by the crowd into finishing the job. It was only completed by his sawing away at the neck with a knife.

Sedgemoor was the last pitched battle fought on English soil. It ended King Monmouth's 25-day reign in the west country. Among all the invasions of England his stands alone in creating a popular movement. William the Conqueror, Robert of Normandy, Empress Matilda, Henry Plantagenet, Henry Bolingbroke, Edward IV, Henry Tudor – all previous invaders were pursuing hereditary rights in dynastic disputes of scant interest to common people. So too, ostensibly, was Monmouth, but he was taken for a messiah and hailed as a liberator of the people, as only Warbeck had been before him. But while Warbeck's short-lived appeal in the west was quickly forgotten,

Mary Queen of Scots after Nicholas Hilliard

Arbella Stuart by William Larkin

The Duke of Monmouth after William Wissing

James Edward Stuart, the Old Pretender, by Louis Gabriel Blanchet

Opposite: James II by Kneller

Charles Edward Stuart as a young man by A. David

Charles Edward Stuart in old age by H. D. Hamilton

Henry Stuart, Cardinal York, after P. Batoni

Monmouth has been long remembered and mourned, not as a royal pretender but as the lost leader of a people's cause. That his popular attraction was strictly personal is illustrated by the tepid reception accorded to William of Orange, the second Protestant hero and invader, three years later: 'The country is not fond of him, nor forward to run in to him'.[27] Monmouth possessed that indefinable quality, the common touch, and it is clear that his contemporaries were dazzled by a charisma which it has been impossible to recapture since the death of those who saw him for themselves.

If account is taken of the hero-worship he inspired, Monmouth's attempt on the crown was not the futile escapade it seems in retrospect. The general insurrection which he had been misled into expecting remained a real possibility if only the idol himself had not had feet of clay. The first step towards success in all rebellions, it has been said, is that a leader 'should inspire his followers with confidence in his courage, determination and ability'.[28] Monmouth failed his on all three counts.

His own dukedom was attainted and there have been no other dukes of Monmouth before or since. But the dukedom of Buccleugh, which became his by marriage, survived unforfeited. As duchess in her own right his widow bore the title for nearly fifty years after his death. Their eldest son, James, Earl of Dalkeith, allowed the claim to the throne to lapse, although in 1692 some loyal adherents of his father, described as 'thirty or forty wild people', proclaimed him king at the cross of Sanquhar in Dumfries-shire. He died of apoplexy before his mother, and it was his son Francis who became the second duke. Francis too had no royal pretensions, marrying a Windsor washerwoman and being buried 'very meanly' at Eton.

In 1698 a Monmouth risen from the dead and said to be living in Sussex was identified as the son of a local innkeeper. Later he became a favourite candidate for the Man in the Iron Mask. But in sober fact his body lies at rest, appropriately beside Queen Jane's, in the chapel of St Peter ad Vincula in the Tower of London.

In the west country he lives on in legend.

IO

James III, Old Mr Melancholy

A DYNASTY which cannot produce heirs condemns itself to extinction. Sterility, not a rival claimant, had put an end to Tudor rule. For the Stuarts Charles II was fertile and virile enough, but none of his children came from the marriage bed. In compensation his brother James II performed well beyond the call of dynastic duty in producing fifteen legitimate children. His tally of six sons and nine daughters should have been ample to insure the family against losing its throne a second time; yet, thanks to the still rudimentary state of medical science, only four survived infancy. Two daughters of his first marriage, to the then Protestant Anne Hyde, succeeded to the throne as Queen Mary II and Queen Anne, but both died childless (Anne having borne seventeen children, of whom sixteen had died in infancy and one at the age of eleven). But the birth of James's sixth son, one of only two surviving children of his marriage to the Catholic Mary of Modena, so far from perpetuating Stuart sovereignty, became the cause of its abrupt termination.

Christened James (after his father), Francis (after his uncle, the Duke of Modena) and Edward (after the Black Prince, on whose feast day he had made his entry into the world), the boy to be known to posterity as the Old Pretender was born on 10 June 1688 to immediate controversy. To his supporters, known as Jacobites (Jacobus being the Latin for James), he became no pretender but King James III (of England) and King James VIII (of Scotland). His life was to be that of a king with a title but no throne, a court but no kingdom.

The Old Pretender was called by other names too. From his Italian mother he inherited black eyes and dark hair and was affectionately nicknamed Little Blackbird and Bonnie Black Laddie. More formally, while his father lived, he was Prince of Wales, and after his father's death, while some recognised him as king and others as The Pretender, he himself adopted the incognito of Chevalier de St George. Later, as a downcast exile, he attracted nicknames such as The Old Chevalier, Jamie the Rover, Mournful Jemmy, Mr James Misfortunate and Old Mr Melancholy. When settled in Rome he was referred to colloquially as *Il Re de quà* (the king here) to distinguish him from *Il Re de là* (the king there, in London). As The King Over the Water his titular reign lasted for nearly 65 years (1701–66). This was a longer stretch than Queen Victoria's 63 or George III's 60 and remains an unbroken record among claimants to the English or Scottish crown.

His lack of a throne and kingdom was due to his father's foolishness. After Monmouth's execution James II adopted measures which fed suspicion that this ardent convert to Catholicism intended to deliver a staunchly Protestant England back into the arms of Rome. He enlarged his standing army at a time when the Catholic King of France was using his to massacre his Protestant Huguenot subjects. He offended the universities by attempting to force Catholics into prominent positions at Oxford and Cambridge. Most crucially, not content with the reform of the discriminatory Test Act, he tackled the Church of England head on.

The arrest of the Archbishop of Canterbury and six other bishops for resisting the reading of James's Declaration of Indulgence in churches was Stuart folly at its height. Their journey to the Tower became a triumphal procession, and when they were tried for seditious libel the jury acquitted them unanimously to universal rejoicing. If Monmouth had delayed his invasion and landed at that moment he would have found all England at his feet.

Condemned as a new Mary Tudor preparing to light faggots on the pyres of a new generation of Protestant martyrs, James was, in fact, endeavouring to move the country in the direction of religious toleration. He was no Torquemada – merely a well-meaning blunderer, tactless, impatient and obtuse, who succeeded in setting back the cause of Catholic emancipation by more than a century. Horace Walpole's sharp reference to the characteristics of the house of Stuart as bigotry, obstinacy and want of judgment is well deserved in James's case, but his good intentions have been overlooked by anti-Catholic

E. STUARTS AND HANOVERIANS

This simplified genealogical tree omits members of the family not relevant to Chapters 9–12.

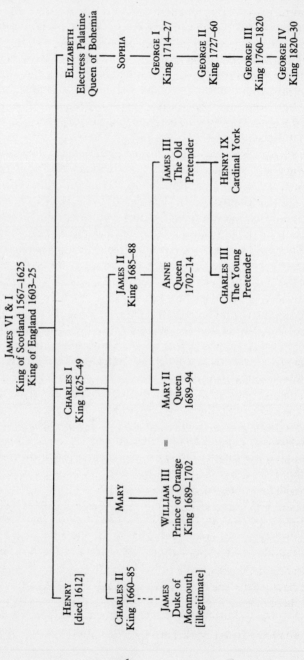

commentators. His reputation has been blackened almost as harshly in the works of Whig historians as Richard III's in the propaganda of Tudor chroniclers, and for much the same reason. Each was the last of a ruling line whose good name fell into enemy hands, to be destroyed by those whose purpose was to justify rebellion against a crowned and anointed king.

Until the birth of James Francis Edward little was keeping James II on the throne except the expectation of a Protestant succession by his elder daughter Mary, married to William, Prince of Orange, himself the Protestant son of a Stuart princess (James's sister Mary). In these circumstances the arrival of a Catholic heir was cataclysmic. It precipitated The Glorious Revolution. Within five months William had launched his invasion to rescue England from the bonds of popery by usurping the throne. A cold, calculating man in the mould of Henry Tudor, he was to become as unpopular a king and die as unlamented.

His expedition was everything Monmouth's had not been: meticulous in preparation and overwhelming in force. He landed at Torbay in Devon and marched unhurriedly towards the capital. No one joined him; no one opposed him. As a shrewd politician, he had made his accommodations with those in power in advance: those not in power were irrelevant. Religion apart, James was the more popular man, and William's accession was to be marked with the same public apathy as had greeted Henry Tudor's. From William the Conqueror to Lenin history teaches that popularity is not an essential ingredient in successful usurpation, whatever subsequent myth-making may allege.

Like Henry Bolingbroke, William of Orange was a usurper who had chosen not to go through the preliminary procedures of pretendership. A claim is, after all, best argued from the throne, and he was soon sitting on it. It can hardly be said that he won the crown; rather, he picked it up where his father-in-law had left it. James's behaviour in conceding a walk-over is hard to explain. He rode to Salisbury to lead a waiting army into battle in defence of his realm, retired with a nose-bleed and returned to London. Was he convinced that his army would never beat William's? It might well have done. Did he distrust his commanders as latter-day Stanleys? Only after he had deserted his army did they show their hand and desert him. Was he haunted by the fate of his father on the scaffold? In the event William went to some lengths to facilitate his escape, rightly reckoning that a royal father-in-law and uncle in captivity would present more problems and attract more sympathy than a craven fugitive.

Like his other nephew, Monmouth, James was a brave man who seemed to have panicked and lost heart when faced with a crisis he could not resolve. In Monmouth's case failure of nerve ended his career as a pretender; for James it spelled the beginning. His obsessive concern was less for his own skin than for that of his son, the cherished cause of his downfall. The baby was despatched to the fleet at Portsmouth for a safe evacuation, but Lord Dartmouth, the commander-in-chief at Spithead, politely returned him to London, fearing to lay himself open to a charge of high treason for taking the heir to the throne out of the country without authorisation from the privy council. So on 9 December 1688, aged six months, the infant Prince of Wales was smuggled out of Whitehall and down the Thames in the arms of his mother. She was dressed as a laundress and he was disguised as a bundle of washed clothes. Pretenders suffer strange humiliations and this was the first of many disguises to which he was forced to resort in the course of a hazardous career.

After an adventurous crossing mother and child were met outside Paris by Louis XIV. The Sun King himself stood in the snow to pay his respects to the queen and kiss the baby prince. He was their cousin, a champion of legitimacy and Catholicism, and an old enemy of the usurping Dutchman. When James II joined them after his escape, Louis gave him the Château of St Germain-en-Laye, on the Seine twelve miles from Paris, and an allowance handsome enough to maintain a court in royal splendour. Until his death in 1715 he remained the firmest ally of the exiled Stuarts and their most promising means of restoration, even though James doggedly declined to drop his display of lilies and the inherited claim to be King of France.

Despite abandoning his realm, he had not abdicated. In his own view he was still king *de jure* and accordingly maintained all his titles and pretensions. In England he enjoyed little support for this constitutional nicety. In attempting the time-honoured ploy of using Ireland as a stepping-stone to the English throne, he disgraced himself at the battle of the Boyne. In Scotland his grounds for hope subsided with the death of Bonnie Dundee at Killicrankie. He then became wholly dependent on Louis, and the more help he received from France the more intense grew the hostility towards him in England. The French king's personal courtesy and generosity were all the more remarkable because they remained unaffected by the policy of his ministers. France's objective was a Britain divided and this was the opportunity.

Would James, they pleaded, not be content with Scotland, wait for England and cede Ireland to France? James would not.

The Stuarts in exile maintained their claim to the three kingdoms for 119 years. But more than religion divided them from the majority of their lost subjects. Through belief in the divine right of kings, they held their title to be inalienable since it was derived from God, not from the people, whose function and duty was to honour and obey. 'Kings being accountable for none of their actions but to God and themselves' run the opening words of the advice bequeathed by James II to his son.[1] But the principles of absolutism and divine right were anathema to most Englishmen, to whom they were now seen as part and parcel of the authoritarianism of Rome. The spirit of Cromwell was still alive in many hearts and minds.

The unEnglishness of Stuart thinking sprang, of course, from their own unEnglishness. James's son, the Old Pretender, was half Italian and a quarter French, with Danish as well as Scottish blood contributing to the remaining quarter. The last infusion of English blood had come from Henry VIII's sister Mary six generations back. He was, however, as he never tired of reiterating, English born, and if he had changed his religion there were occasions when England would have taken him back.

James II's devotion to principle was admirable, but it did not assist him in his new role as pretender. Instead of plotting to subvert William's government, he sought solace in the Cistercian abbey at La Trappe, where he thanked God for depriving him of his kingdoms for the salvation of his soul. Inscrutably, God showed no sign of willing the restoration of the crown He had given to the Stuarts. France failed to win a war against Holland, whose allies included England, and under the terms of the peace settlement at Ryswick in 1697 Louis was placed in the unpalatable position of being bound to recognise William as King of England. He solved the dilemma by according King William *de facto* recognition but refusing to expel King James and his family from French soil. William, never one to miss an opportunity, retaliated by withholding repayment of the Stuart queen's dowry, which had been agreed after a long dispute.

The young James was thirteen when his father died. He had been dubbed spurious or 'supposititious' and the story of his being a changeling, introduced into his mother's bed in a warming pan, was added to the liturgy of anti-Catholic make-believe alongside papist responsibility for the Great Fire of London and the Black Box containing Lucy Walter's marriage certificate. In fact, the Old Pretender strongly resembled both his mother and his father, and estimates of the number of people in the room when he was born vary from 29 to 67. It was nevertheless alleged that the child born had been a girl who was taken into the next room and swapped for a miller's son; alternatively that the queen, who was shy and prudish about her pregnancy, had not been pregnant at all. An inquiry ordered by James II to clear his wife's honour and establish his son's legitimacy had merely served to fan suspicion.

Louis XIV entertained no doubts. Against his ministers' advice, on James II's death in 1701, he had the boy proclaimed King of England, Scotland and Ireland at the gates of his château. The whole Stuart court, headed by his half-brother, the Duke of Berwick, then knelt in homage and swore fealty to him as their sovereign lord. In England Mary II and Anne's only child to survive infancy, the Duke of Gloucester, had died and William was in poor health, a martyr to asthma and gout. A Tory government was in power and a delegation of English non-jurors and Scottish peers begged the newly proclaimed king to abjure Rome. But his pious Italian mother, acting as his regent, returned an unequivocal refusal in his name. 'Never put the crown of England in competition with your eternal salvation,'² had been the dead king's last injunction to his heir.

A promise was made instead that, when crowned and enthroned, James III would not interfere with the established church. This offer was published in a manifesto, dated 3 March 1702, but the French king's highhandedness in taking it upon himself to proclaim a King of England had done the Stuart cause as much harm as a similar action by a previous King of France had done to Mary Queen of Scots. It provoked an Act of Attainder providing for the execution without trial of James Francis Edward Stuart should he set foot in the realms he claimed. The example of Monmouth, who had suffered under the provisions of a similar Act, gave warning that this was no mere formality. Louis' insult and open breach of the Treaty of Ryswick was regarded in England as tantamount to a declaration of war, and the new pretender was in the enemy camp.

A more far-reaching measure was the Act of Settlement of 1701, designed to place a permanent bar to the succession of Roman Catholics. This Act sentenced the Stuarts to pretendership in perpetuity unless they opted for apostasy. In the event of Anne dying childless, the crown was to pass to a grand-daughter of James I, the

Electress Sophia, daughter of the beautiful Winter Queen, Elizabeth of Bohemia, and after her to her descendants, 'being Protestants'. Besides the excluded James III there were 57 other Stuart descendants with a better claim than the Electress, but all were Catholics.

An outlaw as well as a king, James became, like his father, the unhappy victim of the misrepresentations of his enemies in England. Never a religious bigot, he grew into a tolerant man of moderate views. Conscientious and industrious, he bore adversity with the fortitude derived from a firmly held faith. He was not a lecher like his father, nor a drunkard like his son. Indeed his character was a more admirable one in every way than his son's, but he lacked the personal appeal to become a romantic hero like Bonnie Prince Charlie or a popular idol like Monmouth. Reserved and dignified, he would have made a respectable if uninspiring king. If his rival, William III, was a cold fish and slippery, James III was a dull dog but an honest one.

Louis' recognition of him set an example which was followed by Spain, Savoy, the Holy See and, out of family loyalty, Modena. But when William died after a fall from his horse – on the day after signing the Act of Attainder against James – the crown passed without argument to James's half-sister Anne, as it was later to pass successively from Anne to George I, from George I to George II, and from George II to George III while the ageing pretender waited in the wings for a call which never came. In 1702 one solitary act of defiance was performed in his name. Simon, Lord Lovat, first sentenced to death for high treason in 1698 and executed eventually in 1747, dared to proclaim King James VIII in Inverness.

For the next twelve years James was to be on the side of England's enemies during a war in which he took the field in the French army at Oudenarde and Malplaquet, wearing his Garter in a confusion of loyalties. The first serious attempt to put him on the throne came in 1708 when Louis prepared an invasion fleet of seven men-of-war and twenty-one transports to convey several thousand troops from Dunkirk to the Firth of Forth. Characteristically, the resolute but far from dashing Chevalier de St George went down with measles after making his farewells. He had been seriously ill four years earlier, and four years later was to catch smallpox in an epidemic which killed his sister Louisa.

The ill omen was well justified. When the fleet sailed, stormy weather and the British navy both inflicted losses. When it arrived off the coast of Scotland, the French admiral refused to allow James ashore. There had been no pilot to guide them upstream from the mouth of the Forth, and off Inverness heavy gales made a landing too dangerous. Scotland had been reported to be seething with resentment over the Act of Union which had forced the Scots into a junior partnership with the English, but the Jacobites were unorganised and disunited and there was no sign of an army for the pretender to lead.

The true reason for the admiral's rejection of James's insistent demands to be put ashore can only be surmised. Presumably he was reluctant to risk his ships and men in a full disembarcation in unpromising conditions and may have been under orders on no account to risk the loss of such a valuable French asset as James himself. The threat of the expedition had been real enough to cause the withdrawal of English troops from Flanders and a run on the Bank of England, but the abortive outcome was a damaging anti-climax. In Edinburgh there had been 'not four rounds of ammunition'[3] to defend the castle; yet all James had achieved before being returned to Dunkirk was a glimpse of Arthur's Seat through the drizzle.

Marlborough's victories against the French kept Anne's Whig government in power and public esteem. Anne herself was thought to prefer James to an alien Hanoverian as her successor. The Scottish rebels of 1708 were treated with unusual leniency, and she refused to receive Sophia's son, the Electoral Prince, or even to allow him to come to England to take his seat in the House of Lords after his creation as Duke of Cambridge. So when she quarrelled with the Whigs, brought in a Tory administration and dismissed Marlborough, the prospects of a Stuart succession rose sharply and James was urged to make a deal whereby he would recognise her as queen if she would nominate him as her heir. As an inducement he would offer to guarantee religious and civil liberty after his accession. He even considered paying a secret visit to London to persuade her to present him formally to parliament.

Meanwhile the Jacobite movement in Scotland was gaining strength. In Edinburgh James's 24th birthday was celebrated openly with bonfires and fireworks and loyal toasts. The ships in harbour at Leith ran up flags and fired salutes, and crowds thronged to the gates of Holyroodhouse singing 'The king shall enjoy his own again'. In England he could have been assured of a welcome from most Tories – but only if he became a Protestant. The stumbling block was still his religion. 'England,' declared one Tory minister, 'would as soon have a

Turk as a Roman Catholic for king.'[4] Nonetheless, a substantial minority was of the view held by Thackeray's Henry Esmond: 'The desire of the country being unquestionably for an hereditary monarchy, Esmond thought an English king out of St Germain's was better than a German prince from Herrenhausen.'[5]

Under the terms of the Treaty of Utrecht, which ended the War of the Spanish Succession, Louis was at last compelled to expel James from French territory, and the pretender moved his court to Bar-le-duc in Lorraine. The Act of Settlement had not been repealed, and in January 1714 a price of £5000 was put on his head by the British government. When Anne died in August it was raised to a more flattering £100,000. There had been an attempt to kidnap him in France and he lived in fear of assassination. In London the privy council was rumoured to have destroyed a document kept under the dead queen's pillow in which she bequeathed him the crown, but this is hard to believe. She had rejected the deal when he had pleaded that if he was prepared to grant liberty of conscience to his subjects they should surely extend the same indulgence to him, and he had given her no cause to change her mind.

When the news reached Bar-le-duc that Queen Anne was dead it was the long-awaited moment to stir himself into decisive action. But instead of hurrying across the Channel, as Rufus and Stephen had done with such signal success, James hurried to Paris – only to be asked to leave and have to hurry back to Lorraine. From there he announced to the world, not entirely accurately, that he was the sole remaining member of the British royal family and wrote to the Scots assuring them that he would be with them soon. The Electress Sophia, who had set her heart on living long enough to wear the crown (assuring Queen Anne of the truth of an old Dutch saying that 'creaking wagons last long'), had died two months earlier at the age of 84. But in September her son George arrived from Hanover to be acclaimed as the new king in spite of adverse publicity resulting from a wife imprisoned for life and a furiously Teutonic feud with his heir. It has been said that he had nothing to recommend him except his religion, while to James there could be no objection except his religion.[6]

James's chief and best adviser at this time was his half-brother. James Fitzjames, Duke of Berwick was the happy result of a liaison between James II and Arabella Churchill, the future Duke of Marlborough's sister. He became a naturalised Frenchman, a Marshal of France and one of the best European generals of the day, fighting against the English and their allies. When George landed in England he advised James that he must act within three weeks. Six months later James was still awaited in Scotland and his followers there had to be content with a message expressing the hope that he would be with them in the summer. Then summer came and went without him, and so did autumn. The figurehead of The Fifteen, the first of the two major Jacobite uprisings, arrived on 2 January 1716, too late for the fighting or any other useful purpose.

It is hard to avoid the judgment that the lethargic do not deserve crowns but, while admitting his lack of energy and driving force, James's apologists are eloquent in absolving him from blame for such unwarrantable procrastination and dismissing any parallel with the dilatory and pleasure-loving Robert of Normandy. He had no heirs and a madcap venture like Monmouth's would have destroyed the Jacobite movement for ever. Since his life was too precious to be squandered, he needed to be sure of success. That was dependent on French aid, and Louis XIV was old and defeated. His 72-year reign was to end in September 1715, leaving James's expedition, when it at last sailed, to the half-hearted backing of the Regent Duke of Orleans. It must be conceded, though, that James inspired half-heartedness in others: his own lack of zest and confidence was infectious. 'Never,' declared the Jacobite Bishop of Rochester, 'was a better cause lost for want of spirit.'[7]

The Duke of Berwick consented to become James's minister of war in Paris, but adamantly refused the appointment of commander-in-chief. James begged and commanded to no avail, and the absence of a general of Berwick's calibre doomed The Fifteen to failure. The duke argued that as a French subject his loyalty was to France alone and, to prove his point, went campaigning in Spain. The regent, who could have ordered him to Scotland, had need of discretion. With England and France officially at peace, he could hardly authorise one of his marshals to lead the invasion. Yet the most telling reason may have been that neither Berwick nor the regent believed that the invasion would succeed.

James's other advisers were less reliable. The most prominent of his secret supporters in Britain were the Earl of Mar, who had been Anne's Secretary of State for Scotland, and the Duke of Ormonde, who shortly before the queen's death was appointed Captain-General of the forces of the three kingdoms. They confidently reported that nine out of ten Englishmen favoured James. Berwick responded by advising that a day should at once be named for a general rising. Ormonde then replied more cautiously that no rising could be expected until James had landed – with three or four thousand men.

The record of the English Jacobites is not impressive. In 1715 King James was proclaimed in loyalist Manchester by masked horsemen, and in Tory Oxford mobs hailed him and shouted 'No usurpers' in the streets. Demonstrations and riots were widespread – in London, Bristol, Gloucester, Leeds and Wolverhampton – but behind the plotting and the shouting lay no organisation or practical planning. Sporting oak leaves on 29 May (Royal Oak Day) and white roses on 10 June (White Rose Day) and drinking bumpers to the king over the water in privacy was about as far as most Jacobite activity went. While the French baulked at raising an expeditionary force without evidence of solid support in the country, James's English sympathisers sat waiting for the king and his French army to arrive.

Despairing of the French, he was reduced to soliciting aid from the King of Spain, the emperor and even the Protestant King of Sweden. These were not so much friends of James as enemies of George. Charles XII of Sweden, 'the madman of Europe', appeared to offer the best prospect. He was locked in a territorial dispute with Hanover and readily promised to land an army in Newcastle for a down payment of 25,000 crowns. But when it came to the point he was under siege and had need of all the men he could raise nearer home.

The struggle between George's Whig ministers and Anne's ousted Tories came to a head with the arrest of the Earl of Oxford for treason and the flight of Viscount Bolingbroke to Paris to become James's secretary of state. Ormonde at first retired to Richmond under a cloud of suspicion and then followed Bolingbroke to Paris. He claimed to have men ready to seize the arsenals in Bristol, Exeter and Plymouth and take over the towns, but had left them no instructions. Mar fled in the opposite direction. Insulted by King George deliberately turning his back on him at a reception, he sailed from Gravesend to Scotland and without consultation or further ado raised the standard of King James at Braemar on 25 September 1715. His haste cost James any remaining hope of the crown, but the Scots were, understandably, tired of waiting. In addition to the Scottish arms and thistle, the standard bore the words, 'No Union'. In response, nearly all Scotland north of the Tay rose for James: he was proclaimed king in Aberdeen and Dundee, in Inverness and Perth. Scottish Jacobitism was an independence movement; hence its fervour. South of the border

James's appeal sprang from sentiment, a sense of justice and a dislike for German George, and was generally lukewarm, however romantic in retrospect.

The most enthusiastic were the young. At 27 James was not yet the Old Pretender. Of his leading supporters the Marquis of Tullibardine was 26, Lord Strathmore 25, the Earl Marischal 23 and the pretender's English cousin Lord Derwentwater 26. Brave but inexperienced, they would have given a good account of themselves under Berwick, but 'Bobbing John' Mar was among the most incompetent of generals. With Scotland defenceless he hesitated to attack.

After nearly two months of indecision he was confronted by a weak army, led by the Duke of Argyll, at Sheriffmuir near Dunblane on 13 November. He had a three-to-one advantage in numbers (9000 to 3000) and better fighters better positioned; yet the result was a draw, each right wing scoring a victory. Mar's right was larger than Argyll's whole army, but he withdrew without pressing his advantage. In these circumstances a draw was a defeat. He had not opened the road to the lowlands and a junction with the Jacobites in England. Some of his highlanders decided that they had been long enough away from home, while Argyll had won time for reinforcements to arrive from the south. In rebellion attack is the only effective strategy. Monmouth had demonstrated that defensive tactics never win a crown.

In England James was proclaimed at Warkworth in Northumberland by Derwentwater, who then marched to Kelso to join a party of Jacobite borderers under Lord Kenmure. Together they mustered 2000 foot and 600 horse, but had no agreed objective. The Scots wanted to take Dumfries, the English pressed for an assault on Newcastle. After an argument they marched west and then south to gather support in Catholic Lancashire, where no recruits came forward. At Preston they were surrounded and surrendered tamely. The casualty figures speak for themselves: 18 killed, 25 wounded, 1500 taken prisoner. Derwentwater was a Catholic and believed it would prejudice the cause if he became the commander, so the army was led by Thomas Forster, who proved as inept as Mar. Preston was the beginning and end of English Jacobitism as a fighting force. The more the Stuarts became a focus of Scottish nationalism, the less their appeal in England.

Bolingbroke's advice had been that success in Scotland would never restore James to the throne of the three kingdoms, and Berwick concurred: 'to believe that with the Scots alone he will succeed in his enterprise' was 'madness'.[8] He urged that before embarking on an invasion James should first establish the willingness of those in power to receive him, as they had received William, for 'the king should hazard his person, but not fling himself to certain ruin'.[9]

A landing at Plymouth was planned, to rally the disaffected in the west country (like Monmouth) and march from there to London (like William). But by the time Ormonde sailed from St Malo his plot had been betrayed by spies. The Jacobite officers in the Plymouth garrison were under arrest, and a regiment had been sent to reinforce the garrison in Bristol. On receiving this information Ormonde returned from the Cornish coast without even disembarking. James, who had been due to follow him to Plymouth, determined to sail for Scotland instead.

He had spent October 1715 in Lorraine ill-served by poor intelligence and conflicting advice. On the 28th he wrote formally to the heads of all 26 European states to notify them that 'a great part' of his subjects having decided to return to their proper allegiance he was returning home 'to place himself at their head'.[10] In so doing, he asserted, he would not disturb the peace of Europe. Because every move he made was observed by spies and reported to London and Paris, he had to fake illness to account for his disappearance, crossing France in a violet cassock, disguised as an abbé. Even so he was saved from assassination only by the sharpwittedness of a village post-mistress at Nonancourt, who misdirected an Irish ex-officer hired by the British ambassador in Paris to dispose of the pretender once and for all.

He reached St Malo on 8 November only to be disappointed by Ormonde and bad weather. Under pressure from London the Regent of France had ordered his arrest; so still in disguise, this time as a common sailor, he made his way along the coast to Dunkirk. There, frustrated by further delays, he stayed in hiding until 27 December, when he set sail with a handful of followers and a cargo of brandy to brave storms and a watchful British navy which was lying in wait for him. Five days later, weak, seasick and still dressed as an ordinary seaman, he was carried ashore at Peterhead. He had come home after 27 years, but three months too late for the uprising he was to lead. He had arrived with no army and no arms or supplies of any kind (even the brandy was only a cover in case of interception). He was also short of money to buy any, because the bulk of the contributions received from Spain, Lorraine and the pope – 200,000 crowns from Philip V – was lost through shipwreck off Dundee and fell into grateful English hands.

Ill, empty-handed and dispirited, he was greeted by a country deep in the grip of a northern winter such as he had never experienced before, and by the truth about the defeat at Preston and 'victory' at Sheriffmuir. Mar's army of 16,000 was found to number 5000 at most, and sadly in need of the arms and supplies he had failed to bring. Afflicted with snowstorms, high winds, Scottish mist and quartan ague, he was never seen to smile and his despairing gloom depressed all around. 'If he was disappointed in us,' wrote one Scottish Jacobite ruefully, 'we were tenfold more in him.'[11] Although even-tempered in adversity, he lacked an essential quality of leadership: the ability to inspire his followers. The loyal highlanders who were risking their lives for him were puzzled by this grave, pallid, pock-marked king who did not even turn out to inspect their drill or watch their manoeuvres. He was so silent that some had to inquire whether he could speak. They had looked for a messiah and been rewarded with a wet blanket.

James manfully did what he could. He sent urgently to France for men and arms, but none came. He sent urgently to France for a general, but Berwick once more tendered his respects and regrets. A triumphal entry into Dundee and a military review at Perth were consolations, but his coronation at Scone had to be abandoned owing to religious scruples: how could he permit himself to be crowned by a Protestant bishop? After six weeks, threatened by a strongly reinforced government army under Argyll, he departed with as little fuss and ceremony as he had arrived, abandoning his highlanders to Hanoverian retribution and stealing away in a small vessel with Mar. His departure avoided more bloodshed, but the manner of his going cannot be excused. For James, The Fifteen was a shameful episode, even if he was not wholly to blame. His Morton had been a Bolingbroke, his de Chandée and Oxford had been Ormonde and Mar. At least, unlike Warbeck and Monmouth, he lived to fight again. So far from this being the end, more than fifty grim years of hollow pretension still lay ahead.

The fiasco of The Fifteen had left James as an embarrassment to his supporters. Discredited and unwelcome in France and Spain, he was even obliged to leave Lorraine. Bolingbroke, peremptorily dismissed, expressed the hope that his own arm would drop off and his brain fail if he ever again devoted either to the Stuart cause. Heavily in debt, James moved his down-at-heel court of some 500 refugees to Avignon, until once again declared *persona non grata* and required to move on. Fittingly, the pope came to his rescue. In February 1717 he crossed the Alps with a reduced household of 70 to take up residence in a papal palace at Urbino. Except for a few months, he was to spend the rest of his life in Italy as a pensioner of the pope – hardly the most promising situation from which to beguile a Protestant country into accepting him as its king.

Passing through Modena en route, he fell in love with his cousin Benedetta d'Este, the duke's eldest daughter, but the duke was reluctant to offend the British government by giving his consent. James was nearly thirty and marriage for the procreation of lawful heirs was a duty. Disappointed in Modena, he despatched search parties to the various courts of Europe. Optimistically planning an alliance between two arch-enemies, Charles XII of Sweden and Peter the Great of Russia, for a combined assault on England, he negotiated in turn but in vain for the tsar's daughter and niece and the king's sister. Bad breath eliminated the Princess of Hesse, the Princess of Fürstenberg had a red nose, and the Princess of Baden was found in time to be a dwarf.

The final choice seemed to fit all requirements. Princess Maria Clementina Sobieska was the grand-daughter of a king – John III of Poland, a famous warrior who had led Christendom to victory over the Turks. Related to the emperor, the King of Portugal and the Queens of France and Spain, and a god-daughter of Pope Clement XI (after whom she was named), the princess was not only well connected but also pretty, lively and seventeen. The heiress to vast estates, she could bring with her a large dowry. Above all, she came of good child-bearing stock and was to prove it by producing two healthy male pretenders.

To all this was added the romance of a forbidden marriage. The emperor was another ruler chary of giving offence to an increasingly powerful Great Britain, and he ordered Clementina's incarceration in a convent in Innsbruck. From there she was rescued by the subterfuge of changing clothes with a maidservant and smuggled across the Brenner pass in a carriage which, in the course of a hair-raising journey, nearly plunged off the road into a precipice – only one of 'a melancholy Variety of Ugly Accidents'[12] according to the account of her abductor, who made haste to complete the success of his mission by having her married to James in Bologna by proxy. To Stuart historians, accounts of this adventure have proved irresistible: 'From the fastness of Innsbruck her deliverers carried her through storm and peril over the snowy passes of Tyrol to the friendly sunshine of Italy; ultimately to the arms of her king'.[13]

The marriage which began with such great expectations and high drama soon plunged into an abyss of farce and bathos. Urbino was beautiful but remote and boring, and an indulgent Clement XI was persuaded to place the Palazzo Muti in Rome at the disposal of the king and queen (as he recognised James and Clementina to be). Except for a short stay in Bologna, this was to be James's home until his death. There he held court at the very heart of Christendom and from there he conducted his voluminous correspondence as king in exile. His surviving papers, now in Windsor castle, fill 551 volumes.

Clementina enjoyed the title of queen, but her husband and his industrious way of life she found excessively dull. She was a pious girl, but lazy, empty-headed and quarrelsome – and there was plenty to quarrel about in the pretence of a court at the Muti palace. It was a hot-house of dubious characters, a number of whom were spies in the pay of Walpole, the British prime minister. The Earl Marischal in disgust described it as no place for an honest man.

Since it was James's policy not to be seen to be bigoted politically, he surrounded himself with Protestants as well as Catholics, to the affront of the faithful in the Holy City. When Clementina, in interfering mood, demanded the dismissal of his Protestant ministers (the earls of Inverness and Dunbar) she enlisted the support of the pope himself who sent a bishop to remonstrate with James on this and other matters. The king was instructed to dismiss his Protestant chaplains, to stop giving his sons a Protestant education and to stop committing adultery with Lady Inverness (which was a mischievous false charge made by Clementina). Not believing his ears, James told his visitor that he must have misunderstood His Holiness's message; otherwise, he threatened, the bishop would be leaving by the window, not the staircase. The domestic disharmony between king and queen inevitably became public knowledge and the subject of much malicious gossip, and her temporary desertion of him for the company of Ursuline nuns in a convent in the Trastevere was a juicy scandal which delighted the Whig government in London.

The Nineteen was even less glorious than The Fifteen. Britain was at war with Spain, and the Spanish chief minister, Cardinal Alberoni, ordered an expedition of 5000 men to sail from Cadiz under Jacobite leadership and topple the Hanoverian regime. In a concerted two-pronged attack the Duke of Ormonde would head an invasion of England while the Earl Marischal descended on Scotland. Ill, as usual, after a long nightmarish journey from Italy, James made a state

entry into Madrid on 27 March. The following day a storm off Cape
Finisterre wrecked the Spanish armada.

A small force reached Stornaway and made contact with a body of
about 1000 highlanders. An encounter in the pass of Glenshiel with a
numerically inferior government army, fought on White Rose Day
(James's birthday), ended with the highlanders fleeing over the hills
and the Spaniards surrendering. Casualties were as revealingly light as
at Preston. James, who had travelled with Ormonde to Corunna to
embark for England, was stranded without transport and returned
dejected to Rome. However just, the Stuart cause seemed without the
luck or will to prevail.

The Commonwealth which preceded the Stuart restoration in 1660
had been a period of economic decline, but during the reign of George
I and George II England became prosperous at home and unassailable
overseas. In these conditions few looked kindly on the prospect of
another civil war, and the Whigs in power viewed the return of the
Stuarts much as the new Tudor aristocracy would have viewed the
restoration of the monasteries – they had a lot to lose. On the other
hand, the failure of banks when the South Sea Bubble burst shook the
government, and Walpole's corrupt administration made powerful
enemies. The birth of James's sons was an encouragement to restless
Tories, who were reassured by his policy of retaining Protestant
advisers despite the pope's objection.

In Rome James was an object of polite curiosity to English
travellers. 'Were he not the Pretender I should like the man well
enough,' reported one.[14] In 1720 he made plans for another invasion
but issued a Declaration announcing his desire for restoration by
invitation rather than force of arms. He was, he emphasised, English-
born and remained wholly English at heart. But nearly every other
part of him was foreign, and he was not the bold heroic figure to win
English hearts or to seize and exploit every opportunity to send
another uncared-for foreigner packing. For George I was as uninspiring and unEnglish as James and a great deal less couth and kingly. No
one was more conscious of his being a usurper than George himself,
who showed no interest in English customs or concern for English
susceptibilities. Typical of his insensitivity was the notion of
ploughing up St James's Park to grow turnips. When asked the cost,
his secretary of state gravely replied that it would be three crowns –
those of England, Scotland and Ireland.

His death brought a flurry of activity and expectation. On this occasion James was quicker off the mark. He at once travelled north across France to Lorraine to await a summons, but the news from England and Scotland was discouraging and the French were anxious not to jeopardise a new friendship with Britain. Even the pope bowed to pressure from the British government. In 1727, as in 1714, the vacant throne passed to another and the pretender could do nothing but return to Italy and wait for the pendulum to swing. George II was bad-tempered but more popular at first than his father – he even made an attempt to speak English. Ten years later, however, when his wife died, his reputation was at a low ebb and she was mourned with the verse: 'O death, where is thy sting? To take the queen and leave the king?' France and Spain were by that time more amenable to a Stuart alliance, but James had grown disillusioned and suspicious of fair-weather friends.

In January 1744 his elder son made his farewells at the Palazzo Muti, swearing to return with his father's three crowns, otherwise 'your next sight of me shall be in my coffin'.[15] Deeply pessimistic, James had no confidence in The Forty-Five and sat in Rome waiting for the coffin. At 56 he was already an old man, a confirmed invalid, considering abdication in favour of his son. Instead he blessed him for his boldness and created him Prince Regent. 'Though your enterprise should miscarry,' he wrote to him with foreboding after the prince had left, 'the honour you have gained by it will always stick to you.' Warning against rashness, he added: 'My dear child, never separate prudence and courage.'[16]

The Forty-Five duly failed, and James's weary pilgrimage through life still had more than twenty gloomy years to run. He lived on in hope of seeing his heir, his 'dearest Carluccio', again; but never did. Bonnie Prince Charlie had survived but was bonny no longer. In the most poignant of all the Stuart family quarrels his behaviour was callous and implacable. 'Do not deny me, my dear child, the comfort of embracing you before I die.'[17] 'Is it possible you would rather be a vagabond on the face of the earth than return to a father who is all love and tenderness for you?'[18] All such heart-broken pleadings went unheeded.

In 1759 France made preparations for an expedition against England in the Jacobite interest in revenge for Wolfe's capture of Quebec, but this last vision of a crown for poor old Mr James Misfortunate faded away when Sir Edward Hawke sank the French fleet in Quiberon Bay. In the following year the accession of George III took place without a murmur of dissent. He was the first English-born Hanoverian king, and James was to be the last English-born Stuart. The Glorious Revolution of 1688 had become irreversible.

The Old Pretender lived to the age of nearly 78 and for the last 50 of those years had all but given up hope of restoration. A natural equanimity matured into a resigned acceptance of the verdict of God, man and history. His chronic ill health contributed to a deep, unbroken melancholy. Fortune, he was well aware, had rarely smiled on the Stuarts. In successive generations of his Scottish ancestors James I had been murdered, James II killed in an accident, James III murdered, and James IV killed in battle. Mary Queen of Scots and Charles I had been executed. Old Mr Melancholy suffered no violence, but the long-drawn-out misery of the life of a pretender with dwindling expectations has never been more vividly illustrated.

In 1754 a slight stroke had cost him the sight of one eye and the use of one hand. In 1759 he suffered a severe fit of convulsions. In 1760 the doctors gave him up for dead, but he pulled himself through. In 1762 another stroke left him partially paralysed and his speech affected. In 1764 a third stroke rendered him bedridden. In November 1765 his old complaint, quartan ague, returned to the attack. He was making a resolute recovery from this when on New Year's Day 1766 he died quite suddenly.

In his later years, not surprisingly, James grew tetchy and irascible, but he deserves to be remembered not only as a martyr to his faith and ill health but also as an example of the virtues of dutifulness and resignation. In history he has become a split personality. The Old Pretender ridiculed by the Whigs was a dull failure. James III, the toast of the Jacobites, was a devout but tolerant Christian, a man of honour and a rightful king. One obituary written by an apologist contains a good measure of truth: 'That quiet death ended as pure and noble a life as ever man lived in this difficult world. James III had not been called upon to lay down his life in blood for his faith, but he had with firm will and open eyes laid down three kingdoms for it, and chosen a life of poverty, suffering and contempt.'[19]

James's pretensions followed him to the grave. His body was borne in royal state from the Palazzo Muti to the near-by church of Sant' Apostoli and then on to St Peter's for burial. For the grand funeral procession through the streets of the Holy City a crown was placed on his head at last and a sceptre in his hand.

11

Charles III, the Bonnie Prince

ALTHOUGH the prospect of restoration receded with the passage of time, the strength of the Stuart claim to the throne remained undiminished throughout the 18th century. As the 15th-century Duke of York had asserted, right may be put to silence but it does not perish.

In Stuart eyes William of Orange's claim to a parliamentary title to the crown was invalid because only as king could he have summoned a legitimate parliament. Since James II had not abdicated, the so-called parliament of 1688–89 was an illegal assembly summoned by a foreign invader and had no right to dispose of the sovereignty of the realm. William, Mary, Anne and their Hanoverian successors had stolen the crown, like Henry Bolingbroke and his heirs, and time did not condone theft. That was the basis of the legitimist claim of the Stuarts to their *de jure* status as the rightful kings of England, Scotland and Ireland.

Happy in little else, James III, the Old Pretender, was blessed with heirs. His elder son, known at first as the Prince of Wales and the Young Chevalier, succeeded his father in due course as the Young Pretender and *de jure* Charles III. He stands as the only unsuccessful second-generation claimant to the throne – the first-born son of the eldest surviving son of a king – since the death of William Clito.

Prince Charles was born in Rome on 31 December 1720 in the presence of cardinals, ambassadors and a hundred or so other dignitaries. His was a breath of new life which brought a timely surge of hope to a demoralised cause. His birth at a time when thousands of English families had just been ruined by the bursting of the South Sea Bubble seemed a good omen. George I was implicated in the financial skulduggery which lay behind the collapse. Ill-mannered and inconsiderate, he was already shunned for the inhuman treatment of his wife and the suspected murder of her lover, and his two unattractive German mistresses (the Elephant and the Beanpole) made him a laughing stock.

At the moment of the prince's birth, it was reported, a new star appeared in the firmament and a fierce storm over Germany destroyed property in Hanover. But these heavenly portents, like the earthly, proved deceptive. England's government rested in the capable hands of Sir Robert Walpole, whose policies brought prosperity and stilled demands for change. A king like George I who could not even understand the English language suited Walpole well.

In character Charles was very different from his father. A pretty, fair-haired, brown-eyed boy, spoiled and petulant, he grew into a sturdy athletic extrovert, noisy, cheerful and full of charm. Deserted by his mother at the age of five, he was always shy of the opposite sex. Born and bred in Rome, with a Polish mother and a half-Italian father, he learned nothing of English history or literature but was taught to read and speak the language passably: in Scotland his accent was thought to be Irish. His education ended at thirteen and thereafter he pursued no intellectual interests, preferring riding and tennis and golf in the Borghese gardens.

During his career as a pretender he cut a sadder figure than James, his father. Fourteen months of adventurous failure were followed by twenty years of shame and a 22-year 'reign' of unrelieved futility. Unarmed against the arrows of misfortune by the religious faith which sustained his father, as soon as his short-lived glory faded he plunged into dissipation, debauchery and apostasy. His great-great-grandfather, the Protestant Henry of Navarre, thought Paris worth a mass and turned Catholic to become Henry IV of France. Charles, taking the view that 'the Roman Catholic religion has been the ruin of the royal family',[1] reached the reverse conclusion that London was worth 39 Articles. But with characteristic Stuart misjudgment he apostasised five years too late.

A king without a country, he nevertheless achieved a kind of greatness, 'not for what he was, nor even for what he did, but for what he stands for'.[2] As Bonnie Prince Charlie he gave the world a new and enduring romance. He inspired a legend, and Robert Burns and Sir Walter Scott bestowed on him the kiss of immortality, so that little is associated with his name today except heroism. Invading Scotland with seven middle-aged companions, he brought death and the destruction of a whole way of life in the Scottish highlands, but lies enshrined in Scottish hearts. There he remains eternally young and handsome and daring, as though he had died gallantly in battle or pathetically in the arms of Flora Macdonald. What followed The Forty-Five is forgotten, and the Charlie for whom time has stood still is a darling for ever more.

The siege of Gaeta (between Rome and Naples) gave him his first taste of war. His cousin, the second Duke of Berwick, took him there at the age of thirteen to be blooded, and he duly demonstrated his coolness under fire. He was brave and eager for action. A triumphal progress through Italy, as Count of Albany, publicised his pretensions and won some good will. His opportunity came with the victory of George II over the French at Dettingen in June 1743. England and France, although fighting each other as allies of the opposing sides in the War of the Austrian Succession, were formally at peace at the time, and the defeat so angered Louis XV that he ordered a retaliatory invasion of Britain. An army of 13,000 was assembled under the command of his best general, Marshal Saxe.

James, unfit for the expedition, appointed Charles his regent, and the prince, eluding spies and assassins, stole away variously disguised as a Neapolitan courier and a Spanish officer. On arrival in Paris he became 'Chevalier Douglas' and was sped on his way to join the marshal at Dunkirk as a volunteer. Then, not for the first or last time, the weather turned decisively against the Stuarts. At Gravelines news reached him of a storm which had sunk all the ships already at sea and battered those still at anchor against the harbour walls. Saxe was ordered back to Flanders, his men dispersed and the expedition abandoned. With more support than the French had supplied for any pretender to the English throne since Henry Tudor, success had at last seemed within reach, only to be snatched away by what was hard to accept as an act of God.

Back in Paris Charles spent the ensuing months imploring Louis to mount another attempt on England, but the French king's troops were being more usefully deployed elsewhere. In May 1745 Saxe's army in Flanders, led by an Irish brigade in the French service, avenged Dettingen in overcoming George II's son, William, Duke of

Cumberland, at Fontenoy. In July Charles, impatient of delay and finally despairing of French aid, sailed for Scotland in defiance of advice from supporters there that if he could not bring 6000 men he had better not come at all.

One of his two frigates, loaded with arms, ammunition and cash, was intercepted off the Lizard and forced to turn back. The other, the *Du Teillay*, carried him safely to the isle of Eriskay in the Outer Hebrides. He was disguised as an abbé in case of capture at sea, and his army consisted only of advisers, the so-called Seven Men of Moidart, four of whom were Irish, two Scottish and one English. It was even more of a madcap venture than Monmouth's or James's 30 years earlier. No joyful reception committee rushed forward to bid him welcome. Instead the local chief dourly bade him go home. 'I am come home, sir,' was his famous reply.[3]

A night crossing of 60 miles brought him to the mainland, where the clansmen were dismayed at the sight of him without an army. He had brought 1000 muskets and 1800 broadswords but no funds to purchase provisions. Remembering how his father had deserted, they joined him only when he proved his determination to stay by sending the *Du Teillay* back to France. His standard was raised at Glenfinnan at the head of Loch Shiel, and support gathered round him slowly. The magic of the Stuart name did not set the glens ablaze. Out of a total strength of 30,000, no more than 9000 highlanders served in the Jacobite army during The Forty-Five, and an unknown number of those fought unwillingly, conscripted by their chiefs under threat of having their cottages burned about their ears. In the Presbyterian lowlands a Protestant government in London found more favour than a papist from Rome.

Nonetheless, 'who dares wins' has a respectable ancestry. The rashness of Henry Bolingbroke in 1399 and Edward IV in 1471 was rewarded with the crown. In 1745, within five months of landing, Charles was master of nearly all Scotland and leading an army unchallenged into the heart of England. It was a startling achievement which owed much to his leadership and the enthusiasm which his charm and self-confidence inspired. In this respect there was a marked contrast between The Fifteen and The Forty-Five, the Old Pretender and the Young.

Charles's unexpected success also owed much to the opposition or lack of it. George II was absent from his realm, staying where he and his father preferred to be: in Hanover. The Captain-General of his land forces, the Duke of Cumberland, was still in Flanders with most of the army. Walpole was dead and the head of the government in London, the Duke of Newcastle, was incompetent even by 18th-century standards. Regular troops on garrison duty in Scotland totalled fewer than 4000 under an inept commander, Sir John Cope. A smaller force at Newcastle was under the equally maladroit command of General Wade. Mustering some 1400 foot soldiers in Edinburgh, Cope marched out to nip the revolt in the bud; but, wary of an ambush, he chose not to engage the enemy in hilly terrain. He therefore advanced to Inverness without making contact, obligingly leaving the road to the south open to the Jacobite army.

On 4 September Charles was acclaimed as Prince Regent in Perth, which he entered in state on horseback, resplendent in tartan edged with gold lace. There he appointed two lieutenant-generals: Lord George Murray, fifth son of the first Duke of Atholl and a veteran of The Fifteen and The Nineteen, and the young Duke of Perth (a Jacobite dukedom). Both were men of courage devoted to the cause, but otherwise they had little in common. The duke was even-tempered and well-liked, but a weak character exhibiting little talent. Murray was tempestuously quarrelsome and under constant suspicion of treachery, but possessed a natural genius for military strategy. The credit for the Jacobite military successes in The Forty-Five belongs to him, unbearable though colleagues and historians have found his behaviour.

From Perth the prince moved on unopposed to Edinburgh, where his father was proclaimed King James VIII on 17 September. The castle held out for the government, but Charles had the town and the satisfaction of occupying the royal apartments in Holyroodhouse, the main residence of his family as kings of Scotland.

Realising his mistake, Cope brought his men south by sea, disembarking them at Dunbar, east of Edinburgh. They now numbered 2300, rather fewer than the 2500 who marched out of Edinburgh behind the prince to meet them. Cope, however, had the advantage of some cavalry and guns. He camped between the sea and what he believed to be an impenetrable morass, but guided by a local land-owner Charles's army discovered a track, marched through the bog by night and was able to re-form undetected under cover of an early morning mist.

Prestonpans must have broken, and probably still holds, the world speed record for battles. Estimates of the time it took vary from five to ten minutes. Cope's raw levies were surprised and terrorised by a charge of wild highlanders with claymores, scythes and axes. Their casualties were 500 dead; 100 were captured; and the rest fled, the gunners without re-loading. 'They escaped like rabets,'[4] the illiterate prince reported proudly to his father. At the cost of barely 100 dead and wounded he had become *de facto* Regent of Scotland in his father's name. Only the castles of Edinburgh, Stirling and Dumbarton and a few other isolated garrisons held out against him.

For five weeks he held court in regal state at Holyroodhouse. 'The king shall enjoy his own again', a Jacobite chant and aspiration since the days of Charles I, had miraculously become almost true. Autumn sunshine smiled on the first Stuart prince to be seen in the Scottish capital for 63 years. He dined in public and attended balls. Orders were given for the prisoners of war – his father's subjects – to be well treated; the officers were released on parole. He made preparations for a Scottish parliament and issued proclamations, one of which pointedly inquired whether the nation had been happier or more prosperous since James VII and II had been driven from his thrones.

Certainly the much resented union with England had brought little benefit to the northern kingdom, and The Forty-Five has been generally seen as primarily a Scottish nationalist movement. In Edinburgh Charles was urged to abandon the claim to England and settle for an independent kingdom in Scotland, to be protected from the vengeance of the auld enemy by a revival of the auld alliance with France. But Scottish independence was never an item on the Stuart agenda. The prince was not a nationalist, nor even much of a Scot. He had promised his father three crowns, not one, and his next objective was to march south, capture Berwick, defeat Wade's army at Newcastle and take the open road to an undefended London. The triumph of Prestonpans had swollen his army with new recruits, and morale was high.

With counsels divided, the prince's wishes did not prevail over the caution of his advisers. Money was running out and the initiative being lost while they argued. Not until the end of October, with 4500 infantry and 400 cavalry ready for action, did the prince's council agree on an invasion of England. Even then the direct thrust at well-guarded Berwick and Newcastle was ruled out as too audacious: the softer option of Carlisle and a route through Lancashire was preferred. Already, though, it was too late. George II had returned from Hanover, the British regiments had been recalled from Flanders, 6000 Dutch mercenaries were on their way.

By day on the road south Charles led the march on foot; at night he slept in his boots. 'His body was made for war,' wrote one admirer.[5] Carlisle fell to him after a siege of six days. Since the time of James VI and I it had not been in use as a frontier fortress. The defences were run down and the garrison consisted of 80 elderly veterans supported by the local militia. The commander, incapacitated by gout, prudently surrendered without a fight. General Wade had advanced to the rescue as far as Hexham but turned back, complaining of the poor state of the roads. In his professional opinion November was not a proper month for campaigning in the north.

The fall of Carlisle created a panic in London, but Charles was not without problems. His highlanders were reluctant to venture so far from home and 1000 had deserted on the march. His commanders were quarrelling over whether to press on or turn back. Lord George resigned in a huff when his advice was spurned. The Duke of Perth resigned to appease him, and Lord George with an ill grace consented to withdraw his resignation provided that he was entrusted with sole command under the prince. Dissension broke out too between the Scots and Charles's Irish advisers. Colonel O'Sullivan, who held the crucial appointment of quartermaster-general, was particularly disliked and distrusted. The Irish, who were experienced professional soldiers, countered this jealousy with scorn for the Scots commanders as bungling amateurs.

Most ominous of all for the success of the enterprise was the absence of English recruits. Where were all those loyal and oppressed Jacobites who had been reported to be waiting for the army of liberation so that they could rise and throw off the yoke of Hanover? From Northumberland and Cumberland they amounted to a total of seven, one of whom deserted, one went sick and another turned out to be a spy. To the English, Charles was no Monmouth.

Jacobite intelligence in The Forty-Five had not improved since The Fifteen. The employment of spies and go-betweens, so skilfully organised by Henry Tudor's mother, seemed beyond or beneath the Stuart pretenders. On no hard evidence and with little contact with sympathisers in England the illusion was still nursed that as soon as the prince crossed the border the English would welcome him with open arms and as soon as the English rose the French would invade.

In fact, the Stuarts were never loved in England and their adherents in towns and among the squirearchy were those hostile to the government. True Jacobites were few. The general attitude towards the struggle between Guelph and Stuart was much as it had been during the wars between York and Lancaster. Both were arguments in which those not directly involved took sides only out of self-interest. Except among a small Catholic minority, the choice between corrupt and incompetent Whigs and timid and ineffectual Tories did not raise any great issues of principle or passionate partisanship. At a popular level the London mob was violently anti-Jacobite and, in coming to England at the head of a Scottish army, Charles had inevitably aroused the same hostility as Warbeck had encountered during his incursion with James IV. The Scottish highlanders were hated and feared as savages. At their approach valuables were hidden and towns emptied.

Once a decision to continue the march was taken, the highland army moved on unopposed. The occupation of Preston avenged the disgrace of thirty years before. Manchester, a centre of Jacobite sympathies, was taken without resistance by a recruiting sergeant, his mistress and his drummer, who somehow arrived ahead of the main army. King James was proclaimed and a Manchester Regiment loyal to him was formed out of nearly 300 volunteers. At Macclesfield, where it was reported that the road to London was barred by a large force at Lichfield under the command of the Duke of Cumberland, Lord George decided on a feint towards Wales. Cumberland was deceived and the way was left open for Charles to reach Derby with no opposing army between him and the capital.

The battle at Derby was a war of words which has never ceased. On Black Friday the prince's council, led by Lord George Murray, was insistent on the army turning back. The prince himself, in a minority of one, was outvoted. Such a deep penetration into enemy territory – the furthest a Scottish army had ever advanced into England – was a remarkable military exploit, but the decision at Derby rendered it worthless. Both at the time and down the years since, Charles's admirers have denounced Murray as a defeatist who threw away victory by overriding his master's wishes.

'It can hardly be doubted that if Charles had had his way he would have won the throne for his father and what is more, kept it.'[6] That is the opinion of Sir Compton Mackenzie, who added for good measure that the decision at Derby changed world history: with the Stuarts back on the throne there would have been no loss of the American colonies, no French revolution, no martyrdom of Ireland, no decline of Scotland, no exploitation of the poor by industrialists. Even in the 20th century, it seems, the attraction of Bonnie Prince Charlie exercises a powerful hold over the Celtic imagination. It has long been an article of Jacobite faith that a Stuart restoration bringing boundless benefits would have been achieved but for the infamous Lord George.

It is, of course, possible that the prince's bravado in making a dash for London (127 miles away) might have attracted support and won the day. His prospects may be thought not much slimmer than Henry Tudor's on the road to Bosworth. Numbers and logistics, on the other hand, point decidedly the other way, and the backing of the rest of the council for Murray is surely significant. Although billets were ordered for 9000, the Jacobite army at Derby probably numbered no more than 4500. Opposed to them were Wade on the flank (now with 18,000 men), Cumberland in Staffordshire and a new army forming to protect London – a total of not fewer than 30,000, including troops with battle experience in Flanders.

The prince argued that he could reach London without having to fight either Wade or Cumberland, that London would welcome him and the French would land. Certainly there were Jacobite sympathisers among the city fathers in London (they are said to have included eight of the Lord Mayors who held office during the 1740s), and his optimism about the French was not unreasonable. George II was to call off Cumberland's pursuit of the retreating Jacobites after the re-capture of Carlisle because his army was needed in the south to meet the threat of a French build-up at Dunkirk. The French, however, proved content with the handsome dividend already received in return for their cautious investment in The Forty-Five. The withdrawal of English and Dutch troops had enabled them to overrun the Austrian Netherlands.

Murray argued that it would be necessary to fight two or three armies in succession and there would be no chance of defeating them all. Not a single person of rank had joined them since they crossed the border and the common people were openly antagonistic. London would certainly resist if they got as far, and how could it be besieged with Wade and Cumberland unbeaten in their rear? The prince, he confidently predicted, would be in a cell in Newgate within a fortnight.

After winning the argument Murray demonstrated his class as a military commander by organising a withdrawal which has been compared with the retreat of the Ten Thousand recorded in

Xenophon's *Anabasis*. In a masterly exercise, himself commanding the vulnerable rearguard, he took a disconsolate army in an orderly retreat back to Scotland unscathed, crossing the Esk without loss on the still sulking prince's 25th birthday.

They met with a cold reception in Hanoverian Glasgow, and Stirling castle withstood their assault and siege. But they soon had the good fortune to meet another incompetent enemy commander in General Hawley, the government's new commander-in-chief in Scotland. Hawley had occupied Edinburgh in their absence and, before leaving, erected gibbets in the street to hang any rebels captured in battle. He also brought hangmen with him to the battlefield.

At Falkirk his small superiority in numbers (10,000 to 8000) was no compensation for Murray's vastly superior generalship. When Hawley's dragoons advanced, the Jacobite army held its fire until they were within ten yards. Then the highlanders knifed the horses and scattered the enemy left flank with a charge like the one which had carried the day at Prestonpans. On the right three regiments of government veterans stood fast until ordered to retreat, leaving the Jacobites victorious on the field. Back in Edinburgh Hawley had 32 of his infantrymen shot for cowardice and used his gibbets to hang 31 of his own dragoons for desertion. To Cumberland he reported: 'Our left is beat, and their left is beat.' Yet they had won. 'My heart is broke.'[7]

Falkirk was fought in January 1746. On Murray's advice the lowlands were then abandoned for the winter and the army retired to Inverness. By April numbers were down to 5000 with few horses, fewer guns, a shortage of food and an empty money chest. Cumberland meanwhile was preparing for the kill. Once the threat of a French invasion was lifted he returned north with 9000 men, more than a quarter of them cavalry, accompanied by a train of artillery. Well provisioned by a fleet, he advanced towards the highlands with his lines of communication guarded by 5000 Hessians. Over a period of two months his infantry were subjected to an intense course of musket practice to train them to fire three volleys a minute.

Four months younger than Charles, the duke was a veteran of Dettingen, where he had been wounded, and Fontenoy, where he had displayed conspicuous gallantry. At 18 stone – some said 20 – he was monstrously overweight and an ugly customer in every way, fully meriting the nickname of 'Butcher'. To him the Jacobites were rebels and outlaws and to be treated as such. They were not an enemy fit to be granted quarter in battle. Their wounded were to be clubbed or bayoneted to death; fugitives to be pursued by dragoons and sabred. The scourge of marauding highlanders was to be ended by extermination. This brutal policy, it has to be said, was widely applauded in England and the Scottish lowlands.

The death knell of Stuart aspirations was tolled at Culloden, five miles east of Inverness, on 16 April 1746. Outnumbered three to one, professionals versus amateurs, Charles was advised by Murray to follow the example of Monmouth at Sedgemoor and attempt a surprise attack by night. But his men were rain-soaked, exhausted and half-starved before they started – the day's rations were water and, for those who could get it, one biscuit. When daylight broke they were still two miles from the duke's encampment at Nairn and, to the prince's fury, Lord George gave the order to about-turn.

Lord George was furious too. Against his advice and on that of the hated Irishmen, Charles had chosen a flat moor for his battlefield – open ground which would enable the enemy to deploy his guns and horses to maximum effect, instead of rough slopes which gave highlanders the advantage. The prince had indeed made a fatal error. Cumberland's tactics were to inflict as much punishment as possible with his guns before risking hand-to-hand fighting, and his artillerymen enjoyed a clear view. Their opening cannonade decimated the rebel ranks. Charles, waiting for the enemy cavalry to charge first, played into his hands by delaying the order to attack. Then, when the order was given, the messenger who carried it was killed; which led to a further delay while the duke's guns played havoc. Then at last came the wild highland charge, calculated to strike terror into the stoutest of hearts. At the head of the clansmen, as at Prestonpans, was the fiercest of them all – Lord George himself.

On this occasion it encountered strong resistance. There were clans which had refused the prince's call, among them the Campbells, who were mustered in strength among the government forces and had scores to settle with the Camerons. They laid an ambush with enfilade fire from behind a stone wall about which Lord George had expressed unheeded misgivings. On the prince's left the Macdonalds, displeased at being deprived of their rightful place of honour on the right, refused to take part in the charge. Cumberland then unleashed his cavalry and both Jacobite flanks were swept away. The highlanders broke and ran, and their prince fled with them, leaving a scene of carnage which was to haunt him for the rest of his life. He had believed his highlanders invincible, but their blood was on his hands. In the words of Lord Lovat, one of his leading supporters: 'None but a mad fool would have fought that day.'[8]

The survivors re-grouped at Ruthven, but Charles did not keep the rendezvous. A message arrived instead, announcing his return to France. Without either provisions or money he had little choice. Abandoning his men to Cumberland's merciless pursuit, he disappeared into the heather to achieve an extraordinary metamorphosis. Five and a half months as a hunted refugee transformed him into a folk hero, his responsibility for Culloden disregarded or forgiven. A natural adventurer, he revelled in the danger and hardship, in living and sleeping rough. Wet and cold and hunger he endured with patience and good humour, fortified by liberal draughts of brandy and whisky. The price of £30,000 on his head tempted no one to betray him, for he 'won more hearts in his distresses than in his gleam of triumph'.[9]

Charles's judgment was as poor as ever, though. He escaped from the relative safety of the mountainous mainland to the western isles where he was more exposed to capture, and in so doing missed the arrival of two French ships at Borrodale. Sailing under false English colours, they carried 40,000 louis d'or, which were unloaded, but had to make the return journey without him. Instead they took aboard the ailing Duke of Perth, who died at sea.

Government search parties were on the prince's track in the Hebrides. In one of the best-remembered of romantic exploits in history he was rowed by night in a storm for eight hours across the sea from North Uist to Skye. There, dressed in a flowery calico gown as an Irish maid answering to the name of Betty Bourke, he was led away from under the noses of militia men searching for him. Although an old hand at disguise, in this one he was described as 'the worst pretender ever I saw'.[10] His young preserver was Fionnghal (or Flora) Macdonald, who was afterwards sent to the Tower of London but released and lived to the age of 88 to tell the tale. Immortalised in prose and poetry and song, 'her stainless memory will be fragrant while white roses bloom'.[11]

The fugitive was smuggled back to the mainland where he was fortunate to find *L'Heureux*, another French ship sent to rescue him. Embarking almost where he had landed fourteen months earlier and evading British naval patrols thanks to a providential fog, he was taken to Brittany and reached Paris to an ecstatic welcome. The

French king received the royal adventurer with all honour as Regent of England, Scotland and Ireland, and Parisian society lionised him. Practical assistance was another matter. France was now in need of peace with England, and the pension Louis offered him was conditional on his retiring to Switzerland.

Charles contemptuously rejected the offer and asked for 20,000 French troops instead. He was burning to return and reverse his defeat, but succeeded only in offending Louis and his ministers. In gloom and frustration he also quarrelled with his father, his brother, his agent in Paris and other loyal associates and followers. As for Lord George, who had also made good his escape and had written one of his tactless letters pointing out forcefully that the failure of the campaign was entirely due to a series of acts of folly by the prince himself, Charles demanded that he be consigned to the Bastille. Murray, however, was well received by the Old Pretender in Rome and was to die in his bed, an exile in Holland, fourteen years later.

By Article IV of the Treaty of Utrecht the French had long been bound to recognise the Protestant succession in Britain, and it was a stipulation of the Treaty of Aix-la-Chapelle in 1748 that no pretender to the throne of Great Britain should be permitted to reside in France, Spain, Holland or Germany. When the prince was accordingly served notice to quit Paris he ignored the order and threatened to kill himself if forcibly deported. Louis, angry at the insult, had him arrested at the opera, bound hand and foot, thrown head first into a hired coach and driven off to the fortress of Vincennes. Two pistols and a pair of compasses were found on his person, so the suicide threat may not have been an idle one. This defiance of his most valuable ally and the public indignity of his arrest and expulsion did nothing to bring nearer the day of restoration.

On his release after a few days, he sought asylum in Avignon, where his father had formerly held court, but once again, under pressure from Britain, was required to move on. Rome beckoned, but his face was set against his father and the pope. If the countries where he wished to live were closed to him as Prince Regent, he would lead his life incognito. 'What can a bird do that has not found a right nest?' he wrote to his father: 'He must flit from bough to bough.'[12] In February 1749 he left Avignon and vanished for almost 18 years.

At first there were sensational rumours that he was planning to marry the Tsarina of Russia or a princess of Prussia, or to unseat Augustus III and become King of Poland. Sightings were reported from Lithuania (in a castle with the beautiful Princess Radziwill), from Sweden, even from Staffordshire. In fact, he was secretly on the move in Paris and elsewhere in France, in Venice and Berlin, in Ghent, Coblenz, Frankfurt, Liège and Basle, a vagabond dogged by spies and fearful of hired assassins. His letters were written in cipher and he travelled under cover of aliases: James Douglas, Comte John Douglas, Count Johnson, Dr Thompson and even Mr Brown and Mr Smith. Sometimes he was disguised as an abbé, sometimes as a Capuchin friar. His make-up included a long false nose, a false beard, a black eye-patch, a black wig and painted pox marks. How much of this was necessary, how much histrionics, it is hard to unravel. No doubt there were creditors and officials with expulsion orders to be hidden from, as well as British agents.

This was no romantic adventure like being hunted through the highland glens. The rising star of Jacobite hopes had sunk into a furtive life of vice and squalor. The gay Young Chevalier had become a lonely tippler, a broken hero drowning the anguish of his memories and brooding over wrongs and shortcomings and what might have been. He was on the run and out of funds.

In 1750, in an act of bravado, he travelled to England and spent six days calling on astonished supporters in London. He took lodgings in Pall Mall, visited the Tower (noting that a petard would blow in the gate) and in a church in the Strand solemnly abjured Rome and was received into the Church of England 'as by law established in the 39 Articles, in which I hope to live and die' (as he recorded in a draft proclamation nine years later).[13] The real purpose of this secret visit remains a mystery. Was it a personal whim, a purposeful reconnaissance or a crucial consultation to put the finishing touches to a serious plot? Might he again have deluded himself that the whole country would rise once his presence in the capital became known? No one betrayed him by handing him over to the authorities; which might have been an embarrassment, since the government almost certainly had him under surveillance. 'When the gentleman shall have looked about him a little,' George II is reported to have said when the question of his arrest was raised, 'he will no doubt return quietly.'[14] The story may be apocryphal, but not the damning scorn. In the government's view, it seems, the Young Pretender at liberty was doing the Jacobite cause so much harm that it would be unwise to interfere and make a martyr of him. In London his surreptitious meetings served to identify important Jacobite sympathisers, who included noblemen such as the Duke of Beaufort and the Earl of Westmorland.

All the royal nomad's precautions were ineffective because the government had a secret agent among his closest associates. The details of every Stuart intrigue and the names of those involved were betrayed throughout the 1750s by Pickle the Spy, only unmasked more than a century after his death as Alastair Macdonell, chieftain of Glengarry, one of Charles's favourite drinking companions and apparently the most loyal and faithful of Jacobites. The deadliest of the conspiracies aborted on the evidence of this informer was the Elibank Plot to seize the Tower of London and St James's palace and assassinate the entire Hanoverian royal family. Forewarned, the government arrested one of the principal conspirators, Archibald Cameron, and hanged him at Tyburn. The Hanoverian secret service initiated by Walpole was as effective against the Stuart pretenders as Walsingham's had been in contriving the downfall of Mary Queen of Scots. It is largely owing to Glengarry that there were no more Fifteens or Forty-Fives.

Rather than playing a game of European hide-and-seek and plotting in his cups, the least service Charles could and should have rendered to his cause was to marry and produce an heir. Perversely, he chose a mistress to take with him as Countess Johnson, Mrs Thompson etc. during eight years of his wanderings. A Catholic from Lanarkshire by the name of Clementina Walkinshaw, she had a sister in the household of the Hanoverian Princess of Wales in London and was therefore suspected by Charles's companions of being a spy, probably unjustly. She and Charles quarrelled in public during heavy drinking bouts, and he so ill-treated her that in the end she sought refuge from him in a French convent, taking their daughter Charlotte with her. By that time the prince was often drunk from morning to night; he had turned a deaf ear to a heart-rending plea to go to Rome and pay his last respects to his still doting father, who was thought to be on his deathbed; and the Earl Marischal, still the staunchest of Jacobites, declared that he would not give six sous to rescue the dissolute pretender from the bottom of a river.

When James died Charles arrived too late to bid him adieu and shed no tears. Such energy as he still possessed was devoted to securing recognition as *de jure* King of Great Britain in succession to his father. Yet even the Vatican, which had recognised James III to the end, demurred. Apart from the diplomatic inadvisability of offending the *de facto* government in London, the pope felt obliged to point out a religious disqualification: Charles had become a convert to the Church of England, which did not recognise him, the pope, except as Bishop of Rome. Elsewhere the response was no different. In 1766 Jacobitism was seen to have been a dead cause since the uncontested accession of George III – when the house of Stuart received a final consolation prize in the appointment of a Stuart, the Earl of Bute, as chief minister.

In Rome the once Bonnie Prince Charlie, disgraced and down-graded, shut himself up in the Palazzo Muti, home of his boyhood when the future looked bright. He would not go out, he announced, until acknowledged as king. But no one minded, and he had to settle for being Charles III indoors and the Count of Albany outside.

In spite of such insistence on his pretensions it took him six years to do his duty in getting married. Louis XV arranged for a respectable bride from an impoverished family of minor royalty. It was the most a throneless debauchee could expect. Princess Louise of Stolberg-Geldern was an intelligent, blue-eyed blonde with a fetching retroussé nose, aged 19. He was 52 and reported to be consuming six bottles of wine after dinner every day. She found him 'the most insupportable man that ever existed'[15] and the union was not blessed with a child.

To be known as the Queen of Hearts was flattering but little compensation for not being treated as a real queen outside the confines of the Muti palace. In search of recognition for both of them, her ailing and asthmatic, shuffling and smelly, bored and boring sot of a husband took her first to Leghorn, then to Siena and finally to Florence where, however, the Grand Duke of Tuscany would not oblige by receiving them as any other than the Count and Countess of Albany.

In Florence Louise found consolation in the arms of a Piedmontese poet called Alfieri and in 1780 the marriage broke down after eight unhappy years. Charles had brought his celebration of the feast of St Andrew to a climax by raping and half-strangling her in bed. Like James's wife and Charles's mistress before her, she fled for sanctuary into a convent. A sympathetic pope arranged for her return to Rome to enter the religious life in an Ursuline house. It was some time before he learned that the wronged wife was guilty of adultery. The scandal of the assault and the cuckolding of the pretender became a spicy news item in the salons of Europe. Louise left the Ursulines to resume her liaison with her lover, and after Charles's death they lived happily together until Alfieri's. She then returned to Florence and lived to become a legend on her own as Bonnie Prince Charlie's widow alive and well nearly eighty years after The Forty-Five.

Marital disharmony was the only event of note in Charles III's 22-year reign. When brought to accept the breach as irreparable, he sent for his daughter Charlotte, with whom he had had no communication for 20 years. As a reward for becoming his housekeeper she was legitimated and created Duchess of Albany. This proved to be one of his few good moves. She was sweet-natured and sensible, nursed him through his dropsy and asthma, and refrained from telling him about her three illegitimate children by the Archbishop of Bordeaux.

Charles had always been fond of music and, living now more at ease than at any time since that never-to-be-forgotten day at Culloden, he found consolation in playing the cello. Beneath the surface, though, the wounds had not healed. When one day a visitor incautiously referred to the fate of the highlanders, he collapsed in a fit, still incapable of coming to terms with the butchery of the brave and faithful for which in his heart he could blame no one but himself.

Destiny had cast a well-meaning man in the role of pretender and thereby destroyed him – not in body, but in mind and character. Even towards the end there were flickers of hope for a Stuart revival. In the 1770s Jacobites in the American colonies were intriguing to make Charles III a transatlantic king, following the example of their forefathers during the Protectorate who had invited Charles II to become King of Virginia. In London, according to Dr Johnson, 'if England were fairly polled, the present king would be sent away tonight and his adherents hanged tomorrow'.[16] The good doctor, admittedly, was prone to dogmatic assertions of doubtful validity but, whatever the truth, Charles had long since ceased to be what his dignified and principled father had always been: in modern terms, a viable alternative.

He died in Rome in 1788 on 31 January, the anniversary of Charles I's execution. His brother had hurried to his bedside to ensure that he received the last rites of the church he had renounced. His body was honoured as a king's in a magnificent ceremony in Frascati cathedral. After a period of waiting (and negotiation) it was laid at rest beside his father's in St Peter's.

It is kindest to remember this pretender as the Bonnie Prince of highland legend. Charlie is not here a diminutive of the English name, Charles; it derives from English pronunciation of the Gaelic name, Tearlach. Years afterwards, veterans of The Forty-Five known to Sir Walter Scott broke down and wept at the mention of his name; for, whatever his shortcomings, he was their prince. While alive he was theirs alone. Since his death he has become everybody's darling. In the lowlands, and south of the border too, there is a tear in the eye and a catch in the throat when the mournful Jacobite melodies are played and sung and the pretender who brought death and disaster is implored: 'Will ye no come back again?'

12

Henry IX, King Cardinal

THE LAST of the three Stuart legitimist pretenders was Henry Benedict Thomas Edward Maria Clement Francis Xavier. Born in Rome in 1725, the younger son of the Old Pretender, James III and VIII, and Clementina Sobieska, he was baptised by the pope himself – his father's friend, Benedict XIII – and created Duke of York, the traditional title of a second son of the King of England.

In his family and court circle of exiles in the Palazzo Muti James insisted on English being spoken, partly perhaps by way of pointing a contrast with the custom of the Hanoverian usurpers occupying St James's palace in London, who continued to converse in German. But Henry was no more English than the Hanoverians and never became fluent in the language. He spoke and wrote it eccentrically and had difficulty in understanding. His temperament, with its sudden squalls of rage, owed more to Polish than Scottish ancestry, and in appearance he was swarthy and Italianate, like his father and his ancestor Charles II. In a long life he never set foot in England or Scotland: more than eighty of his eighty-two years were spent in Italy, where he was seen as the very model of an 18th-century Roman patrician.

As a boy he was pretty and lively, his father's favourite, and although never healthy and robust like his brother Charles, he enjoyed an active life, dancing and hunting. When he was eight it was suggested that he might one day become a successful candidate for the crown of Poland, and three years later it was thought that he would make a suitable King of Corsica. Clearly, in other people's opinions as well as his own (for he was not noted for modesty), his royal blood, upbringing and personal qualities well qualified him for a throne. He gave himself extravagantly princely airs and was, in his brother's words, not much loving to be contradicted.

In adolescence the high-spirited boy matured into a solemn young man, and it became apparent that Henry had inherited his mother's extreme piety and obsession with religious observance. At the age of seventeen he was on his knees in prayer for more than three hours every day as well as finding the time to attend two or three masses. This was not a passing phase: he had found his vocation. His devotion embraced music, but other activities in education and sport were all but abandoned. Although later a a bibliophile, he never became more than an indifferent scholar and the books he collected so avidly were most cherished for the beauty of their bindings.

In 1744, to his great grief and humiliation, Henry was forbidden by his father to accompany his elder brother on the historic expedition to Scotland to regain the family's lost kingdoms. It took eighteen months of pleading before he was granted leave to follow. His mission was to persuade the French government to supply him with the reinforcements without which his brother was doomed.

In Paris he quickly discovered that the authorities took as gloomy a view of Charles's prospects as his father did in Rome. He arrived incognito as the Count of Albany in September 1745, earnest and determined but young for his twenty years: in papal circles he was still known affectionately as *il Duchino di York* – the little Duke of York. He was handicapped by inexperience in politics and lacked his brother's charm. His audience with Louis XV, the Stuarts' paymaster, was not a success.

In these circumstances he had no resources to fall back on except importunity. During this period, as later in life, his most valuable asset in adversity was a generous share of the well-attested Stuart obstinacy: the refusal to take 'no' for an answer which was to sustain them in exile for almost 120 years. His next audience, with the French queen, was more encouraging. Marie Leczinska was a fellow Pole, but she proved to have little influence at court, and the Duc de Richelieu, a notorious philanderer, took a strong dislike to what he judged to be a pompous, puritanical and priggish princeling. The Minister of War, the Marquis d'Argenson, not only found him absurdly religious and insufferably Italian but even condemned him as miserly, cowardly and deceitful – accusations which could hardly be justified. Henry may have been husbanding inadequate funds and painting an optimistically rosy picture of calamitous events in Britain, but he was no coward; rather a frustrated combatant, frantic to join the fray.

As a supplicant at the French court, his real flaw, which the loose-living found hard to forgive, was his devoutness. In an unhappy misjudgment of priorities he once kept an important council of war waiting while he attended mass. When at last he arrived, Richelieu rebuked him with words which he may well have taken to heart: 'Your royal highness may perhaps win the kingdom of Heaven by your prayers, but never the kingdom of Great Britain.'[1] Henry was soon to make his choice and opt for the kingdom of Heaven.

In the end, sweetened by a liberal financial contribution from the pope, the French reluctantly agreed to supply him with a fleet and 11,000 men to sail to Scotland from Dunkirk. It was a triumph: no one cleverer or more diplomatic could have achieved more. Eagerly Henry set off for action at last, only to have his hopes dashed. Reports of Charles's retreat from England into the highlands gave the half-hearted French an excuse for prevarication. Month after month throughout a dismal winter Henry kicked his heels on the coast at Dunkirk or Boulogne or between, waiting and praying for permission to set sail. At last came the news of Culloden and the expedition was finally called off.

On the other side of the Channel Henry was identified as The Youngest Pretender, and the navy had orders to intercept ships sailing from French ports and search for him. There were constant rumours of his having landed secretly in England. If true, his life would have been worth little. One Jacobite captive, the young Charles Radclyffe, mistaken for him while being marched through the city of London, was almost torn to pieces by the mob. Such was the hatred for the Stuarts engendered by the Jacobite highlanders' invasion of England.

Instead of obeying his father's order to return to Rome, Henry stubbornly maintained his determination to salvage his honour in battle. Granted leave to serve with the French army under Marshal Saxe at the siege of Antwerp, he had the satisfaction of taking the field against an English army under the command of the Duke of Cumberland, the Hanoverian prince who had butchered his brother's army. Even the critical D'Argenson conceded that at Antwerp Henry behaved with 'a valour both natural and hereditary'.[2]

This brief spell of campaigning was to be his only military experience. He returned to Paris to join in the hero's welcome which awaited Charles after his escape from Scotland. The reunion was joyous, but the brothers' affection for each other was destined to be short-lived. Charles was scarred by his defeat and haunted by the horrors of a campaign in which Henry had taken no part. In sheer relief at survival he and his companions plunged into a life of debauchery, and Henry's austere disapproval marked him down as sanctimonious. When James wrote once more ordering him back to Rome, Henry was ready to obey.

The final breach between the brothers occurred in April 1747, when Henry invited Charles to supper at his house in Paris. On arrival, the guest was told that the host had disappeared three hours earlier. Henry had left behind him a letter of apology and explanation, but with instructions that it was not to be delivered until three days later. During that time Charles could only imagine that his brother had been kidnapped or assassinated. When the letter did reach him it contained the information that Henry had left in secret in obedience to a summons recalling him to Rome. But why secretly and why the calculated insult?

A further explanation arrived shortly afterwards in the form of a long letter from Rome, written to Charles by his father to notify him that the pope had offered Henry a cardinal's hat and that Henry had accepted with his father's blessing. They had decided not to tell Charles until the matter was a *fait accompli*. This was, presumably, the reason for Henry's mysterious and inexcusable behaviour in Paris: it seems that he feared violence and, possibly, a pursuit. Since Charles was James's heir apparent and Henry was Charles's heir presumptive – the last of the Stuart line – Charles should certainly have been consulted, and his father admitted as much, but 'the duke and I were unalterably determined on the matter and . . . we foresaw you might probably not approve of it'.[3]

That proved a considerable understatement. In Charles's eyes Henry's acceptance of a cardinal's hat was the act of a traitor. It was a fatal blow to his own aspirations and those of the whole Stuart succession. How could a Protestant country where anti-popery was rife ever be expected to accept as king a man whose brother and heir was a cardinal? In bitter fury Charles replied tersely to his father that the news of Henry's cardinalate was like 'a Dager throw my heart'.[4] He gave orders that Henry's health was never again to be drunk at his table, that Henry's name was never again to be spoken in his house.

For the rest of his life he remained adamant in refusing to meet his father ever again, and it was to be more than eighteen years before the brothers were reconciled.

Charles may have over-reacted but he was not the only person to see Henry's decision as a betrayal. While George II expressed delight at the news, Jacobites everywhere behaved as though it was as great a calamity as Culloden. The rector of the Scots College in Paris voiced a common view when he denounced Henry's 'late change of condition' as 'a mortal deadly stroke to the cause'.[5] It made clear to the world that after sixty years of exile and the failure of The Forty-Five both James and his younger son had given up all hope of a Stuart restoration. While continuing to maintain their claims and pretensions, they had in effect conceded defeat. Henry had chosen to exchange the empty life of 'a proscribed, disowned, rarely recognised English prince'[6] for real dignity, real honour, real power. If that was treachery, he could at least dispute the accusation that he alone had sealed the fate of the Stuarts. All his brother Charles had had to do to retrieve the situation was to marry and produce heirs of his own.

When Benedict XIV presided over his admission to the Sacred College in July 1747 Henry was aged twenty-two and not in holy orders. The pope was at pains to point out that there were precedents for young cardinals: others had received their red hats at sixteen and even at twelve. And the rank or dignity of cardinal did not necessitate priesthood: there had been many examples of political cardinals, filling secular posts, who were in minor orders. Benedict was well satisfied that Henry was a holy young man, even if he had other failings. His Holiness – a witty man – is on record as remarking that if all the Stuarts were as boring as Henry it was no surprise that the English had got rid of them.

Certainly the new cardinal was not popular among his colleagues. As a prince of the blood royal he immediately took precedence over all of them except the most senior. His mantle was trimmed with ermine; in the pope's presence he wss permitted to sit on a golden cushion instead of a bare wooden stool; and he was addressed as Royal Highness and Eminence, no one being allowed to forget the Royal Highness, for Henry was haughty and a stickler for protocol.

Thus, while his invalid father was sunk in melancholia and his brother became an alcoholic, Henry enjoyed a successful and satisfying career as a churchman. In September 1748 he was ordained a priest and thereafter his progress was spectacular. There were no scandals in his public life and his father was continually urging his advancement on successive popes. In 1758 he became *camerlengo* or chamberlain of the papal court, and as such presided over the conclave which elected Benedict's successor. In 1759 he was Archbishop of Corinth. In 1761 he was enthroned as Bishop of Tusculum, a see including Frascati, which became his favourite residence for nearly half a century. Later he was appointed Vice-Chancellor of the Holy Roman Church and in the end Dean of the Sacred College. Few others have lived to enjoy the eminence of a cardinalate for sixty years.

At first, however, he continued to live at the Palazzo Muti with his father, although taking little interest in the maintenance of the Stuart claim. His time was devoted to his duties and to music, to the fabric of his church (Santa Maria in Campitelli) and to the poor of his parish. Inevitably there were quarrels with his father. Bickering was a persistent feature of Stuart family life and both father and son were touchy and in poor health. James was a martyr to dyspepsia and Henry had consumptive symptoms – a weak chest, fainting fits and some coughing of blood. There were outbursts of temper on both sides, and tense periods of not speaking to each other.

The rift became serious when James objected to the dismissal of his son's English chamberlain and his replacement by a young Genoese priest called Lercari, whom Horace Walpole maliciously described as Henry's minion. When Henry left Rome in a furious sulk the pope was forced to intervene, insisting on Lercari's dismissal and ordering the cardinal to return. Recognising that living with father at the age of twenty-six was the real trouble, the ever obliging Benedict gave Henry a lucrative Vatican appointment with a house of his own. There Henry began his long career as a collector, spending his vast church revenues on furniture, pictures, rare books and manuscripts. None of his annual income of some 30,000 crowns went to his brother or the Jacobite cause.

Yet when his father died Henry was tireless in harassing the pope and the crowned heads of Europe into recognising Charles as a king. Because his brother would not enter Rome until the pope had recognised him as Charles III, King of Great Britain, France and Ireland, Henry performed the office of chief mourner at their father's funeral, ensuring that James's body was borne to St Peter's properly adorned with the insignia of the Garter and the Thistle as well as crown and sceptre.

Afterwards the brothers met at an inn outside the city. Henry was handsome and splendid in Roman purple, magnificently jewelled. His income had risen to 60,000 crowns a year, the fruits of a multiplicity of preferments and sinecures which he held in Italy, Spain, France, Flanders, Mexico and South America. Charles was poor, seedy, bloated with drink and unable to walk without assistance. The cardinal escorted this sad relic of a once Bonnie Prince to the Palazzo Muti but was unable to persuade the pope to change his mind about recognising him as a king.

Later the brothers quarrelled again, this time over Charles legitimating his bastard daughter and making her his heir. In a rage Henry sent a long, pompous, formal Protest to Charles and the pope. But by the time of Charles's death they were reconciled again, and there was no disagreement over Henry, not Charlotte, being the legitimate Stuart successor.

At 63 the proud cardinal could style himself Henry IX, but with no prospect of recognition and, it seems, no real intention of attempting to seize his crown from the usurping George III. Although Cardinal Pole, a grandson of the Duke of Clarence, had been considered a serious candidate for King of England as Mary Tudor's consort and a monk had once become King of Poland, a cardinal on the throne of a Protestant nation was scarcely a practical proposition.

Nevertheless, Henry had no hesitation in asserting his rights. A Memorial was issued in which he made it plain, on behalf of his heirs, that he was renouncing no claims. To celebrate his accession he struck silver medals proclaiming himself *Henricus Nonus*; *Magnae Britanniae Rex*. On the reverse they bore wistful inscriptions: *Dei Gratia sed non voluntate hominum* (by the grace of God but not the will of men) or *Non desideriis hominum sed voluntate Dei* (not by the wishes of men, but by the will of God).

The problem of what to call himself was neatly solved. He announced that he would continue to use the name 'Duke of York', but as an incognito title only. Previously styled 'Cardinal Duke of York', he would now be known as 'Cardinal called Duke of York' and continue signing himself 'Henry Cardinal' instead of 'Henry R' in the style adopted by his father and brother. His purpose in all this was to avoid snubs and formal rejections of his claim.

In other ways his royalty was made manifest. The prince's coronet on his armorial bearings was replaced by a royal crown. The members of his household were obliged to address him as Majesty and he was careful always to refer to George III as the Elector of Hanover. He could not resist reviving the practice of offering a miraculous cure to the sick by touching for the king's evil (with a beautiful silver-gilt touch-piece): the Hanoverians had abandoned this custom, which dated from Saxon times, and Henry was its last practitioner. When in 1792 Pius VI's fear of republican France forced him into a somewhat tardy recognition of George as King of Great Britain the cardinal reacted with one of his most vehement protests: 'O God, what a blow! What anguish of soul . . . I myself . . . betrayed.'[7]

Heavier blows were to follow – blows which destroyed the tranquil affluence of the royal state in which the king cardinal indulged himself. In 1793 his Bourbon cousin, Louis XVI, was guillotined. In 1796 Napoleon's armies invaded Italy and occupied the Papal States. Henry contributed family jewels including the famous Sobieski ruby, valued at £50,000, towards an indemnity to buy them off, but two years later the French marched into Rome itself, a republic was proclaimed, and the pope taken into captivity in France. Suffering the same fate as John of Gaunt's Savoy palace in an earlier revolution, Henry's magnificent palaces in Rome and Frascati were ransacked and he had to flee for his life to Naples. In his seventies His Majesty and Eminence had overnight become a penniless fugitive.

The Neopolitan court lay under the protection of Austria, but this proved too weak a shield against the French advance, and towards the end of the year Henry was once more on the run. In a perilous adventure on storm-tossed seas it took him more than three weeks to reach Messina. From Sicily he painfully made his way to Corfu, then from Corfu to Austrian territory in Padua, and finally to Venice, where he arrived exhausted, destitute and with a serious leg injury. He was down but, being a Stuart, not out.

Aid came from an unexpected quarter, for George III's kindly nature was touched when he learned of his rival's misfortune. Diplomatic negotiations resulted in Henry receiving a civil list pension of £4,000 a year from the British government. At King George's insistence it was to be paid in a manner which would cause the cardinal least embarrassment. 'I confess I am at a loss to express my feelings,' Henry wrote in grateful acceptance of this unexpected bounty.[8] And well he might have been, for this exceeded even Stephen's generosity to the young Henry Plantagenet. It must be the only instance of a king, freely and out of the goodness of his heart, paying a pension to a pretender to his throne.

Jacobites, however, were not slow to suggest that George III was doing no more than making inadequate reparation for a long outstanding debt. Not surprisingly, the British government had never seen fit to honour payment of the jointure of £50,000 a year to which James II and after him his widowed queen, Mary of Modena, were legally entitled from 1688 until her death in 1718. More surprisingly, parliament had never bothered to repeal this grant, and it could therefore be argued that James II's heirs were owed one and a half million pounds.

When Pius VI died a prisoner in Valence the French Directory determined that there should be no more popes, but Henry's misadventures and illness had not affected the stubbornness of his will and he determined otherwise. Since Rome was still in French hands he defiantly arranged for the other cardinals to be summoned to Venice and the thirty-four (out of forty-six) who were able to answer the call held a conclave on the island monastery of San Giorgio. After three and a half months of deliberation a new pope was elected and crowned as Pius VII. He was to be engaged in a long and humbling but, in the end, triumphant struggle against Napoleon. Despite his seniority and self-importance, Henry himself never became a candidate for the papacy; it is not likely that he would have attracted many votes.

The impact of the French revolution and Napoleon's assault on the old order of church and state throughout Europe transformed relations between the Roman Church and a Protestant England which had become the last bastion of resistance to the Corsican iconoclast. In the past the Stuart exiles, including Henry himself, had not hesitated to take up arms in a French cause against men they claimed as their own subjects. But when he learned of Nelson's victory over the French in the battle of the Nile Henry particularly charged the British envoy in Naples to make it known in England that no man rejoiced in the success of British arms more than he did. For his part Napoleon, frustrated by Britain's intransigence, threatened to turn the house of Hanover off the throne and restore the Stuarts. One can only speculate with some interest whether, in the event of a successful invasion of England, Napoleon would in fact have offered the crown to one of his bitterest enemies and whether, if he had, Henry would have succumbed to temptation and accepted it from such hands.

In 1800 the cardinal was able to return to Rome and his beloved Frascati in the Alban hills. His health was frail and his great wealth irrecoverable, but he found peace of mind and an income adequate to support old age in dignity and style. Distinguished and saintly, he resumed the life of a grand old man who had become, along with St Peter's and the Trevi fountain, one of the sights of Rome for visitors from Great Britain. Their curiosity to glimpse this handsome historic relic was insatiable. In 1764 when a rival Duke of York (George III's brother Edward) paid a visit to Rome Henry had beaten a hasty retreat, leaving town discreetly to avoid embarrassment. But in 1792 he remained to receive in audience one of George III's sons (Prince Augustus, afterwards Duke of Sussex) and to be rewarded by the prince courteously addressing him as Royal Highness. After 1800 he became a legendary figure and when he died in 1807 English society and newspapers were loud in their praises.

A fulsome obituary in the *Gentleman's Magazine* acknowledged him to have been 'a sincerely pious prelate'; he was 'a compassionate benefactor', especially to British visitors; 'his purse was always open to suffering humanity'. *The Times* judged his life to have been 'humane and temperate'. He was also a respected advocate of legitimacy and a worthy representative of an *ancien régime* which had passed away for ever. A snob and a bore, it must be added, he was also, as the last of the Stuarts, an unregenerate upholder of the outworn doctrine of the divine right of kings. That he should have survived into the nineteenth century was a freak of history.

The king cardinal was buried with due honour in the crypt of St Peter's beside his father and brother, their tombs proclaiming them to have been Jacobus III, Carolus III and Henricus IX. In the church above, they are touchingly remembered in a fine marble memorial by Canova. In his will Henry gracefully returned to the *de facto* King of England some crown jewels which James II had taken with him into exile. They were bequeathed to George III as 'remembrances'. Right to the crown was another matter. That was not Henry's to bequeath. It passed to 'the nearest lawful heir', who was Charles Emmanuel IV, Duke of Savoy and King of Sardinia, the great-great-grandson of Henrietta, Duchess of Orleans, the youngest daughter of Charles I. Down the generations this claim was to pass through Charles Emmanuel's niece to Francis V, Duke of Modena, and through his niece to the ducal house of Bavaria, where it now rests.

Like Robert of Normandy, Cardinal York lived for more than eighty years, belying the general rule that pretenders' lives are nasty, short and brutish. In a more civilised period than the middle ages or Tudor England all three Stuart pretenders were permitted a long innings, and Henry's career as a pious prelate, like the innocent faith of Lady Jane Grey, brought some dignity and sympathy to the name and status of pretender – a word too often associated only with rank impostors or down-at-heel refugees.

CONCLUSION

Although Henry Stuart was the last serious pretender to the British throne, the pretensions of his ill-fated family lingered on and still appeal to sentiment. When King Victor of Savoy, the then heir to Stuart claims, died in 1824 Lord Liverpool, the prime minister, ordered public mourning on the grounds that many people in Britain regarded him as their rightful king. The reigning monarch, George IV, sitting securely on the throne, took an indulgent view of the outcast line. As Prince Regent he had been one of the principal contributors to the cost of erecting Canova's monument, which serves to this day to persuade believers in St Peter's of the rightful kingship of the Stuart pretenders.

In 1886 the Order of the White Rose was revived. This badge and symbol of Yorkist royalty had been adopted by a Jacobite secret society in 1710, and White Rose Day was celebrated on the anniversary of James III's birth. On Queen Victoria's death in 1901 members of the order boldly proclaimed a new queen, to massive public indifference. Instead of Edward VII they recognised Mary IV and III. This representative of the Stuart senior female line was Archduchess of Austria-Este-Modena and the wife of Prince Louis of Bavaria. The archduchess herself, like the other Heads of Name and Line since Henry's death, advanced no claim, and waning British enthusiasm for the cause evaporated during the first world war when the next heir, Rupprecht of Bavaria, became a field-marshal in the imperial German army. Today the Stuart claim to the crowns of England and Scotland rests with Duke Albrecht of Bavaria (b. 1905) and his son Prince Franz (b. 1933), who are reported to wear kilts and white roses and lay wreaths at the foot of a statue of James VI and I in Munich on appropriate anniversaries. Diplomatically, Duke Albrecht (King Albert to the faithful) 'neither presses nor denies' his Stuart claim.[1]

These are the legitimists, but there has also been a final flurry of imposture. The Young Pretender's queen, it has been suggested, gave birth to a son in February 1773, and the long looked-for heir, so far from being proclaimed to the world, was smuggled out of Italy in secrecy for fear of kidnapping or murder at the hands of agents of the usurping dynasty. The precious baby was handed to Captain (later Admiral) John Carter Allen, a British naval commander whose ship was at anchor in Leghorn harbour. Brought up as the admiral's own child, he became Lieutenant Thomas Allen RN, concealing his true identity until it was revealed after his death by his two sons: the self-styled John Sobieski Stuart, Count d'Albanie (c. 1794–1872) and Charles Edward Stuart (1797–1880).

Presumably bearing some facial resemblance to real Stuarts, the so-called Sobieski Stuarts were well endowed with charm and religious zeal – as Anglicans, Presbyterians and Roman Catholics successively. Patronised by a descendant of the Jacobite Lord Lovat, they commended themselves to the credulous without a shred of evidence to support an unlikely tale. After a period in the highlands their royal abode was a modest lodging house in a district which was not the most fashionable in Victorian London. From darkest Pimlico they emerged, wearing Stuart tartans or exotic uniforms liberally sprinkled with purchased decorations, to enliven the reading room of the British Museum or the drawing room of a gullible hostess.

The last recorded claimant of this line made an appearance in a London law court in 1925, seemingly for the purpose of reviving the spurious claim. A grandson of the Count d'Albanie, he was Colonel Alfred von Pratt, a Czechoslovak subject holding honorary rank in the Czech army. With the death of Von Pratt the age of impostors appears to have drawn to an unseemly close, but who knows what surprises lie ahead? An alleged descendant of George III from his supposed secret marriage as a young man to Hannah Lightfoot (a Wapping shoe-maker's daughter playing the role of Lucy Walter) may yet emerge from obscurity to stake a claim superior to that of Elizabeth II.

Meanwhile it may be noted that the growth of democratic institutions in Britain has spelt death to all serious pretenders; first, because at the head of constitutional governments kings have become relatively powerless and their job correspondingly less attractive to the ambitious; and, secondly, because in a parliamentary democracy the opposition is a loyal one, intent on forming an administration under the same, not a different, monarch. This has been the British experience since the Jacobite threat receded in the second half of the 18th century.

A general acceptance of agreed rules of inheritance and succession, the development of a standing army, improvements in communication and the spread of knowledge are other factors contributing to the end of imposture and the elimination of the pretender as a significant figure in public affairs. Outside Britain, by contrast, the obsolescence of monarchy and its replacement by republics in a modern world has created a boom in pretendership among the descendants of crowned heads. Rule independent of the will of the people is no longer the divine right of kings. In the 20th century it has become the prerogative of military dictators and communist party secretaries.

A backward glance suffices to establish the narrowness of the line of division between king and pretender. Matilda and Jane might well have won their contests for the crown. They would then have been known in history as queens and Stephen and Mary as pretenders. Henry Tudor, later Henry VII, spent a long enough period as a claimant in exile to qualify as both pretender and king. Similarly, if one of the Stuart uprisings had ultimately succeeded in enthroning James III or Charles III they would still be remembered also as the Old or Young Pretender.

Other kings who might be thought to qualify as pretenders were claimants only briefly, and some may be more appropriately designated usurpers. Such were William, Duke of Normandy, Henry Bolingbroke, Edward, Earl of March, Richard, Duke of Gloucester and William, Prince of Orange, who dethroned incumbents to become William I, Henry IV, Edward IV, Richard III and William III. The usurped, on the other hand, undoubtedly qualify as pretenders if, like Henry VI and James II, they survive to maintain their claim.

Usurpers and pretenders have this in common: their claim to the crown may be better than their rivals', as William, Edward and Richard vehemently asserted. But whether Harold or William was the rightful king, whether Henry VI or Edward IV, whether Edward V or Richard III or Henry VII, whether James II or William III, one distinction is clear. Kings and usurpers occupy thrones; pretenders do not. Pretenders *qua* pretenders are always losers, they are nearly always tragic figures, and the tragedy is seldom of their own making. They are bound by birthrights or destined to be marionettes dancing on puppet-masters' strings.

To avoid the fate of Prince Perkin, Queen Jane, Mary Queen of Scots and King Monmouth on the scaffold, pretenders need luck, an independent power base or steadfast allies. Henry Tudor had the luck. Robert of Normandy's dukedom was his consolation prize and springboard. Matilda's husband was Count of Anjou. John of Gaunt's immense wealth lay beyond his Spanish rival's reach. The exiled Stuarts owned no territory or resources of their own, but the protection of the French crown and the Roman church enabled them to die in their beds. The only unsuccessful pretenders on whom providence chose to smile were Lambert Simnel and Henry Stuart, who found their respective vocations at the opposite ends of the social scale as falconer and cardinal.

The Sobieski Stuarts lower a comic-opera curtain on scenes of tragedy in English history. They were pretenders of the kind which has given all pretenders an undeservedly bad name, for most merit our pity and some our respect. The worthiest were innocent victims of the harsh doctrine that might is right and history's unappealable verdict that the king who rules reigns. But, to their own supporters at least, the sovereignty of pretenders is not in doubt. When met at Sedgemoor with the challenge 'Who are you for?' Monmouth's men replied boldly: 'For the king.' This necessitated a further question: 'Which king?' and brought the confident rejoinder: 'King Monmouth'.

The sentiment of a Jacobite poet furnishes a similarly open-minded conclusion:

God bless the King, I mean the Faith's Defender;
God bless – no harm in blessing – the Pretender;
But who Pretender is, or who is King,
God bless us all – that's quite another thing.[2]

SELECT BIBLIOGRAPHY

A complete bibliography would fill a second volume. The titles listed below form only a small selection of the more important primary sources and of books likely to appeal to the general reader interested in further study. Dates refer to editions and are not necessarily the dates of first publication.

General

The Compact Edition of the Dictionary of National Biography 1975
The Complete Peerage of England, Scotland, Ireland, Great Britain and The United Kingdom 1910–59

Introduction

SHAKESPEARE, Nicholas: *The Men Who Would Be King* 1984

Chapters 1 and 2

Anglo-Saxon Chronicle ed. B. Thorpe (Rolls Series) 1861; tr. G. N. Garmonsway 1960
Anglo-Saxon Chronicle, The: A Revised Version ed. D. Whitelock with D. C. Douglas and S. I. Tucker 1965
BARLOW, Frank: *William Rufus* 1983
BROOKE, Christopher: *The Saxon and Norman Kings* 1963
CHAMBERS, James: *The Norman Kings* 1981
CRONNE, H. A.: *The Reign of King Stephen* 1970

DAVID, C. W.: *Robert Curthose, Duke of Normandy* 1920

DAVID, R. H. C.: *King Stephen* 1967

DOUGLAS, D. C.: *William the Conqueror* 1964

EADMER: *Historia Novorum in Anglia* ed. M. Rule (Rolls Series) 1884

English Historical Documents II, 1042–1189 ed. D. C. Douglas and G. W. Greenway 1981

FLORENCE OF WORCESTER: *Chronicon ex Chronicis* ed. B. Thorpe 1848–9

FREEMAN, E. A.: *The History of the Norman Conquest of England* 1869–75

FREEMAN, E.A.: *The Reign of William Rufus* 1882

Gesta Stephani Regis Anglorum ed. & tr. K. R. Potter 1955

HENRY OF HUNTINGDON: *Historia Anglorum* ed. T. Arnold (Rolls Series) 1879

HIGDEN, Ranulph: *Polychronicon* Vol. VII ed. J. R. Lumby (Rolls Series) 1879

KNIGHTON, Henry: *Chronicon Henrici Knighton* Vol. I ed. J. R. Lumby (Rolls Series) 1889

LE HARDY, Gaston: *Le Dernier des Ducs Normands* 1882

MAP, Walter: *De Nugis Curialium* ed. T. Wright 1850

ORDERIC VITALIS: *The Ecclesiastical History of Orderic Vitalis* ed. & tr. M. Chibnall 1969–81

PAIN, Nesta: *Empress Matilda* 1978

RICHARD OF HEXHAM: *De Gestis Regis Stephani* ed. R. Howlett (Rolls Series) 1886

RUNCIMAN, Steven: *A History of the Crusades* Vol. I 1951

WILLIAM OF JUMIEGES: *Gesta Normannorum Ducum* 1914

WILLIAM OF MALMESBURY: *De Gestis Regum Anglorum* ed. W. Stubbs (Rolls Series) 1887–9

WILLIAM OF MALMESBURY: *Historia Novella* ed. & tr. K. R. Potter 1955

WILLIAM OF NEWBURGH: *Historia Rerum Anglicarum* ed. R. Howlett (Rolls Series) 1884

WILLIAM OF POITIERS: *Gesta Willelmi Ducis Normannorum et Regis Anglorum* in *Scriptores Rerum Gestarum Willelmi Conquestoris* ed. J. A. Giles 1845

Chapter 3

ADAM OF USK: *Chronicon Adae de Usk AD 1377–1421* ed. & tr. E. M. Thompson 1904

ARMITAGE-SMITH, Sydney: *John of Gaunt* 1904

BENNETT, H. S.: *Chaucer and the Fifteenth Century* 1948

Chronicon Angliae ed. E. M. Thompson (Rolls Series) 1874

COLLINS, Arthur: *The Life of Edward Prince of Wales; also The History of John of Gaunt* 1740

COULTON, G. G.: *Chaucer and his England* 1963

English Historical Documents IV 1327–1485 ed. A. R. Myers 1969

FROISSART, Jean: *Chronicles* tr. & ed. G. Brereton 1968

GODWIN, William: *Life of Geoffrey Chaucer (including memoirs of John of Gaunt, Duke of Lancaster)* 1804

HIGDEN, Ranulph: *Polychronicon* Vol. IX ed. J. R. Lumby (Rolls Series) 1886

John of Gaunt's Register 1371–75 ed. S. Armitage-Smith (Camden Third Series Vols. XX & XXI) 1911

John of Gaunt's Register 1379–1383 ed. E. C. Lodge & R. Somerville (Camden Third Series Vols. LVI & LVII) 1937

KNIGHTON, Henry: *Chronicron Henrici Knighton* Vol. II ed. J. R. Lumby (Rolls Series) 1895

McKISACK, May: *The Fourteenth Century 1307–1399* 1959

RAMSAY, Sir James: *Genesis of Lancaster 1307–99* 1913

SOMERVILLE, Robert: *History of the Duchy of Lancaster Vol. I 1265–1603* 1953

STEEL, Anthony: *Richard II* 1962

WALSINGHAM, Thomas: *Historia Anglicana* ed. H. T. Riley (Rolls Series) 1863/64

WORKMAN, H. B.: *John Wyclif* 1926

Chapters 4, 5 and 6

Accounts of the Lord High Teasurer of Scotland Vol. I: 1473–1498 1877

BACON, Francis: *The History of the Reign of King Henry the Seventh* 1622

BROOKE, Richard: *Visits to Fields of Battle in England of the Fifteenth Century* 1857

BRYAN, Donough: *Gerald Fitzgerald, The Great Earl of Kildare (1456–1513)* 1933

BUSCH, Wilhelm: *England Under the Tudors Vol. I: King Henry VII* 1895

Calendar of Patent Rolls AD 1476–1485 (1901) and *AD 1485–1494* (1914)

Calendar of State Papers (Milan) Vol. I ed. A. B. Hinds 1912

Calendar of State Papers (Spain) Vol. I ed. G. A. Bergenroth 1862

Calendar of State Papers (Venice) Vol. I ed. Rawdon Brown 1864

CHASTELAIN, J.-D.: *L'Imposture de Perkin Warbeck* 1952

CHRIMES, S. B.: *Henry VII* 1972

CHRIMES, S. B.: *Lancastrians, Yorkists and Henry VII* 1966

CONWAY, Agnes: *Henry VII's Relations with Scotland and Ireland 1485–1498* 1932

CURTIS, Edmund: *A History of Mediaeval Ireland from 1110 to 1513* 1923

Exchequer Rolls of Scotland, The: Vol. X, AD 1488–1496 ed. G. Burnett 1887

FABYAN, Robert: *The New Chronicles of England and France* 1811

FORD, John: *The Chronicle Historie of Perkin Warbeck: A Strange Truth* 1634

GAINSFORD, Thomas: *The History of Perkin Warbeck, proclaiming himself Richard the Fourth* 1618

GAIRDNER, James: *History of the Life and Reign of Richard the Third* 1898

GRAFTON, Richard: *Continuation of John Hardyng's Chronicle* 1543

Great Chronicle of London, The: ed. A. H. Thomas and I. D. Thornley 1938

GRIFFITHS, Ralph A. and THOMAS, Roger S.: *The Making of the Tudor Dynasty* 1985

HALL, Edward: *Hall's Chronicle,* ed. H. Ellis 1809

HUTTON, William: *The Battle of Bosworth Field* 1813

INGULPH: *Chronicle of the Abbey of Croyland* tr. H. J. Riley 1854

JACOB, E. F.: *The Fifteenth Century 1399–1485* 1978

KENDALL, Paul Murray: *Richard the Third* 1955

LANDER, J. R.: *Conflict and Stability in Fifteenth-Century England* 1977

Letters and Papers Illustrative of the Reigns of Richard III and Henry VII ed. J. Gairdner 1861/63

LEVINE, Mortimer: *Tudor Dynastic Problems 1460–1571* 1973

MADDEN, Sir Frederick: *Documents relating to Perkin Warbeck* (Archaeologia XXVII) 1838

MYERS, A. R.: *England in the Late Middle Ages* 1952

POLLARD, A. F.: *The Reign of Henry VII from Contemporary Sources* 1914

RAMSAY, Sir James: *Lancaster and York* 1892

Register of the Privy Seal of Scotland, The: Vol. I, AD 1488–1529 ed. M. Livingstone 1908

ROSS, Charles: *Edward IV* 1974

ROSS, Charles: *Richard III* 1981

ROTH, Cecil: *Perkin Warbeck and his Jewish Master* (Trans. Jewish Hist. Soc. of Eng. IX) 1922

ROTH, Cecil: *Sir Edward Brampton* (Trans. Jewish Hist. Soc. of Eng. 16) 1952

Rotuli Parliamentorum Vols. V (1439–1468) & VI (1472–1503) 1783

RYMER, Thomas: *Foedera 1475–1502 Vol. XII* 1711

SEYMOUR, Willima: *Battles in Britain Vol. I 1066–1547* 1975

SHELLEY, Mary Wollstonecraft: *The Fortunes of Perkin Warbeck* 1830

Statutes of the Realm Vol. II (1377–1509) 1816

VERGIL, Polydore: *Three Books of Polydore Vergil's English History* ed. H. Ellis 1844

WERNHAM, R. B.: *Before the Armada* 1966

WILLIAMS, Neville: *The Life and Times of Henry VII* 1973

Chapters 7 and 8

ANDERSON, James: *Collections Relating to the History of Mary Queen of Scots* 1727–28.

ARMSTRONG DAVISON, M. H.: *The Casket Letters* 1965

ASCHAM, Roger: *The Scholemaster* 1570

BRADLEY, E. J.: *Arabella Stuart* 1889

Calendar of State Papers (Domestic: Edward VI, Mary and Elizabeth 1547–1580) ed. R. Lemor 1856

Calendar of State Papers (Foreign: Elizabeth) 1863–1936

Calendar of State Papers (Scotland 1547–1603) 1898–1969
Calendar of State Papers (Spanish: Mary and Elizabeth) 1892–1954
CHALMERS, G.: *Life of Mary Queen of Scots* 1818
CHAPMAN, Hester W.: *Lady Jane Grey* 1962
CHAPMAN, Hester, W.: *The Last Tudor King* 1958
Chronicles and Political Papers of King Edward VI ed. W. K. Jordan 1966
COOPER, E.: *The Life and Letters of Lady A. Stuart* 1866
COWAN, Ian B.: *The Enigma of Mary Stuart* 1971
DURANT, David N.: *Arbella Stuart* 1978
FLORIO, M.: *Historia de la Vita . . . Giovanna Graia* 1607
FOXE, John: *Actes and Monuments (The Book of Martyrs)* 1563
FRASER, Antonia: *Mary Queen of Scots* 1969
FROUDE, J. A.: *History of England from the Fall of Wolsey to the Death of Elizabeth* 1893
GODWIN, Francis: *Annals of England* 1630
GRAFTON, Richard: *Grafton's Chronicle* 1809
HENDERSON, T. F.: *Mary Queen of Scots* 1905
HOLINSHED, Raphael: *Chronicles of England, Scotland and Ireland* 1577
HOWARD, George: *Lady Jane Grey and Her Times* 1822
LANG, Andrew: *The Mystery of Mary Stuart* 1912
MATHEW, David: *Lady Jane Grey* 1972
NEALE, J. E.: *Elizabeth I and her Parliaments 1559–1581* 1953
NEALE, J. E.: *Elizabeth I and her Parliaments 1584–1601* 1957
NEALE, J. E.: *Queen Elizabeth* 1934
NICHOLS, J. G.: *Literary Remains of King Edward the Sixth* 1857
NICOLAS, N. H.: *Memoirs and Literary Remains of Lady Jane Grey* 1825
POLLINI, G.: *L'Historia Ecclesiastica Della Rivoluzion d'Inghilterra* 1594
PRESCOTT, H. F. M.: *Mary Tudor* 1952
READ, Conyers: *Mr Secretary Walsingham and the Policy of Queen Elizabeth* 1925
RIDLEY, Jasper: *The Life and Times of Mary Tudor* 1973
SKELTON, John: *Maitland of Lethington and the Scotland of Mary Stuart* 1894
STOW, John: *The Annals of England* 1601
STRICKLAND, Agnes: *Lives of the Queens of England Vols. V and VI* 1842/3
STRYPE, John: *Life of Sir John Cheke* 1821
STRYPE, John: *Memorials of Thomas Cranmer* 1812
TYTLER, P. F.: *England under the Reigns of Edward VI and Mary* 1839

Chapter 9

ASHLEY, Maurice: *James II* 1977
Calendar of State Papers (Domestic: James II, Vol. I) 1960
CLARKE, J. S.: *Life of James the Second* 1816
CLIFTON, Robin: *The Last Popular Rebellion* 1984

D'OYLEY, Elizabeth: *James, Duke of Monmouth* 1938

DRYDEN, John: *Absalom and Achitophel* 1681–82

EARLE, Peter: *Monmouth's Rebels* 1977

EMERSON, W. R.: *Monmouth's Rebellion* 1951

English Historical Documents VIII 1660–1714 ed. A. Browning 1953

EVELYN, John: *The Diary of John Evelyn* ed. E. S. de Beer 1955

FEA, Allan: *King Monmouth* 1902

KENYON, John: *The Stuarts* 1958

LITTLE, Bryan: *The Monmouth Episode* 1956

MACAULAY, Lord: *The History of England Vols. I and II* ed. C. H. Firth 1913–14

PEPYS, Samuel: *The Diary of Samuel Pepys* ed. R. Latham and W. Matthews 1976–83

ROBERTS, George: *The Life, Progresses and Rebellion of James, Duke of Monmouth* 1844

SCOTT, Lord George: *Lucy Walter: Wife or Mistress* 1947

SEYMOUR, William: *Battles in Britain Vol. 2 1642–1746* 1975

TRENCH, Charles Chenevix: *The Western Rising* 1969

TURNER, F. C.: *James II* 1948

The Western Martyrology 1705

WYNDHAM, Violet: *The Protestant Duke* 1976

Chapters 10, 11 and 12

BEVAN, Bryan: *King James the Third of England* 1967

BROWNE, James: *A History of the Highlands and the Highland Clans* 1845

Calendar of State Papers at Windsor Castle (HMC) 1902–23

CHAMBERS, Robert: *History of the Rebellion of 1745–6* 1847

DAICHES, David: *Charles Edward Stuart* 1973

D'ARGENSON, Marquis: *Mémoires* 1857/58

DUKE, Winifred: *Lord George Murray and the Forty Five* 1927

EWALD, A. C.: *The Life and Times of Prince Charles Stuart* 1883

FORBES, Rev. Robert, Bishop of Ross & Caithness: *The Lyon in Mourning* ed. H. Paton 1895–96

FORSTER, Margaret: *The Rash Adventurer* 1973

FOTHERGILL, Brian: *The Cardinal King* 1958

HAILE, Martin: *The Old Chevalier* 1907

LANG, Andrew: *Pickle the Spy* 1897

LANG, Andrew: *Prince Charles Edward Stuart, The Young Chevalier* 1903

LEES-MILNE, James: *The Last Stuarts* 1983

MACKENZIE, Compton: *Prince Charlie* 1932

McLYNN, F. J.: *The Jacobite Army in England 1745* 1983

MAHON, Lord: *History of England 1713–1783* 1853–54.

Memoirs of the Chevalier de Johnstone 1870

Memorials of John Murray of Broughton 1740–47 1898
MILLER, Peggy: *James: Old Pretender* 1971
OMAN, Carola: *Prince Charles Edward* 1935
PETRIE, Sir Charles: *The Jacobite Movement* 1959
PLUMB, J. H.: *The First Four Georges* 1956
PREBBLE, John: *Culloden* 1967
RUVIGNY & RAINEVAL, Marquis de: *The Jacobite Peerage* 1904
SEYMOUR, William: *Battles in Britain Vol. 2 1642–1746* 1975
SHIELD, Alice: *Henry Stuart, Cardinal of York* 1908
SHIELD, Alice and LANG, Andrew: *The King Over the Water* 1907
STUART MSS, Royal Archives, Windsor Castle
TAYLER, A. & H.: *The Old Chevalier* 1934
TAYLER, A. & H.: *1715: The Story of the Rising* 1936
TAYLER, A. & H.: *1745 and After* 1938
TAYLER, A. & H.: *The Stuart Papers at Windsor* 1939
TAYLER, H.: *Jacobite Epilogue* 1941
TRENCH, Charles Chenevix: *George II* 1973
WILKINSON, Clennell: *Bonnie Prince Charlie* 1932
WOGAN, Charles: *Female Fortitude* 1722

Conclusion

Burke's Royal Families of the World 1977

SOURCES AND REFERENCES

Full details of the author and title of the books referred to can be found in the Select Bibliography except where given below.

Chapter 1:
Duke Robert and William Clito

1. Ord. Vit. V p. 25
2. Ord. Vit. IV pp. 93/95
3. *E.H.D.* II p. 29
4. Ord. Vit. IV p. 115
5. Ord. Vit. IV p. 199
6. Ord. Vit. IV p. 93
7. Ord. Vit. V p. 291
8. Flor. of Worc. ii p. 48
9. Ord. Vit. V p. 301
10. Ord. Vit. VI p. 79
11. Ord. Vit. VI p. 99
12. Will. of Malm., *De Gestis* ii p. 482

Chapter 2:
Empress Matilda, Lady of England

1. Pain p. 21
2. *Gest. Steph.* p. 13
3. *A-S. Chron.* in *E.H.D.* p. 210
4. Will. of Malm., *Hist. Nov.* p. 16
5. Orderic Vitalis
6. Hen. of Hunt. (Pain p. 78)
7. *Gest. Steph.* p. 153
8. *A-S. Chron.* in *E.H.D.* p. 211
9. Bishop of Lisieux
10. *Gest. Steph.* p. 123
11. *Gest. Steph.* p. 123
12. *Gest. Steph.* p. 139.
13. *Gest. Steph.* p. 135

Chapter 3:
John of Gaunt, King of Castile

1. Froissart: cf. Brereton p. 114
2. Armitage-Smith p. 215
3. Jean le Bel, *Chroniques* I pp. 155/6
4. Godwin II pp. 108/9
5. Collins p. 24
6. Collins p. 49

7. Shak., *Ric. II* Act II Sc. 1, line 150
8. Godwin II p. 540
9. Ingulph p. 353
10. Godwin II p. 536
11. Steel p. 21

Chapter 4:
Yorkists, Lancastrians and Henry Tudor

1. Chrimes, *L., Y. and H. VII* p. 33
2. Froissart p. 466
3. *Rot. Parl.* V p. 377
4. Rymer XII p. 185
5. *York Civic Records* ed. Raine pp. 73/4
6. Cornwallis, *Encomium of Richard III* 1977 p. 9
7. *Paston Letters* ed. Gairdner III pp. 317/8
8. Vergil p. 224
9. *Rot. Parl.* VI p. 270

Chapter 5:
Lambert Simnel, Ireland's King

1. Bacon p. 20
2. *Rot. Parl.* VI p. 397
3. Hall p. 432
4. Curtis p. 392
5. Holinshed p. 79
6. Bryan p. 108
7. Hall p. 433
8. Hall p. 431
9. *Rot. Parl.* VI p. 397
10. Bacon p. 67
11. *Rot. Parl.* VI p. 397
12. Hall p. 433
13. Hall p. 434
14. *Rot. Parl.* VI p. 502
15. Hall p. 435
16. Ford, opening lines

Chapter 6:
Prince Perkin

1. Hall p. 462
2. Bacon p. 138
3. Bacon p. 23
4. Bryan p. 130
5. *Letters & Papers* II p. 55
6. *Great Chron. Lond.* p. 285
7. *ibid.*
8. *ibid.*
9. *Cal. P.R. 1476–85* p. 481
10. *Cal. P.R. 1485–94* p. 274
11. *Cal. S.P. Venice* I 799
12. Hall p. 462
13. Hall p. 461
14. Ford, Act I Scene 1
15. Hall p. 462
16. Hall p. 463
17. Hall p. 465
18. *ibid.*
19. Hall p. 469
20. *Cal. S.P. Venice* I 650
21. Gainsford p. 55
22. Bryan p. 187
23. Hall p. 471
24. Gainsford p. 73
25. Bacon p. 148
26. *Cal. S.P. Milan* I 490
27. *Cal. S.P. Venice* I 665
28. *Carew MSS (Book of Howth)* p. 180
29. Hall p. 484
30. *Great Chron. Lond.* p. 281
31. Gainsford p. 95
32. Gainsford p. 101
33. Gainsford p. 102
34. Hall p. 486
35. *ibid.*
36. *Cal. S.P. Spain* I 221
37. *Cal. S.P. Venice* I 760
38. *Cal. S.P. Spain* I 221
39. Gainsford p. 111
40. *Cal. S.P. Spain* I 249

41. Gairdner p. 385
42. Hall p. 473
43. Bacon p. 150
44. Pollard I p. 108
45. Madden p. 156
46. Shelley, preface p. vi
47. Speed, *History of G.B.* 1611 p. 738
48. Bacon p. 193

Chapter 7:
Queen Jane

1. *Cal. S.P. Spain* I 456
2. Grafton II p. 225
3. Nichols I p. 207
4. Strype, *Cheke* p. 88
5. Strype, *Cranmer* p. 206
6. Godwin p. 255
7. Froude V p. 171
8. Chapman, *Lady Jane Grey* p. 106
9. Nicolas p. xlix
10. Nicolas p. liii
11. Nicolas p. xlix
12. Nicolas p. l
13. *Acts of Privy Council* IV p. 317
14. Stow p. 1039
15. Strype, *Cranmer* p. 915
16. *Cal. S.P. Spain* XI p. 168
17. Holinshed p. 1733
18. Grafton II p. 543
19. B. L. Harl. MSS 2342
20. Grafton II p. 543

Chapter 8:
The Queen of Scots

1. Froude XII p. 257
2. Anderson I p. i
3. Anderson I p. lv
4. Fraser p. 162
5. *Cal. S.P. Foreign 1572–4* 93
6. Read II p. 399

7. Morris, *Poulet Letter Books* pp. 359–61
8. Durant p. 207, quoting post-mortem

Chapter 9:
King Monmouth

1. Macaulay II p. 566
2. Roberts II p. 143
3. *West. Mart.* p. 163
4. Dryden, lines 29, 30
5. Dryden, line 312
6. Turner p. 161
7. Evelyn, *Diary* II p. 456
8. Pepys, *Diary* III p. 191
9. Roberts I p. 88
10. Pepys, *Diary* VI p. 170
11. Fea, p. 49
12. *Poem of the Clyde*
13. Dryden, lines 27, 28, 31, 32
14. Dryden, lines 173, 174
15. Ashley p. 147
16. Fea, p. 335
17. Roberts I p. 248
18. Roberts I p. 320
19. Roberts I p. 333
20. Trench, *Western Rising* p. 185
21. Emerson p. 19
22. Clarke II p. 43
23. Clarke II p. 32
24. Roberts II p. 153
25. Clarke II p. 25
26. Evelyn, *Diary* IV p. 456
27. B. L. Sloane 4194 f. 3686
28. Wolseley, *Marlborough* I pp. 335/6

Chapter 10:
James III, Old Mr Melancholy

1. Clarke II p. 619
2. Bevan p. 68
3. Shield & Lang p. 103

4. Trench, *George II* p. 36
5. *The History of Henry Esmond, Esq.*
6. Petrie, Intro. to Bevan (p. 12)
7. Trench, *George II* p. 36
8. Miller p. 156
9. Miller p. 155
10. Tayler, *Old Chevalier* pp. 69, 70
11. Trench, *George II* p. 49
12. Wogan p. iv
13. Shield p. 1
14. B.L. C115.i.3. 55 p. 7
15. Ewald p. 49
16. *Stuart MSS* 275. 26
17. *Stuart MSS* 386. 30
18. *Stuart MSS* 413. 115
19. Shield p. 184

Chapter 11:
Charles III, The Bonnie Prince

1. Lang, *Prince C.E.S.* p. 451
2. Wilkinson p. 3
3. Lang, *Prince C.E.S.* p. 95
4. Oman p. 51
5. Lang, *Prince C.E.S.* p. 200
6. Mackenzie p. 73

7. Ewald p. 201
8. Prebble p. 65
9. Lang, *Prince C.E.S.* p. 289
10. Oman p. 95
11. Lang, *Prince C.E.S.* p. 311
12. Lang, *Prince C.E.S.* pp. 356/7
13. Lang, *Prince C.E.S.* p. 452
14. Mahon IV p. 9
15. Lees-Milne p. 103
16. Mackenzie p. 143

Chapter 12:
Henry IX, King Cardinal

1. Shield p. 92
2. D'Argenson III p. 70
3. Shield p. 112
4. Tayler, *Stuart Papers* p. 209
5. Tayler, *Stuart Papers* p. 210
6. Shield p. 116
7. Fothergill p. 205
8. Lees-Milne p. 166

Conclusion

1. Burke p. 148
2. John Byrom, *To an Officer in the Army*

Index

Abingdon, Abbot of 86
Act of Settlement (1701) 164–5, 167
Adela of Normandy, Countess of Blois 16, 34
Adelisa of Louvain, queen of Henry I 31, 38
Afghanistan, exiled king of 12
Aix-la-Chapelle, Treaty of (1748) 190
Albania, claim to throne of 12
Albemarle, Christopher Monk, Duke of 151
Alberoni, Cardinal 174
Albrecht of Bavaria, Duke 207
Alexius I, Emperor 22
Alfieri, Vittorio, Count 193
Alfonso V, King of Portugal 96
Alfonso VI, King of Spain 27
Allen, Admiral John Carter 207
Allen, Lieutenant Thomas 207
Alton, Treaty of (1101) 26, 29, 44
American colonies 185, 194
Angus, Earl of 116
Anjou, counts of see Fulk; Geoffrey Plantagenet
Anne, Queen 158, 160, 164, 165, 166, 167, 168, 178
Anne, daughter of Thomas, Duke of Gloucester 66
Anne of Beaujeu, Regent of France 75
Anselm, Archbishop of Canterbury 21, 25, 32

Antioch 22–3, 34
Ap Meredith, Owen 69
Ap Thomas, Rhys 77
Ap Tudor, Owen 69
Argyll, Archibald Campbell, Duke of 170, 172
Argyll, Archibald Campbell, Earl of 147, 148, 151–2, 154
Armada, Spanish 135
Artevelde, Jacob van 49
Arthur, Prince of Wales 29–30, 107, 108, 116
Arthur of Brittany 11–12
Arundel castle 38
Ascalon, battle of (1099) 23
Ascham, Roger 117
Astley, John 105
Atholl, Duke of 182
Audley, James Touchet, Lord 105
Augustus III, King of Poland 190
Austria-Este-Modena, Mary, Archduchess of ('Mary IV and III') 206
Austro-Hungary, claim to throne of 12

Babington, Antony 134
Babington plot 133, 134
Bacon, Francis (quoted) 86, 112
Baden, Princess of 173
Baldwin, Count of Flanders (grandfather of Robert, Duke of Normandy) 14

Ball, John 150
Barton, Andrew 103
Barton, Robert 103
Bavaria, ducal house of, and Stuart claim to throne 205, 206–7
Beauchamp, Edward, Lord 116
Beaufort, Henry Somerset, 1st Duke of 151
Beaufort, Charles Somerset, 4th Duke of 192
Beaufort, Lady Margaret 66, 69, 73–4, 75, 86, 120, 184
Beaulieu abbey 91, 106
Becket, St Thomas 45
Bedford, Duke of *see* Tudor, Jasper
Benedict XIII, Pope 196
Benedict XIV, Pope 199, 200, 201, 202
Berwick, James Fitzjames, 1st Duke of 114, 164, 167–9, 170–1, 172
Berwick, James Francis, 2nd Duke of 180
Black Box, the 139–40, 163–4
Blake, Robert 151
Bloody Assizes, the (1685) 155
Blount, Sir James 75
Bodrugan, Sir Henry 87
Bohemond, Prince of Taranto 22
Bolingbroke, Henry St John, Viscount 169, 170, 172
Bordeaux, Archbishop of 194
Bosworth, battle of (1485) 77–9, 80, 82, 84, 86–7, 88, 89, 90, 91, 96, 100, 186
Bothwell, James Hepburn, Earl of 132
Bothwell Bridge, battle of (1679) 142
Bouillon, Godfrey, Duke of 23
Bourbons 12
Bowhill 138
Boyne, battle of the (1690) 162
Bradgate 118
Braganza, house of 12
Brampton, Sir Edward (Duarte Brandao; Edward Brandon) 94–7, 109
Brampton, Lady 94, 96
Brémule, battle of (1117) 28
Brétigny, Treaty of (1360) 53–4
Bristol 151, 152–3
Bristol castle 27, 38
Broughton, Sir Thomas 86, 87, 89
Buccleugh, Francis, 2nd Duke of 157
Buccleugh, Walter, 5th Duke of 140
Buccleugh, dukedom of 157

Buccleugh, Anne, Countess of *see* Monmouth, Duchess of
Buccleugh and Queensberry, Duke of 138
Buchan, James, Earl of 102
Buckingham, Henry, Duke of 66, 73, 74, 114
Buckingham rebellion (1483) 73
Burghley, Lord *see* Cecil, William
Burgundy, Margaret, Duchess of *see* Margaret
Burgundy, dukes of *see* Charles the Bold; Philip I, King of Castile; Philip the Bold
Burns, Robert 180
Bute, John Stuart, Earl of 193

Calais, siege of (1346–47) 51, 53
Calixtus II, Pope 28–9
Cambrai, Bishop of 110
Cambridge, Richard, Earl of 66, 67
Cameron, Archibald 192
Camerons 188
Campbells 147, 188; *see also* Argyll
Cardiff castle 27
Carlisle, fall of (1745) 184
Casket Letters, the 132
Catherine of Braganza, queen of Charles II 143
Catherine of Valois, queen of Henry V 68–9, 110
Cecil, William (Lord Burghley) 117, 132, 133, 134
Chandée, Philibert de (Earl of Bath) 79, 90
Chandos, Sir John 54
Charles I 30, 137, 144, 160, 161, 177, 183, 205
Charles II 12, 137–46, 148, 151, 155, 158, 160, 194, 196
Charles IV, King of France 11
Charles V, King of France 56
Charles VI, King of France 11, 62, 68
Charles VIII, King of France 75, 91, 97–8, 104, 109
Charles V, Emperor 114
Charles XII, King of Sweden 169, 173
Charles Edward Stuart, the Young Pretender ('Bonnie Prince Charlie', 'Charles III') 11, 137, 160, 165, 175, 176, 178–95, 196, 197, 199–200, 201–2, 208

Charles Emmanuel IV, Duke of Savoy, King of Sardinia 205
Charles the Bold (the Rash), Duke of Burgundy 82, 95–6
Charlotte, Duchess of Albany 192, 194, 202
Chaucer, Geoffrey 47
Cheke, John 117–18
Chester, Ranulf, Earl of 39, 44
Cheyney, Sir John 78
Churchill, Arabella 167
Clarence, Albert, Duke of 30
Clarence, George, Duke of 66, 71, 81, 82, 84
Clarence, Lionel, Duke of 49, 50, 61, 66, 68
Clarendon, Edward Hyde, Earl of (quoted) 139
Clement VII, Anti-pope 62
Clement XI, Pope 173, 174
Clement XIII, Pope 192–3
Clifford, Lady Margaret 115, 116
Clifford, Sir Robert 99
Cogna, Peter Vacz de 94
Constantinople 21, 22, 23
Cope, Sir John 182–3
Corpus Christi College, Cambridge 60
Courtenay, Peter, Bishop of Exeter 74
Courtenays 74, 126; *see also* Exeter, Marquess of
Coventry, Sir John 141
Coverdale, Miles 119
Cranmer, Thomas, Archbishop of Canterbury 118, 119
Crécy, battle of (1346) 47, 49, 51, 53, 57
Crèvecoeur, Philippe de 76–7
Crofts, James 139
Crofts, Lord 139
Cromwell, Oliver 12, 144, 149–50, 152, 163
Cromwell, Richard ('Tumbledown Dick') 12
crusade, first 13, 21–3
Culloden, battle of (1746) 188–9, 194, 198, 200
Cumberland, William, Duke of 180–1, 182, 185, 186, 187–9, 198
Cumberland, Eleanor, Countess of 115, 116

D'Albanie, John Sobieski Stuart, Count 207
Dalkeith, James, Earl of 157

D'Argenson, Marquis 197, 198
Darnley, Henry Stuart, Lord 116, 130–2, 134
Dartmouth, George Legge, Lord 156, 162
David, King of Scotland 32, 37–8, 40, 42, 44
Davison, William 134
De la Forse, Anthony 96
Delamere, Lord 148
De la Pole, Edmund *see* Suffolk, Earl of
De la Pole, John *see* Lincoln, Earl of; Suffolk, Duke of
De la Pole, Richard 11, 114
De la Pole, William 114
De Montfort, Simon 50
Derby, Robert Ferrers, Earl of 50
Derby, withdrawal from (1745) 185–7
De Redvers, Aveline 50
De Redvers, Baldwin 37
Derwentwater, James, Earl of 170
Desmond, Maurice Fitzthomas, Earl of 97, 101, 102, 105
Desmonds 92
D'Este, Benedetta 173
Dettingen, battle of (1743) 180, 187
De Veres 75; *see also* Oxford, earls of
Devizes castle 27, 42
Devon, Edward Courtenay, Earl of 74, 126
Dorset, Thomas, Marquess of 74, 86
Dorylaeum, battle of (1097) 22
Dover, Treaty of (1670) 142–3
Drummond, Margaret 103
Dryden, John 138
    Absalom and Achitophel 138, 143
Dudley, Lord Guilford 120, 121, 122, 125, 126
Dudley, John *see* Northumberland, Duke of
Dudley, Robert *see* Leicester, Earl of
Du Guesclin, Bertrand 54

Edgar Atheling 11, 20, 22
Edgecombe, Sir Richard 93
Edinburgh, Treaty of (1560) 130
Edith (Matilda), queen of Henry I 31–2
Edmund Ironside 20
Edward the Confessor 20
Edward I 46, 48
Edward II, 46, 48, 50–1, 72–3
Edward III 11, 47–51, 53–4, 57–8, 66–8, 73, 82

Edward IV (Earl of March) 66, 68–73, 76, 80, 81, 86, 90, 91, 95, 109, 114, 156, 181, 208–9

Edward V (Prince of Wales) 66, 71–3, 81, 95, 96, 110, 111, 113, 209

Edward VI 10, 115–18, 119, 120–1, 123, 124

Edward VII 206

Edward VIII 29

'Edward VI' *see* Simnel, Lambert

Edward, Prince of Wales (the 'Black Prince') 47, 48, 49, 50, 53, 54, 55, 58, 66, 158

Edward, son of the 'Black Prince' 55

Edward of Middleham, Prince of Wales 75, 82

Elibank plot (1752–53) 192

Elizabeth I 87, 115, 116, 117, 119–20, 121, 125–6, 128–36, 138, 155

Elizabeth II 47, 207

Elizabeth, Electress Palatine, Queen of Bohemia 160, 165

Elizabeth Woodville, queen of Edward IV 71–4, 85–6, 118

Elizabeth of York, queen of Henry VII, 25, 47, 66, 72, 74–5, 80, 81, 86, 109, 116

Enrique, King of Castile 54, 56

Enrique, Infante of Castile 63

Essex, Geoffrey de Mandeville, Earl of 39

Etaples, Treaty of (1492) 98

Eustace, son of King Stephen 44

Evelyn, John (quoted) 139

Exeter, Henry Courtenay, Marquess of 114, 126

Fairfax, Sir Thomas 149

Falkirk, battle of (1746) 187

Faro, Katharine de, alleged mother of Perkin Warbeck 96, 109

Feckenham, Dr, Dean of St Paul's 126

Ferdinand, King of Aragon 100, 103, 107, 109

Fernando, son of King Juan of Castile 63

Feversham, Louis de Duras, Earl of 153, 154

Fifteen, the 168–72, 181, 182, 184, 192

Fitzgerald, Sir Thomas 85, 89

Fitzgeralds 84; *see also* Desmond and Kildare, Earls of

Fitzwalter, Lord 99

Flambard, Ranulf, Bishop of Durham 19, 25–6

Fontenoy, battle of (1745) 180–1, 187

Forster, Thomas 170

Forty-Five, the 176, 180–9, 192, 195, 197–8, 200

Fotheringhay castle 128, 134

Foxe's *Book of Martyrs* 143, 149

France, claims to throne of 11, 12, 49, 53, 68, 76

Francis I, King of France 114, 130, 164

Francis II, King of France 116, 129

Francis, Duke of Brittany 70, 71, 73, 74, 75

Francis, Duke of Modena 205

Franz of Bavaria, Prince 207

French revolution 185, 203, 204

Frion, Stephen 97

Fulk, Count of Anjou 28, 29, 33

Fürstenberg, Princess of 173

Gaeta, siege of (1734) 180

Gardiner, Stephen, Bishop of Winchester 126

Garth, Thomas 97

Gaveston, Piers 51

Geoffrey, son of Henry II 11

Geoffrey, Bishop of Coutances 19

Geoffrey of Conversano, Lord of Brindisi 23

Geoffrey Plantagenet, Count of Anjou 33, 34, 37, 42, 43, 44, 209

George I 160, 165, 166, 167–8, 169, 170, 175–6, 179

George II 160, 165, 175, 176, 180, 181, 183–4, 186, 191, 200

George III 159, 160, 165, 176–7, 193, 202–4, 205, 207

George IV 160, 206

George V 30

Gerberoi, battle of (1078) 15, 17

Gesta Stephani 41

Glenshiel, battle of (1719) 175

Glorious Revolution (1688) 150, 161, 177

Gloucester, Humphrey, Duke of 72

Gloucester, Thomas of Woodstock, Duke of 63, 64, 66, 72, 73

Gloucester, William, Duke of 164

Gloucester, Robert, Earl of 27, 32–44, 132, 140

Gloucester cathedral 13

Good Parliament, the (1376) 58

Gordon, Lady Catherine, 'queen' of 'Richard IV' 102, 107

Grafton, Henry Fitzroy, Duke of 153

Great Fire of London (1666) 163
Great Schism 61–2
Greece, exiled king of 12
Gregory VII, Pope 32
Grey, Lady Catherine (Countess of Hertford) 115, 116, 130, 136
Grey, Ford, Lord 147, 154, 155
Grey, Henry *see* Suffolk, Duke of
Grey, Lady Jane (Queen Jane) 10, 11, 114–27, 128, 137, 138, 139, 156, 157, 205, 208, 209
Grey, Lady Mary 115, 116
Gustavus Adolphus, King of Sweden 149
Gwladys the Dark 69
Gwynne, Nell 141

Habsburgs 12
Hall, Edward – *Hall's Chronicle* 112
Hamiltons 131
Hardwick, Bess of (Elizabeth Talbot, Countess of Shrewsbury) 135
Harold, King 10, 20, 208–9
Hawke, Sir Edward 176
Hawley, General Henry 187
Helias of Saint-Saens, Count of Arques 28
Henrietta Maria, queen of Charles I 140
Henry I 14, 16, 24–36, 38, 40, 58
Henry II (Henry fitzEmpress; Henry Plantagenet) 16, 34, 43–6, 74, 79, 84, 156, 203
Henry III 46, 48, 50
Henry IV (Henry Bolingbroke) 46, 48, 64, 65–7, 69, 72, 156, 161, 178, 181, 208
Henry V 11, 47, 48, 67, 68, 142
Henry VI 11, 48, 67, 68, 69, 70, 72–3, 208–9
Henry VII (Earl of Richmond; Henry Tudor) 10–11, 25, 47, 66, 68–71, 73–94, 97, 99–100, 102–9, 111–14, 116, 120, 130, 135, 140, 149, 150, 156, 161, 180, 186, 208, 209
Henry VIII 13, 30, 47, 66, 87, 114–18, 122, 126, 130, 135
Henry IV, King of France 179
Henry IV, Holy Roman Emperor 32
Henry V, Holy Roman Emperor 32, 46
Henry, Prince of Portugal ('the Navigator') 46–7
Henry, Prince, son of James VI and I 30, 137, 160
Henry, Bishop of Winchester, Abbot of

Glastonbury, grandson of William I 16, 35, 36, 38, 39, 40, 41
Henry Benedict, Duke of York, Cardinal York ('Henry IX') 11, 160, 175, 190, 194, 196–205, 206, 209
Heron, John 105
Hertford, Catherine, Countess of *see* Grey, Lady Catherine
Hertford, Edward Seymour, Earl of 130
Hertford castle 52, 60
Hesse, Princess of 173
Historia Novella (William of Malmesbury) 41
Holinshed, Raphael – *Chronicles* 112
Huntingdon, Henry Hastings, Earl of 130

Innocent VII, Pope 85
Iran, claim to throne of 12
Isabella, Queen of Castile 47, 107, 109, 111
Isabella, queen of Edward II 11, 68
Italy, claim to throne of 12

Jacobites 158, 166, 168–72, 174–5, 176, 177, 181–9, 191–3, 194, 200, 201, 203–4, 206, 208, 209
James I (and VI) 116, 132, 133, 134, 135–6, 137, 160, 164, 207
James II (Duke of York) 138, 140, 141, 143–9, 151–2, 154, 155–6, 158, 159–64, 165, 167, 178, 183, 204, 205, 208–9
James I, King of Scotland 177
James II, King of Scotland 177
James III, King of Scotland 102, 177
James IV, King of Scotland 91, 97, 99, 102–3, 108, 110, 116, 177, 185
James V, King of Scotland 116, 129
James Francis Edward Stuart, the Old Pretender ('James III and VIII') 11, 158–77, 178, 179, 180, 181, 182–3, 185, 190, 192, 196, 197, 198, 199, 201, 206, 208
Jane, Queen *see* Grey, Lady Jane
Jeffreys, Sir George (Judge) 155
Jerusalem 23, 25
Joan, Princess of Wales, wife of Edward, the 'Black Prince' 61
Joan of Arc 74, 125
Joanna, Queen of Castile 113
Joao II, King of Portugal 96

John, King 11–12, 46, 90
John III, King of Poland 173
John, son of Richard III 94
John of Gaunt *see* Lancaster, Duke of
John of Montfort, Duke of Brittany 56
Johnson, Dr Samuel (quoted) 194
Juan, King of Castile 62–3

Katharine, Queen of Castile 46, 48, 63
Katharine of Aragon, queen of Henry
   VIII 47, 107, 114, 115
Katharine Parr, queen of Henry VIII
   118–19
Kenilworth castle 50, 52
Kenmure, William Gordon, Viscount
   170
Kildare, Gerald, Earl of (the Great Earl)
   84–5, 92–3, 97, 101, 104–5, 108
Knollys, Sir John 56
Knox, John 119

Lalain, Roderic de 102
Lancaster, Blanche, Duchess of 47, 48,
   49–50, 54–5
Lancaster, Constance of Castile,
   Duchess of 48, 56, 60, 61, 62, 63, 64
Lancaster, Henry the Good, Duke of 48,
   49, 51, 52
Lancaster, John of Gaunt, Duke of 11,
   46–64, 66, 67, 69, 149–50, 209
Lancaster, Alice Lacy, Countess of 51
Lancaster, Edmund Crouchback, Earl of
   48, 51, 53
Lancaster, Henry, Earl of 48, 51
Lancaster, Thomas, Earl of 48, 50–1
Landois, Peter 75, 76
Lanfranc, Archbishop of Canterbury 17,
   21
Leicester, Robert Dudley, Earl of 120,
   131
Leicester castle 52, 64
Lennox, Elizabeth, Countess of 135
Lennox, Lady Margaret Douglas,
   Countess of 115, 116, 131, 135
Lennox, Charles Stuart, Earl of 116, 135
Lennox, Matthew Stuart, Earl of 131
Lightfoot, Hannah 207
Limoges, siege and massacre of (1370) 55
Lincoln, John de la Pole, Earl of 82–9,
   90, 92, 96, 98, 112, 113
Lincoln, Bishop of 38
Liverpool, Earl of 206
Llewellyn the Great 69

Louis VI, King of France 28, 29
Louis XI, King of France 70, 73, 76
Louis XII, King of France 114, 116
Louis XIV, King of France 142–3,
   162–4, 165, 167, 168
Louis XV, King of France 180, 190,
   193, 197
Louis XVI, King of France 203
Louis of Bavaria, Prince 206
Louisa, daughter of James II 165
Louise of Stolberg-Geldern, Princess,
   Countess of Albany, 'queen' of
   'Charles III' 193–4, 207
Lovat, Simon, Lord 165, 207
Lovel, Francis, Viscount 77, 80–1, 82,
   86, 87, 89
Lovell, Sir Thomas 90

Maastricht, siege of (1673) 142
Macaulay, Lord (quoted) 137
Macdonald, Flora (Fionnghal) 180, 189
Macdonalds 188
Macdonell, Alastair, chieftain of
   Glengarry ('Pickle the Spy') 192
Mackenzie, Sir Compton (quoted) 185
'Magdalen' (impostor of Richard II) 65
Malcolm, King of Scotland 15, 20
Manchester, taking of (1745) 185
Man in the Iron Mask 157
Mar, John Erskine, Earl of ('Bobbing
   John') 168, 169, 170, 172
March, Edmund, Earl of 66, 67, 83
March, Roger, Earl of 66, 67, 68
Margaret, queen of James IV of Scotland
   103, 115, 116, 130, 131
Margaret, Duchess of Burgundy 66, 82,
   83, 84, 85, 96, 97, 98, 100, 102, 109,
   110
Margaret of Savoy 103
Maria Clementina Sobieska, Princess,
   'queen' of 'James III' 173–4, 179, 193,
   196, 197
Marie Leczinska, queen of Louis XV 197
Marischal, George Keith, Earl 170, 174,
   192
Marlborough, John Churchill, Duke of
   152, 153, 166, 167
Mary I, Queen (Mary Tudor) 10, 47,
   115, 116, 119, 120, 121, 122–6, 129,
   130, 135, 143, 149, 159, 202, 208
Mary II (Mary Stuart; Princess of
   Orange) 47, 138, 146, 158, 160, 161,
   164, 178

Mary, Queen of Scots (Mary Stuart) 11, 114, 115, 116, 128–36, 155, 156, 164, 177, 192, 209
Mary, queen of Louis XII (Duchess of Suffolk) 115, 116, 118, 163
'Mary III and IV' *see* Austria-Este-Modena, Mary, Archduchess of
Mary, Princess of Orange (wife of William II of Orange) 160, 161
Mary of Modena, queen of James II 143, 158, 162, 163–4, 204
Matilda (Maud), Empress 11, 16, 31–45, 46, 70, 74, 79, 115, 151, 156, 208, 209
Matilda, queen of William I 14, 15–17, 24
Matilda (Edith), queen of Henry I 31–2
Matilda, queen of King Stephen 41
Maude, Duchess of Zealand 48, 50, 51
Maximilian, Emperor 91, 99, 101, 102, 103, 104, 108, 110, 113
Meno, Pregent (Pierre Jean) 94, 97
Merciless Parliament, the (1388) 63
Minster Lovell skeleton 89
Monmouth and Buccleuch, Anne, Duchess of 141, 146, 157
Monmouth and Buccleuch, James, Duke of 11, 137–57, 159, 160, 161, 162, 164, 165, 168, 170, 171, 172, 181, 184, 188, 209
Monypenny, Lord 98
Moray, James Stuart, Earl of 132–3, 134
More, Sir Thomas 108
Mortimer, Anne 66, 68
Mortimer, Ralph 69
Morton, John, Bishop of Ely 73, 74, 75
Mountford, Sir Simon 99
Murray, Lord George 182, 184, 185–7, 188, 190

Najera, battle of (1367) 54, 57
Napoleon I 203, 204
Nelson, Horatio, Viscount 204
Nevill, Sir George 98
Nevills 86; *see also* Warwick
Newcastle, Thomas Pelham Holles, Duke of 182
Newcastle-upon-Tyne 13, 15
Nile, battle of the (1798) 204
Nineteen, the 174–5, 182
Norfolk, John Howard, Duke of 77–8
Norfolk, Thomas Howard I, Duke of (Earl of Surrey) 103

Norfolk, Thomas Howard III, Duke of 133
Norfolk, Hugh Bigod, Earl of 35
Northumberland, John Dudley, Duke of (Earl of Warwick) 119–21, 122–4, 125, 126
Northumberland, Henry Percy, Earl of 77–8, 86
Northumberland, Thomas Percy, Earl of 133

Oates, Titus 144, 146
O'Connells 92
Odo, Bishop of Bayeux, Earl of Kent 18, 19, 22, 39
O'Donnell, Hugh Roe 102, 105
O'Neills 92
Orleans, Henrietta, Duchess of 205
Orleans, Duke of, Regent of France 168, 171
Ormonde, earls of 85
Ormonde, James 97
Ormonde, James Butler, Duke of 168–9, 171, 172, 174, 175
Osbeck, Piers *see* Warbeck, Perkin
O'Sullivan, Colonel John William 184
Oxford, John de Vere, Earl of 75, 77, 87, 88, 95, 108
Oxford, Robert de Vere, Earl of 61
Oxford, Robert Harley, Earl of 169
Oxford castle 43

Paget, William, Lord 123
Parry, Dr 133
Paulet, Sir Amyas 134
Peasants Revolt (1381) 60, 149–50
Pedro the Cruel, King of Castile 54, 55–6
Pembroke, Thomas Herbert, Earl of 151
Pembroke, William Herbert, Earl of 69–70
Pembroke castle 68, 69–70
Pepys, Samuel (quoted) 141
Perrers, Alice 54
Perth, James Drummond, Duke of 182, 184, 189
Peter the Great, Tsar of Russia 173
Peter the Hermit 21
Peterborough cathedral 134
Philip I, King of France 15
Philip IV, King of France 11
Philip I, King of Castile (Archduke Philip, Duke of Burgundy) 99, 100, 113–14

Philip II, King of Spain 47, 125, 131, 133, 135
Philip V, King of Spain 171
Philip the Bold, Duke of Burgundy 57
Philippa, Queen of Portugal 46, 48, 62
Philippa, queen of Edward III 47, 54
Philippa, daughter of Lionel, Duke of Clarence 66, 68
'Pickle the Spy' *see* Macdonell, Alastair
Picquiny, Treaty of (1475) 70, 71, 76
Pilgrimage of Grace (1536) 87
Pius VI, Pope 203, 204
Pius VII, Pope 204
Poitiers, battle of (1356) 47, 53, 57
Poix, Walter Tirell, Count of 23
Pole, Reginald, Cardinal 202
Pontefract castle 51, 52, 60, 65
Portugal, claim to throne of 12
Poynings, Sir Edward 99
Pratt, Colonel Alfred von 207
Preston, battle of (1715) 170, 172, 175
Prestonpans, battle of (1745) 182-3, 187, 188
princes in the Tower *see* Edward V; York, Richard, Duke of (son of Edward IV)

Radclyffe, Charles 198
Radziwill, Princess 191
Ramsay, James 102
Ratcliffe, Sir Robert 99
Raymond, Count of Toulouse 22
Reading abbey 30, 49
Riccio, David 131
Richard I 11
Richard II 46, 48, 56, 58, 60-1, 63, 64, 65, 66, 67, 72-3, 92
Richard III (Duke of Gloucester) 46, 66, 69, 71-83, 86, 87, 88, 94, 95, 102, 110-11, 128, 161, 208-9
'Richard IV' *see* Warbeck, Perkin
Richard, son of William I 14, 16, 23
Richard, son of Robert, Duke of Normandy 23
Richelieu, Duc de 197, 198
Richmond, Henry Fitzroy, Duke of 120
Richmond, Edmund Tudor, Earl of 68-9
Robert, Duke of Normandy (Robert Curthose) 11, 13-30, 33, 36, 38, 40, 45, 62, 70, 142, 148, 156, 168, 205, 209

Robert, Count of Flanders 21, 22
Robert Guiscard, Duke of Apulia 14, 22
Robert of Mortain 19
Robsart, Amy 120
Rochester castle 42
Roger, Bishop of Salisbury 35, 37, 38
Romanovs 12
Royal Oak Day 169
Rupert of the Rhine, Prince 141
Rupprecht of Bavaria, Prince 206-7
Russell, William, Lord 146
Russia, claim to throne of 12
Rye House plot (1683) 146, 147
Ryswick, Treaty of (1697) 163, 164

St James's Park or turnips 175
St John of Jerusalem, Grand Prior of the Order of 99
St Margaret of Scotland 31
St Paul's, Dean of 99
St Paul's cathedral 54-5, 59, 62, 63, 83, 125
St Peter ad Vincula 157
St Peter's, Rome 177, 194, 205, 206
Salic law 67, 68
Salisbury, Margaret, Countess of 66, 130
Savage, Sir John 77
Savoy, house of 12
Savoy, Peter, Count of 50
Savoy palace 50, 52, 53, 59, 60
Saxe, Maurice de, Marshal of France 180, 198
Scandalum Magnatum 59
Schwartz, Martin 83, 88, 89, 90
Scott, Sir Walter 142, 180, 195
Sedgemoor, battle of (1685) 154-5, 156, 188, 209
Seven Bishops, the trial of the (1688) 159
Seven Men of Moidart, the 181
Seymour, Edward *see* Somerset, Duke of
Seymour, Thomas 119
Seymour, William *see* Somerset, Duke of
Shaftesbury, Anthony Ashley Cooper, Earl of 143, 144
Shakespeare, William 108
Shelley, Mary Wollstonecraft (quoted) 112
Sheriffmuir, battle of (1715) 170, 172
Shrewsbury, George Talbot, Earl of 87
Shrewsbury, Roger of Montgomery, Earl of 19, 26
Sibyl, wife of Robert, Duke of Normandy 23, 28

Sidney, Algernon 146
Simnel, Lambert 11, 13, 80–90, 91, 92, 93, 94, 96, 98, 107, 112, 156, 209
Simons, Richard 82, 83, 84, 90
Skelton, Richard 105
Sluys, battle of (1340) 51, 57
Somerset, Edward Seymour, Duke of (Protector) 118, 119, 120, 123, 130
Somerset, John, Duke of 66, 69
Somerset, William Seymour, Duke of 116, 136
Sophia, Electress of Hanover 160, 165, 166, 167
Sosa, Ruy de 109
South Sea Bubble (1720) 175, 179
Stafford, Humphrey 81, 86
Stafford, Thomas 81, 86
Stanley, Thomas, Lord (Earl of Derby) 73, 74, 77–9, 87, 89, 161
Stanley, Sir William 77, 78, 89, 99–100, 161
Stephen, King 16, 32, 33, 34–45, 78, 79, 167, 203, 208
Stephen, Count of Blois and Chartres 34
Stoke, battle of (1487) 88–9, 90, 91, 92, 96
Stow, John 84
Strange, George Stanley, Lord 87, 89
Strathmore, Earl of 170
Stuart, Arbella 11, 116, 135–6
Stuart, Charles Edward 207
Stuarts, Sobieski 11, 207, 208
Suffolk, Elizabeth, Duchess of 82
Suffolk, Frances, Duchess of (Marchioness of Dorset) 115, 116, 118, 120, 121, 122, 124, 125
Suffolk, Mary, Duchess of *see* Mary, queen of Louis XII
Suffolk, Henry Grey, Duke of 118, 121, 122, 123, 124, 125
Suffolk, John de la Pole, Duke of 113
Suffolk, Edmund de la Pole, Earl of 11, 113–14
Surrey, Thomas Howard I, Earl of *see* Norfolk, Duke of
Sussex, Augustus, Duke of 205
Swynford, Katharine 53, 64, 69

Talbot, Gilbert 77
Taunton 151, 152
Taylor, John 97
Tewkesbury, battle of (1471) 68
Thackeray, William – *Henry Esmond* 167

Theodore, Count of Blois 16, 34, 35
Throckmorton, Lady 125
Tinchebrai, battle of (1106) 27
Tories 144, 145, 146, 166, 169, 175, 185
Tudor, Edmund *see* Richmond, Earl of
Tudor, Jasper (Duke of Bedford) 69, 70, 71, 79, 87
Tullibardine, Marquis of 170
Turenne, Marshal 142, 153
Tyler, Wat 150
Tyrell, Sir James 113

Urban II, Pope 21
Urban VI, Pope 61–2
Utrecht, Treaty of (1713) 167, 190

Victor, King of Savoy 206
Victoria, Queen 31, 140, 159, 206

Wade, General George 182, 183, 184, 186
Walkinshaw, Clementina 192, 193
Walpole, Horace 159, 201
Walpole, Sir Robert 174, 175, 179, 182, 192
Walsingham, Sir Francis 133, 134, 192
Walter, Lucy 139–40, 145, 164, 207
Warbeck, Perkin 11, 13, 91–112, 125, 140–1, 154, 156, 172, 185, 209
Warham, Dr William 99
Warwick, Edward, Earl of 11, 66, 81–3, 84, 90, 94, 96, 107–8, 112; *see also* Simnel, Lambert
Warwick, John Dudley, Earl of *see* Northumberland, Duke of
Warwick, Richard Nevill, Earl of ('the Kingmaker') 47, 68, 70, 82
Wentworth, Lady Henrietta 146
Werbecque, Jehan 93, 94, 96, 109–10
Werbecque, Pierre (Pierrechon, Peter, Peterkin) *see* Warbeck, Perkin
West, Robert 146
Westminster Abbey 135
Westmorland, Charles Nevill, Earl of 133
Westmorland, John Fane, Earl of 192
Whigs 144, 145, 148, 161, 166, 169, 175, 177, 185
White Rose, Order of the 206
White Rose Day 169, 175, 206
William I (the Conqueror; the Bastard; Duke of Normandy) 10, 13, 14–15, 16, 17–19, 20, 24, 31, 36, 80, 140, 156, 161, 208–9

William II (Rufus) 14, 16–25, 35, 36, 58, 167

William III (Prince of Orange) 47, 138, 139, 144–9, 156, 157, 160–5, 171, 178, 208–9

William I (the Silent), Prince of Orange 133

William, son of Adela 16, 34

William, son of King Stephen 44

William, Count of Holland and Hainault 47

William Atheling, son of Henry I 16, 29, 31

William of Breteuil 24

William Clito, Count of Flanders 11, 13, 16, 28–9, 33, 36, 178

William of Hatfield, son of Edward III 49, 66

William of Wykeham 59

William of Ypres 41

Winchester 24, 35, 38, 40, 41

Winchester, Bishop of 59

Wolfe, James 176

Wolsey, Thomas, Cardinal 114

Wolvesey castle 41

Woodville, Sir Edward 95

Woodville, Queen Elizabeth *see* Elizabeth Woodville

Woodville, Lionel, Bishop of Salisbury 74

Wulford, Ralph 107

Wyatt, Sir Thomas 125

Wyclif, John 47, 59, 117

York, Anne Hyde, Duchess of 158

York, Edmund, Duke of 66, 68

York, Edward, Duke of 205

York, Richard, Duke of (father of Edward IV) 66, 67–8, 83–4, 86, 178

York, Richard, Duke of (son of Edward IV) 66, 71, 72, 73, 81, 83, 90, 113; *see also* Warbeck, Perkin

York, Henry, Cardinal *see* Henry Benedict